DATE DUE

The Battered Woman

The
Battered Woman

Lenore E. Walker

1817

HARPER & ROW, PUBLISHERS
New York, Hagerstown, San Francisco, London

FIRST EDITION

Designed by Eve Kirch

Library of Congress Cataloging in Publication Data

Walker, Lenore E.
  The Battered Woman
    1. Wife abuse—United States. 2. Abused wives—
Services for—United States. I Title.
HV6626.W34 1979   362.8′2   77–11538
ISBN 0–06–014582–X

---

79 80 81 82 83 10 9 8 7 6 5 4 3 2 1

this book is dedicated to
my father
David Auerbach
and
my husband
Morton Flax
in loving memory of their
teaching me how men can
love women gently and
without violence

Contents

Part III The Way Out

Introduction

The problem of battered women has only come into the limelight in the past few years, its progression toward public awareness paralleling the growth of the women's movement. Historically, there has never been any public outcry against this brutality. But now we are learning that the problem is far more pervasive—and terrible—than it was ever thought to be and that the myths which had previously rationalized why such violence occurred between men and women who supposedly loved each other are untrue. Jokes about wife beating no longer seem so funny (if they ever did). Some observers, including myself, estimate that as many as 50 percent of all women will be battering victims at some point in their lives. Contrary to popular belief, these women do not remain in their relationships because they like being battered, but rather because of complex psychological and sociological reasons I have detailed in this book. Most people label these women "masochistic" for not leaving the relationship, unaware of or preferring to ignore the battered woman's inability to help herself.

The whole spectrum of intrafamily violence is perplexing. After all, families are supposed to provide a tranquil refuge from the strains and stresses of the outside world. In order to maintain this idyllic concept of the family, society has been guilty of sweeping the entire range of domestic violence under the rug.

As more studies continue to be made, we learn that there is a relationship between battered women and child abuse. Men who beat their women reportedly were themselves beaten as children. And there are reports of a high incidence of girl child incest occurring in families where there is violence. Some studies have raised the question of whether large numbers of men are being beaten by their women—but this situation has no reliable supportive facts to date. However, the pervasiveness of all violence in society has finally become a cause for alarm.

Many theorists have regarded aggressiveness as the natural order of things in the world, pointing to animals where survival of the fittest has produced highly aggressive species. Interestingly, comparative studies have found that while male animals often dominate females through the use of violence, this is not always so. Sometimes it is the female who is dominant and is responsible for committing similar brutality against the male. I believe that only where there is true equality between males and females can there be a society that is free from violence. Although I believe that aggressiveness is not an innate trait but one which is learned early in life, I do not believe we can eliminate violence from our world without also eliminating discrimination on the basis of sex.

The women's movement has pointed out the huge amount of violence which seems to be committed by men against women in general. So many of society's institutions are set up with men responsible for taking care of women, including the family, it is only natural that these male-dominated institutions have been unresponsive to the female victims of their own aggressiveness. Is it really necessary to have all of this violence in order to keep one half of the population under domination? My feminist analysis of all violence is that sexism is the real underbelly of human suffering. Men fight with other men to prove that they are not "sissies" like women. Women show passive faces to the world while struggling to keep their lives together without letting men know how strong they really are for fear of hurting their men's masculine image. And men beat up women in order to keep themselves on the top of this whole messy heap. Little girls and little boys learn these sex-role expectations through early socialization. Unless we strive for equal power relationships between men and women, women will continue to be victims of the kinds of assaults I share with you in this book.

When I became interested in studying battered women's problems in early 1975, no other psychologists were doing similar research. Several sociologists, such as Murray Straus, Richard Gelles, and Susan Steinmetz, were documenting some of the social causes of violence in the family. Feminists like Susan Brownmiller were studying the history of rape as a means for men to control women. Feminist psychologists like Phyllis Chesler were re-evaluating the usefulness of traditional psychoanalytic therapy for women because of its strong anti-woman theoretical basis. No one, however, was studying the psychology of battered women as victims. I decided to begin at the original source, the battered women themselves.

In early 1975, I was a practicing psychologist on the faculty of Rutgers Medical School in New Jersey. I also held a joint faculty appointment at the Rutgers Graduate School of Applied and Professional Psychology. My private psychotherapy practice reflected my feminist views. Many of my clients were women in transitional periods of their lives. As I began to work with these women, often using new techniques such as assertiveness training, some of them began to report abuse by their men—both physical and psychological abuse. Some of these men and women were married, some not. My first fear was that critics of the women's movement might be right.

Perhaps violence erupted because women began to make their own decisions to control their lives. Feminism was indeed having a profound impact on the family by changing power relationships. Would strong, assertive women be able to live in harmony and equality with those men whom they loved? Fortunately, a further investigation proved these fears to be groundless: in those relationships where battering was occurring, coercion between the partners had existed from the beginning of the relationship. The psychotherapy these women were receiving gave them the strength not only to begin talking about their experiences to others, but to end the battering relationship as well.

These early cases stimulated my curiosity, and I began to ask my colleagues on the medical and psychology faculties about their women patients who were reporting physical or psychological abuse by men. Slowly, these colleagues began to refer such women to me. The feminist network provided another rich source of volunteers for this research. Before long I was inundated with such women, and I began the long, hard task of interviewing. All of them were willing to talk with a woman psychologist if anonymity was guaranteed. I found that my feminist point of view and my willingness to listen without blaming the victim were my greatest assets. When I began, I did not know what questions to ask, so I let them tell their stories in their own ways. Although this was time-consuming, it proved to be an effective way to gather the information. These women told me how rare it was to be able to tell their entire stories to someone. Most listeners would cut them off as soon as they got to some of the more ghastly details. Either they were not believed or they were told that it could only be assumed that they liked what was happening to them, since they had not left the violent situation that they were in. But the pain these women experienced in retelling their stories was testimony enough that none of them had a deep psychological need to be battered.

In the summer of 1975, I moved to Denver, Colorado, and brought my research with me. My faculty appointment at

Colorado Women's College facilitated this work. Newspaper articles, radio shows, a few television specials, and plenty of word-of-mouth brought out more battered women who were ready to talk. Volunteers for subjects and interviewers quickly outgrew my need and my ability. When I had begun, very little publicity was given to this age-old problem. Once the media began to publicize its existence, battered women felt freer to tell their stories. When one newspaper article reported a speech that I gave to the American Psychological Association, over fifty battered women called within the week to volunteer their stories. Six months after this article had appeared, several women called stating that they had saved the phone number until they had the courage or opportunity to use it. An appearance I made on an all-night radio talk show also brought volunteers who were fearful of using the telephone during the day.

To date, I have collected over 120 detailed stories of battered women. I have listened to fragments of over 300 more stories. I have interviewed dozens of helpers who have offered their services to battered women. These women came from all over this country, as well as from England, where I spent some time visiting refuges for battered women during the summer of 1976. This is a self-volunteered sample. These women were not randomly selected, and they cannot be considered a legitimate data base from which to make specific generalizations. Therefore, throughout this book I have attempted not to use statistics to analyze any of the data. Rather, I have concentrated on the commonalities expressed by the battered women and generalized from them. The stories reported here are typical examples of stories heard in my interviews with battered women. I believe it will only be through listening to what battered women say that we will be able to understand what happens to a battered woman, how she is victimized, and how we can help a society change so that this horrible crime can no longer be perpetrated upon women.

One of the first tasks that faced me early in the interviews was the problem of learning just what it meant to be a battered woman. Women who were uncertain whether they were really being battered would call and ask me to make a determination. While it was perfectly evident that women suffering physical mutilation were battered, some women reported incidents which did not produce physical damage. It became difficult to distinguish between those women living in unfulfilling and unhappy marriages and those in battering relationships. The differentiation was not well defined until about midway through this project. The commonality was the life-threatening incidents that continuously occurred in battered women's lives. Early on, I decided that a woman's story was to be accepted if she felt she was being psychologically and/or physically battered by her man. Although there were many women who wished to tell of being battered by their fathers, children, or grandchildren, they were only included if they were also being battered by their current or past husbands or lovers. I listened for incidents of coercive abuse. After I had identified the battering cycle, I relistened to the tapes for confirmation. In every case, the woman's self-definition was accurate. Battered women themselves are the best judges of whether or not they are being battered. I soon learned that if a woman has reason to suspect she is being battered, she probably is. If she errs in her judgment at all, it is in denying or minimizing the battering relationship. Battered women rarely exaggerate.

Defining battering also has caused problems for others dealing with the syndrome. The primary definition most researchers have used is physical violence resulting in bodily injury. Physical violence also has been the accepted research standard in the area of child abuse. I could not, however, ignore the pleas of battered women who insisted that psychological abuse was often more harmful than the physical. Thus, I began to collect data on both physical and psychological coerciveness. I found that both forms of violence exist in battering couples and they cannot be separated, despite the difficulty in documentation. It is relatively easy to count black eyes and broken ribs and assign severity ratings according to medical standards. To measure psychological abuse, the severity must be estimated with both the frequency with which it occurs and the subjective impact it has upon the woman. Most of the women in this project describe incidents involving psychological humiliation and verbal harassment as their worst battering experiences, whether or not they had been physically abused. Furthermore, the threat of physical violence was always present: each believed the batterer was capable of killing her or himself. When using this expanded definition of battering behavior as both physical and psychological, the previously invisible battered woman becomes much more identifiable. Thus, the definition used in this research for battered women is as follows:

A battered woman is a woman who is repeatedly subjected to any forceful physical or psychological behavior by a man in order to coerce her to do something he wants her to do without any concern for her rights. Battered women include wives or women in any form of intimate relationships with men. Furthermore, in order to be classified as a battered woman, the couple must go through the battering cycle at least twice. Any woman may find herself in an abusive relationship with a man once. If it occurs a second time, and she remains in the situation, she is defined as a battered woman.

Throughout this book at times, I have substituted the word "wives" for "women" and "husbands" for "men" in the interest of readability, although the battering relationship exists outside of marriage, too. However, it is important to note that battering relationships are more frequent among married couples. The marriage license in our society also seems to serve as a license to violence.

I think this research has raised more questions for me than it has answered. As a trained researcher, I felt uneasy about stating some of my conclusions in this book. They seemed too tentative to write down in the positive manner which I have used. Yet they are confirmed repeatedly by all the available data so far. Furthermore, once the psychological theories are understood by the victims, offenders, and helpers, then effective means of stopping the battering can be implemented. Our culture believes that strong individuals can overcome their circumstances. We retain an illusion that we work against our own probabilities, and if we are good enough we have a chance successfully to overcome the odds against us. Thus, when battered women lose by continuing to be victimized, we all blame it on their inadequacies and go on believing there is a right way but we just have not found it yet. My conclusions shatter this comforting yet false belief. Understanding the phenomenon of wife abuse is murky, at best. But it is clear that psychosocial factors bind a battered woman to her batterer just as strongly as "miracle glues" bind inanimate substances. Battered women are victims and it is from that perspective I tell their stories.

I have divided the book into three parts. The first deals with the description of the sample and refutation of the stereotyped myths that have prevented our seeing the battered woman as a victim. It presents in detail the psychosocial theory of learned helplessness as it applies to battered women, a theoretical construct that I have deduced from these interviews. My second theoretical construct, the cycle theory of violence, is presented in Chapter 3. Together, these three chapters formulate the psychological perspective for viewing the battered woman as a victim.

In Part II of the book, I attempt to define the various coercive techniques reported by these battered women. These include physical, sexual, and economic abuse, as well as social battering and disruption through family discord. This is the section in which the women tell their own stories. They have been edited to protect the women's anonymity, but the details of each story are real. This is important to remember as you read these stories, because some of the violence is so bizarre you may wish to believe it did not happen.

Part III examines the legal, medical, psychological, and other services that have continued to keep battered women as victims. On a more hopeful note, I try to indicate what services the battered women themselves say would be more helpful. The final chapter attempts to look toward a society that could eliminate such violence among its citizens.

I am aware that this book is written from a feminist vision. It is a picture of what happens in a domestic violent act from the perspective of only one of the two parties. The men do not have equal rebuttal time. Rather, I view women as victims in order to understand what the toll of such domestic violence is like for them. Unfortunately, in doing so I tend to place all men in an especially negative light, instead of just those men who do commit such crimes. Perhaps when more is known about batterers, we will need to view them also as victims. Certainly those whom I have known did not commit their crimes without severe psychological distress. They, too, are caught in a bind placed upon them by their socialized need to maintain dominance. It is my plea that you, the reader, do not get defensive in reading these women's stories—but do get angry. Let your anger spur you on to some kind of positive action to remedy the injustices committed against such women. If both men and women take collective action, we cannot fail to change our society for the better.

There were many people who were essential in assisting me in writing this book. Without the love and support of my late husband, Morton Flax, I could not have been free to create. His ability to give both the intimacy and the space I needed taught me that it can be done. From him and many of my male friends, I have learned that the men's revolution which will correspond to the women's movement has begun. I hope that our children, Michael, Karen, Jeffrey, Wendy, Douglas, and Stacey, will reap its many benefits. I especially thank Mike and Karen for sharing Mom with the book.

I also want to thank my editorial assistant, Bonnie Downing, for her friendship, organizational skill, ability to keep me meeting deadlines, and extraordinary competence. Many a day, Bonnie's good cheer and good sense kept me on task. I have had several typists who have worked on the manuscript. Shirley Downs put her incredible skill into making it look like a book. Vickey Talbert and Carol Casperson diligently typed earlier versions. Special thanks go to Karen Schreiber for beginning together and to my interviewers, Diana Huston, Carol Casperson, Sally Wilson, Lorraine Hagar, Gayle Costello, Madeline Millensifer, Sharon Morikawa, and Mickey Gudet. Mary Yost, my literary agent, must be credited for always believing in me. Her early support was invaluable. And special acknowledgments go to Kitty Benedict, my former editor at Harper & Row, and Elisabeth Jakab, who inherited me when Kitty went elsewhere. Elisabeth's keen sensitivity to women's issues and superb editorial skill have made it a joy to work with her.

Anonymous thanks must go to all the helpers who have shared their concerns with me as I traveled through this country and England. They helped shape this work. And finally, I must thank all the battered women who have been courageous enough to share their stories. Without them, this book could not have been written.

Prologue
The Story of Anne

The following story of a battered woman comes from my interviews with such women in my psychotherapy practice. The story has been edited and certain details have been changed to protect the woman's anonymity.

The reason I'm telling you this story is to help other girls so that they don't make the kind of mistake I did, because I never dreamed in a million years that *I* would.

I was married in 1970 on my eighteenth birthday, and I thought I was very much in love. I had known my husband for about nine months. My mother agreed with anything I wanted to do; but my dad was against my getting married. My husband's father worked for my dad, so that kind of made it touchy, too.

The first year that we were married, we got along really well and did a lot of things together. I had no idea that he was physically violent until about six months into our marriage. Before we were married, he had threatened to burn down my house and kidnap me if I didn't marry him. He also threatened to kill my parents. In a way I believed him, and in a way I didn't. I knew he was capable of real cruelties, but I never thought that he would inflict them upon me. The first time I realized he would was one night when one of my girl friends called, who he knew didn't like him. She wanted to go out to lunch and go shopping. Making my own decision, I said that was just fine. Later, I told him who it was and what I had said, and we got into a violent argument, which ended up with him throwing me across the room. He didn't do that much physical damage; I mean, he bruised me, but I think my ego was hurt more than anything. I threatened him: "Never again will you do this to me!" and he swore up and down that he never would. Thinking about all this, it's something that I did suppress in my memory. It's hard to dig it all up, although there are episodes that will always be in my mind.

He turned out to be an alcoholic, and he didn't work. He'd drink all day and smoke dope while I supported him. Good reason for leaving, huh? Anyway, one morning I wanted him to take me to work. He'd been out real late carousing around, and he just didn't want to. I reminded him that he had said he would take me to work, and I got mad. I'd really try to hang on to my patience and my tolerance until there was just nothing left but to get mad. Then the same thing happened. He gave me a really mean, nasty look, and slammed me against the wall.

I can remember a couple of other times where I would wear a short-sleeved dress to work, and people would say, "What's that big bruise on your arm, Anne?" I was real defensive and nervous about it. A couple of guys who knew me pretty well asked, "Did Doug do that to you?" and I would say, "No, no, no." I'd deny everything.

I had not told my parents or his parents what was going on. Anyway, this one particular time, I called my mom and asked her to take me to work because I could see that he was stronger than I was and that there was no use arguing with him. I had a bloody nose and I was crying, so my mom wanted to know what had happened. I finally told her that Doug had done it. Of course, her little girl is her pride and joy, and she was hurt. So she went up and talked to him. He was still hung over and he tried to knock her down the stairs. She was really shocked and had gotten hurt in the incident, but neither of us told my dad about it. He'd been against the marriage from the start. It was my mother who allowed me to get married. After Doug realized what he had done, he calmed down and apologized. As usual, he talked his way out of it and smoothed everything over.

At this time, we were living in Ohio, but Doug and I had always talked about moving to California, so I compromised and agreed to go back to California with him. I didn't have a job there, and I was depending completely on my dad's connections in his business to pull me through. I'm hesitating here because I can remember a few other times that he had hurt me, but it's so far down in my memory that it just comes up every once in a while. Sometimes when I try to recall things, I can't, but the times in San Francisco I remember really well.

There was a long period of time when he didn't hurt me. When we first got to California, I always was the one that had to go out and get things taken care of and make money and have the world look better for Doug. That was a pretty rough way to grow up. He started drinking in Ohio, but it got really bad in California. The more he drank, the more violent he got.

A few times I would slug him back, but I learned that he could hit harder and it was no use because he would use it as an excuse to hurt me by saying, "Oh, you hit me first." I would "nag" him (as he called it) to straighten up and try to do something with himself. I meant well, but this would also make him very violent. He wouldn't let me associate with any of my friends that he didn't like. He would threaten to hurt me if I did. If I'd write letters, he'd want to read them before I mailed them to make sure I wasn't blabbing that he was hurting me. He used the threat of hurting me physically more and more to get me to stay. At one point, he took his belt to me and put welts on me. Luckily, I had a friend at work whom I could talk to. He was a teacher and was married, so he had a way with kids, me being the kid. I showed him the welts and started crying, and he told me I was really crazy for sticking around. He said he was very tempted to stick me on a plane back to Ohio that very minute; but, I don't know, once I started something, I wanted to give it every effort I could before I'd give up.

I did go back home by myself on a couple of vacations, thinking things would work out once I got back. I went to visit my sister and came back with all sorts of enthusiasm, self-will, and, you know, "I'm going to do what I want. Nobody is going to think for me." Doug noticed that I started telling him no, and told him to stop doing my thinking for me.

Once a friend bought me a really pretty sweater, and he literally ripped it off of me while I screamed. As usual, he was drunk. I don't remember what the argument was about, but I remember what happened. As before, he threw me on the hard wood floor and up against the wall. At that point, after having my clothes ripped off and hearing threats on me and my family's lives, I decided to run out the door. He grabbed me, stuck me in the shower, and started dousing me with cold water. It was such a shock that I cried hysterically. The neighbors probably couldn't imagine what was going on, all this screaming, all this crying. One of them called the police. When the next thing he did was to turn on the hot water, I ran out of the room, out of our apartment, and went flying down the stairs, naked and dripping wet. All of the neighbors were out of their apartments, looking up at our apartment, wondering what in hell was going on.

At this point, you're probably saying, "Oh, that poor girl." It's hard to laugh about. It's something I think about once in a while, but I learned my lesson. That's all I could do was to learn from it and decide not to go through that again. Anyway, the police came. There was a complaint filed. They wanted to make sure I was O.K. What could I say? I said, "Sure, I'm fine," because I knew if I didn't, he would probably hurt me again.

At this point, I was completely fed up, and I could see no future for this marriage. Life was too beautiful to go on in this depression, this way of life. I knew there were a lot of nicer people out there. I talked to his parents and to my parents without his knowing it. I told them, with lots of tears, the whole story. It was pretty traumatic for them, and my mom told me that they'd send me a plane ticket. I was seriously considering leaving.

Communication between Doug and me was pretty bad. I couldn't tell him the way I felt, because if I did, he would threaten to kill me. He had taken a gun to me before and told me that if I didn't straighten up, this was going to be it. The time that I went flying out of the apartment, I was really, really scared, but afterward he acted like "You thought I was going to kill you? Oh, you're crazy. Where did you ever get an idea like that?" You know, playing Mr. Innocent. I know I've made mistakes, too. Between the ages of eighteen and twenty-two, I went through a lot of changes, and I can see where I made the mistake of being a little girl in my marriage. He treated me like one by not letting me have my name on the checking account, which had my money in it, and giving me a two-dollar-a-week allowance.

Sex with my husband was more like rape, if you can imagine rape by your husband. I did not enjoy sex with him. He did some really weird things to me. Like in the middle of the night, he held me down and cut off all my pubic hair. I know some men dig that, a hairless pubic area, but to forcefully hold somebody down is strange. He would also want me to perform sexual services such as oral intercourse, which I just despise. He tried sometimes to drag me out on the flat roof on a cold night to make love, while I cried and kept saying no. My parents, my mom especially, gave me that whole Victorian picture of sex, but I had feelings and was an affectionate person. It was just that he totally turned me off. He even bought me a vibrator, but that didn't do anything for me except make me mad.

Toward the end of our marriage, he wanted me to have an affair with somebody else; but I wasn't raised that way, and I just couldn't do that. I had lots of chances, but I couldn't. About a year ago, he brought one of his pool-hall friends home with him and asked him to stay overnight. I could tell that this guy was attracted to me, and I was scared. While Doug was out, his friend started putting the moves on me, kissing me, and so on. He held me down and started unzipping my pants. I kept saying, "No, please don't do that," and finally I said, "Look, you're hurting me!" At that point, my husband had been listening at the door, and he came inside and told this guy to leave.

Later that night, he wanted to make love to me, and he kept wanting to repeat what this guy had done to me because it turned him on. He really made me feel like a piece of meat, like a receptacle. My husband had told me that all a girl was was a servant who could not think, a receptacle, a piece of meat.

The next day I wasn't feeling very well, so I stayed home. I thought over what had gone on the night before while I sat there making macramé Christmas presents. I sat there by myself saying, "Wow, you know, this is unreal. I can't believe all this has happened. I don't have to put up with this. I'm not that type of person." So the following day, I called my friend at work, "my father confessor," and told him what had been going on. He had been just wonderful to me this whole time and kept my faith in mankind from becoming pretty sour. This time he told me, "Anne, you're a fool. You're blind in one eye. You can't see what's going on. You'd better take your plane ticket and get going home." That really shook me up, and I thought back to all the nights that I had taken such shit, such physical and psychological damage, and I knew that this couldn't go on any longer. I couldn't live like this for the rest of my life, in constant fear that my husband would fly off the handle and start throwing me around for who knows what. I really respected my friend's opinions, so I said, "Sure, O.K., I'll come down to meet you at work and I'll leave."

It was a hard decision that I had had trouble making for a long time. Pride got in my way, and I hadn't wanted my parents to know what was going on. I was also afraid that if I left him and told my parents what was going on, later on I might be still so in love that I might go back to him, and he would really hurt me if he knew I had told anyone what was going on.

A little dog that I have was also one of the things that had kept me from leaving, believe it or not. One time when I went up to see my sister, he kept my dog hostage. Another thing which kept me from leaving were my possessions, which filled the house. Everything was mine. My parents gave me everything. I knew how much everything was worth, and it was hard for me to part with it.

But all of a sudden, as I looked around the house, I realized that everything was breakable except me, everything was replaceable except me. So I took my little dog, and I left. It was raining outside. It was December. My heart was pounding, and, oh, my adrenalin must have been going crazy. As I was going out, I saw my husband and his friend coming toward the apartment, but they didn't see me, so I turned and went the other way. I walked in the rain with my dog. My heart was pounding. All the way downtown, I took all of the side streets for fear that he would come after me. As I turned each corner, I was really, really terrified. I just couldn't believe what was happening, and I thought back to seeing my husband and his friend walking and talking in the rain.

Doug had said something before about how I should have an affair with whoever turned me on, and how I should work in a massage parlor. He had even talked about how much money I could get if I wanted to become a call girl. I put two and two together and figured that he was taking money to have his friend sleep with me.

Another thing about Doug is that he is bisexual. I knew that he had had homosexual experiences before we were married, but I thought that he would change. When we lived in San Francisco, one of my best friends asked if I would make my husband quit pinching his rear. I guess I just didn't want to believe that it was really happening.

Before I left, I had told him that I was going to leave if

things didn't get better, and he threatened me with how easy it would be for him to hire someone to kill me and my parents. He said that he had somebody following me, and that he was going to call the president of my father's company to tell him horrible things about my dad. One of the first steps I had taken in making my getaway (I know I probably sound like a prison escapee, but that's just about how I felt) was to tell him to go ahead and call my father's boss. He had never even talked to my dad because he was so scared of him. He couldn't believe I had called his bluff, and he just laughed.

I was really afraid that he was going to come after me, the whole way downtown, where I was going to meet my friend at work. He drove me over to a girl friend's house, where I stayed overnight, wondering the whole time, When is he going to come for me? I was really, really scared, just terrified. The next morning, I flew back home to Ohio with my dog. During a layover between connections, I hid in the bathroom in the airport, thinking that somebody might be after me.

I was really relieved to be back with my parents. They were really very, very happy to see me, and, wow, I knew how much they loved me. I just can't tell you in words the fear that was instilled in me because of the beatings and physical abuse, and I knew my dad would never even touch my mom and never has, because he's a gentleman. My parents are both very sweet people, who never spanked me when I was a child, I never had to be, because that's the way they brought me up. I lived with my parents for ten months after I had left my husband, before I moved here.

Right now, I am living by myself and am learning to really enjoy it. I am much happier now than I was when I was married, as many of my friends who have known me over the years have noticed and commented on. I am really enjoying school, studying to be an art major. It will probably take a while for my wounds to heal, but I really have come a long way through the support of my parents and friends.

I do know that I suffered more psychological damage than physical. One time I had the flu and was really sick, and he still made me drive through a blizzard up to Cheyenne, Wyoming. I was really scared, because the roads were icy and we didn't have snow tires. I was amazed to find out what extremes I would go to when he would force me to in these situations. Another time, when we were coming back from the grocery store, he had the grocery cart trailing behind him up the three flights of stairs to where we lived. When the mayonnaise broke, he got so mad that he threw the cart all the way down the stairs, spilling the groceries all over, and he made me clean it up. It was very humiliating, with everyone looking at me, like "Who is this madman?"

As for psychological effects, I'm afraid of men, and if I see any type of temper in a man that denotes physical violence, my first reaction is to cringe, and then I won't have anything to do with him. I am more aware of what men are out to get from me and am never sure if I can distinguish who the "nice guys" are. I usually don't talk to too many people about having been battered, because I still have some problems with self-esteem when I think that I actually put up with so much abuse. I still don't feel that I measure up sometimes; and I have a low opinion of myself, probably because I look at too many people as authority figures. I think it will take me a while to really build up my self-image. The child part in me was very frightened by my husband's violence. I was also kept from "growing up" because he did all of my thinking for me. Even though I had a job and had to handle a lot of important things which he wouldn't, I can see where he really retarded my maturing.

My mother is also having some psychological effects from my battering incidents, because she blames herself for giving consent for me to marry Doug against my father's wishes. Since I've always been friends with my mom, I finally told her everything that happened, which I realize now maybe I shouldn't have done. It hurts her to think that she allowed this to happen, and I am dealing with her guilt problem now by telling her that I probably would have gotten married anyway, whether she had let me or not. My father adds to her guilt feelings, and I don't think he will ever forgive her.

I still get scared a lot of times. Not that I live in constant fear of my ex-husband, but the first couple of months of living on my own were really rough. When I saw a black Volkswagen with a Rolls-Royce front, like the one Doug had, I literally froze and thought, This is it, or when does he show up? For a long time after I had moved back home, I was not allowed to answer the phone, but my parents had security patrol and my dad was a sharpshooting trapshooter, who had also taught me, so I gradually got braver and realized how ridiculous it all was. But still, Doug himself has admitted that he's crazy, and I just never knew what he might do. Like I said, the first couple of months were rough, and I had many depressions, living alone with my fears, memories, and self-rejection.

I have talked to Doug on the phone since I left him. He called and said that he had lost his job, is still drinking, and is seventy pounds overweight. It's really too bad, you know. He really is, believe it or not, a very smart person, with an I.Q. of 152. He always talked about plans and goals that made a lot of sense to me, and I believed him. I think he really could have done well if he had tried, but he thought the whole world was against him. I sometimes felt that it was a compliment to be considered his friend, but there was the other side of Doug, too. All of the things I've been talking about really did happen. When he got drunk and showed his temper, his mean, ugly side would surface, and I just couldn't believe that someone could be like that.

I just didn't want to believe that any of these things I've been talking about really happened. A lot of my problem was that I kept thinking that things would change and get better. From listening back over my story, I know it sounds unreal that anybody would put up with all the things that I did, but it wasn't for quite a while before I realized how stupid it was to hope for a change for the better.

PART I

Psychology of the Battered Woman

Introduction

Wife abuse has an ancient history. Susan Brownmiller's research on the history of rape provides a description of the trade-offs women historically made to obtain economic and physical security. In her book *Against Our Will,* Brownmiller suggests that women preferred to cope with one man's arbitrary discipline rather than be ravaged by many men, and that from Biblical days women have traded freedom for security by mating with one man to protect themselves from the assaults of many men. Women were actually purchased and became the legal property of men. Men believed it was their duty to defend their women, but they also believed they had a right to discipline their "property" as they saw fit. Man's physical and economic strength reinforced woman's acceptance of this "right of discipline." Terry Davidson, in a chapter in *Battered Women: A Psychosociological Study of Domestic Violence,* edited by Maria Roy, claims that prior to the creation of the Bible, women were not treated this way; rather, women were worshiped as the Goddesses of Life.

In those cultures where women were sovereign in religious

and other matters, they did not batter men. Men and women gave pleasure to each other and believed that ancestral spirits fathered their children. Davidson states that once men realized the significance of their participation in the creation of life, things began to change. Man became the patriarch in religious and other matters and a repressive mode of living ensued, resulting in harsh cultural attitudes toward women. There are many, myself included, who believe that we are entering into a new social order which will overthrow patriarchy and replace it with an egalitarian society. Probably the reason the women's movement has elicited such great fear is that it is correctly perceived as the beginning of this revolution. A cornerstone, then, of the creation of a new egalitarian social order would be to reverse the tides of violence committed against women.

Today, many men still believe their rights to rule their women are primary. This notion has been supported not only by religion but by the law, beginning with the century-old right of a husband to beat his wife with a stick "no thicker than his thumb." Early in the nineteenth century, English and American courts acknowledged wife beating as a husband's right. This ruling was later modified to suggest noninterference or "benign neglect" in marital fighting, unless the violence was excessive.

Although these laws have not been enforced for a while, the attitudes which permitted them to be written in the first place still exist. In some states the "stick rule" remained on the books until quite recently. Many states still have an informal stick rule they follow in deciding whether or not to arrest and prosecute an offender by counting the number of stitches the victim's wounds need. Batterers will cite the right to discipline their wives as justification for their abusive behavior. One man in New York City reportedly told a woman judge sentencing him to prison for assaulting his pregnant wife that he was astounded that the judge thought she could interfere in the way he ran his home. In a recent television documentary, a batterer asserted that anytime his wife did not behave, he had the right to beat her up. Another batterer in a different film also claimed that it was his right to discipline his wife in any way he saw fit. If she did something minor, he claimed, then he would beat her up a little. If she did something that he really did not like, then he would beat her up a lot. The women interviewed in my study all stated that their men felt it was their right to discipline them. Most of these women did not question this "right." They were socialized to believe that they must be doing something wrong if their men were constantly beating them.

Wife beating has been considered an acceptable resolution to marital disagreements as long as the violence is confined to the home. Party jokes such as "Hey, Jack, have you beaten your wife lately?" or, "Where did Helen get her black eye?" or, "Are you beating her again, Jim?" demonstrate these attitudes. A recent social psychology experiment was conducted by psychologists Darryl and Sandra Bem to see whether strangers would come to the assistance of a woman who was being physically and verbally abused by a man outside on a sidewalk. Passersby at different times saw two men in an argument, two women in an argument, and a man and a woman in an argument. The severity of the verbal and physical activity was the same in all three instances. The strangers intervened with the two women and the two men far more often than with the man and the woman. When questioned about their behavior, the strangers said they did not feel they had the right to interfere in a marital dispute. The assumption was that if a man and a woman are arguing in public they must be married, and this gives the man license to abuse the woman.

One woman in my study related a similar violent incident. She reported for work after suffering a severe physical beating by her husband the night before. Her face was bruised, swollen, and disfigured. No one at work asked her how she had been injured, not did she volunteer any information. A compassionate co-worker brought her some soup for lunch, as it was obvious that she could not open her lips wide enough to chew anything substantial. Then her husband arrived at the office to demand that she return home with him. She did not wish to go, as she was afraid that he would injure her further. In front of two co-workers, her husband twisted her arm behind her back and dragged her out of the office. The co-workers did not interfere. Nor did they call the police or anyone else to make sure that she was not in danger. When this story was told to several other people, they all stated that they could understand why the co-workers did not intervene. It was a marital dispute and thus off limits, despite the criminal nature of the batterer's behavior.

In my research, I have attempted to look at battered women as victims of battering behavior rather than as the causes of the violence. Although these women often did or said things to make the batterer angry, it was obvious that he would have beaten her anyway. Something in her behavior told him that she accepted his right to discipline her through violence. I label her a victim because I believe that society, through its definition of the woman's role, has socialized her into believing she had no choice but to be such a victim. Why some women reject this cultural norm while others fall prey to it is partially explained by the psychological theories I put forth here. First, however, it is necessary to understand the process of victimization.

Psychologist William Ryan originally applied the term "blaming the victim" to those experiencing racial discrimination. In his book *Blaming the Victim,* he discussed how prejudicial attitudes affected both the perpetrator and the victim of discrimination, preventing those who held them from dealing adequately with the situations. Rather, these attitudes serve to maintain the status quo and prevent the kind of open dialogue necessary to eliminate racial prejudice. They also keep the victim in a clearly prescribed role bounded by the stereotypical myths and allow the bigots to maintain their misconceptions.

So, too, is the situation for all women who have been victims of violence committed by men against them, individually or collectively. By perpetuating the belief that it is rational to blame the victim for her abuse, we ultimately excuse men for the crime. According to research being conducted at the University of Colorado by Dr. Margie Leidig, such prejudicial myths exist in seven areas of violence against women: (1) battering women, (2) rape, (3) girl child incest, (4) pornography, (5) prostitution, (6) sexual harassment on the job, and (7) sexual harassment between client and professional (including doctors, therapists, lawyers, and so on).

Blaming women for causing men to batter them has resulted in their shame, embarrassment, denial, and further loss of self-esteem. The batterer feels justified in his violent behavior because society says it is really the woman's fault, not his. It perpetuates his notion that he should beat her because she did something to make him angry. What gets lost in this victim precipitation ideology is the fact that such violence is not acceptable behavior. Although some researchers have tried to understand the offender's behavior by studying the possible provocative behavior of the victim, this research leads up blind alleys and simply encourages continuance of such crimes through its rationalization. The violence will only cease when every person, man or woman, stops defensively rationalizing and begins to understand just how such acts come about in our culture and why they continue.

From the beginning of my research, it seemed to me that these women were physically and psychologically abused by men and then kept in their place by a society that was indifferent to their plight. Thus, they were both beaten and then blamed for not ending their beatings. Told they have the freedom to leave a violent situation, they are blamed for the destruction of their family life. Free to live alone, they cannot expect to earn equal pay for equal work. Encouraged to express their feelings, they are beaten when they express anger. They have the same inalienable right to the pursuit of individual happiness as men do, but they must make sure their men's and children's rights are met first. They are blamed for not seeking help, yet when they do, they are advised to go home and stop the inappropriate behavior which causes their men to hurt them. Not only are they responsible for their own beatings, they also must assume responsibility for their batterer's mental health. If they were only better persons, the litany goes, they would find a way to prevent their own victimization. Hence, there is a need to examine the stereotypical myths that prevent real understanding of this problem.

As I began to interview battered women, I noted how deeply affected they were by society's dictum that they were to blame for what was happening to them and therefore should be able to stop it. This further lowered their self-esteem, which had already been lowered enough by their experiences. It helped to immobilize them rather than spur them on to change their situations. The question "Why do battered women remain in these relationships?" has continually been asked. As the epidemiological nature of the problem became evident, I began to realize that I needed to look for psychosocial causation rather than to individual psychopathology. The phenomenon was too widespread. The learned helplessness phenomenon seemed a logical fit. I was struck by the similarities I saw in the battered women's descriptions as compared to the experimental victims of learned helplessness described in Chapter 2. The women's passivity and inability to leave a situation even when shown the way out were strikingly similar to that of the experimental dogs discussed in that chapter. It is entirely possible that sex-role socialization in young children leaves women vulnerable to becoming victims of men who are socialized into committing violence against them. Why one woman is battered and another not is still not clear. Perhaps the amount and kind of sex-role stereotyping that existed in her family of origin is an explanation. Pairing up with a batterer must be considered *purely accidental* if *one out of two women* will be battered in their lifetimes. Why one man batters his woman while another finds a more acceptable alternative is also still a puzzle. From the social-learning theoretical perspective, I would suspect that the answers lie in better understanding of how violent behavior is learned and passed down from one generation to another. Thus, the second chapter, on psychosocial theories, must be read as a beginning, a framework on which further research can be constructed.

The maintenance of violent behavior, once it occurs, also became an imperative issue/question in this research. While I knew it did not continue because either the men or the women liked it, the specifics of why a woman stayed in the relationship needed response. Discovery of the cycle theory of violence came through deduction from the empirical evidence. It is presented in Chapter 3 as an important and practical construct. Much of my treatment alternatives are based on making clear the reinforcements for battering relationships. Once the spurious nature of its short-term rewards are made more widely known, I believe women will no longer continue to be victimized. Let us hope, then, that such interpersonal violence will become a thing of the past.

1

Myths and Reality

The battering of women, like other crimes of violence against women, has been shrouded in myths. All of the myths have perpetuated the mistaken notion that the victim has precipitated her own assault. Some of them served as a protection against embarrassment. Others were created to protect rescuers from their own discouragement when they were unsuccessful in stopping the brutality. It is important to refute all the myths surrounding battered women in order to understand fully why battering happens, how it affects people, and how it can be stopped.

The battered woman is pictured by most people as a small, fragile, haggard person who might once have been pretty. She has several small children, no job skills, and is economically dependent on her husband. It is frequently assumed she is poor and from a minority group. She is accustomed to living in violence, and her fearfulness and passivity are emphasized above all. Although some battered women do fit this description, research proves it to be a false stereotype.

Most battered women are from middle-class and higher-income homes where the power of their wealth is in the hands of their husbands. Many of them are large women who could attempt to defend themselves physically. Not all of them have children; those who do do not necessarily have them in any particular age group. Although some battered women are jobless, many more are highly competent workers and successful career women. They include doctors, lawyers, corporation executives, nurses, secretaries, full-time homemakers, and others. Battered women are found in all age groups, races, ethnic and religious groups, educational levels, and socioeconomic groups. Who are the battered women? If you are a woman, there is a 50 percent chance it could be you!

MYTH NO. 1: THE BATTERED WOMAN SYNDROME AFFECTS ONLY A SMALL PERCENTAGE OF THE POPULATION.

Like rape, the battering of American women is a seriously underreported crime. Data on wife beating are difficult to obtain because battering generally occurs at night, in the home, without witnesses. The statistics on battered women are buried in the records of family domestic disturbance calls to police departments, in emergency room records in hospitals, and in the records of social service agencies, private psychologists, and counselors. The United States Commission on Civil Rights recently completed an investigation which supports the suspicion that police records on battered women are inaccurately low owing to poor police reporting techniques. My personal estimate is that only one in ten women report battering assaults.

Marjory Fields, a New York City attorney who specializes in battered women, reports that of 500 women represented in divorce actions in Brooklyn in 1976, 57.4 percent complained of physical assaults by their husbands. They had suffered these assaults for approximately four years prior to seeking the divorce. Of 600 divorcing wives in Cleveland, according to a study by Levinger, 36.8 percent reported physical abuse by their husbands. The first epidemiological study of battered women undertaken in this country, by sociologists Murray Straus, Richard Gelles, and Susan Steinmetz, reported that a physical assault occurred in 28 percent of all American homes during 1976. This statistic, nearly one third of all families, is certainly evidence that the battered woman problem is a widespread one.

MYTH NO. 2: BATTERED WOMEN ARE MASOCHISTIC.

The prevailing belief has always been that only women who "liked it and deserved it" were beaten. In a study of battered wives as recently as twenty years ago, it was suggested that beatings are solicited by women who suffer from negative personality characteristics, including masochism. "Good wives" were taught that the way to stop assaults was to examine their behavior and try to change it to please men: to be less provocative, less aggressive, and less frigid. There was no suggestion that provocation might occur from other than masochistic reasons, that aggressiveness might be an attempt to ward off further assault, and that frigidity might be a very natural result of subjection to severe physical and psychological pain. The burden of guilt for battering has fallen on the woman, and the violent behavior of the male has been perpetuated. The myth of the masochistic woman is a favorite of all who endeavor to understand the battered woman. No matter how sympathetic people may be, they frequently come to the conclusion that the reason a battered woman remains in such a relationship is that she is masochistic. By masochism, it is meant that she experiences some pleasure, often akin to sexual pleasure, through being beaten by the man she loves. Because this has been such a prevailing stereotype, many battered women begin to wonder if they are indeed masochistic.

MYTH NO. 3: BATTERED WOMEN ARE CRAZY.

This myth is related to the masochism myth in that it places the blame for the battering on the woman's negative personality characteristics. Battered women's survival behaviors have often earned them the misdiagnosis of being crazy. Unusual actions which may help them to survive in the battering relationship have been taken out of context by unenlightened medical and mental health workers. Several of the women in this sample reported being hospitalized for schizophrenia, paranoia, and severe depression. One woman who told of hearing voices which told her to kill her husband had received numerous electroshock therapy treatments. But just listening to her describe her husband's brutal treatment made her hallucination very understandable. Many women reported being given heavy doses of anti-psychotic medications by doctors who were responding to their overt symptoms rather than attempting to understand their family situations. It is not clear whether these women were overtly psychotic at the time of their reported diagnoses. As a clinical psychologist, I can state that at the time I interviewed these women, there was insufficient evidence of such disorders. One woman was interviewed shortly after being released from a state hospital. Arrangements had been made for her to go to a temporary shelter, legal assistance was provided to initiate divorce proceedings, and her batterer was refused knowledge of her whereabouts. Her mental health improved markedly within days. I wonder how many other women who have been mislabeled as mentally ill were really attempting to cope with a batterer. After listening to their stories, I can only applaud their strength in retaining their sanity.

MYTH NO. 4: MIDDLE-CLASS WOMEN DO NOT GET BATTERED AS FREQUENTLY OR AS VIOLENTLY AS DO POORER WOMEN.

Most previously recorded statistics of battering have come from lower-class families. However, lower-class women are more likely to come in contact with community agencies and so their problems are more visible. Middle- and upper-class women do not want to make their batterings public. They fear social embarrassment and harming their husbands' careers. Many also believe the respect in which their husbands are held in the community will cast doubt upon the credibility of their battering stories. The recent public focus on battered women has brought many of these middle- and upper-class women out of hiding. The publicity being given the problem is creating a climate in which they think they will finally be believed. They report an overwhelming sense of relief once they have told their stories and find that others will now believe them.

MYTH NO. 5: MINORITY-GROUP WOMEN ARE BATTERED MORE FREQUENTLY THAN ANGLOS.

The battered women interviewed in this study were Hispanic, native American, black, Asian, and Pacific American, as well as Anglo. Although each grew up in a culture with different values and different attitudes about male and female roles, none of them was able to make any impact on the kind of violence she experienced. Anglo and minority women alike told similar battering stories and experienced similar embarrassment, guilt, and the inability to halt their men's assaults. Minority women, however, spoke of having even fewer resources than Anglos to turn to for assistance.

MYTH NO. 6: RELIGIOUS BELIEFS WILL PREVENT BATTERING.

The Catholic, Protestant, Mormon, Jewish, Eastern, and other religious women in this study all indicated that their religious beliefs did not protect them from their assaultive men. Most of the women in my study held religious beliefs. For some, belief in a deity helped them endure their suffering, offering comfort and solace. Sometimes attending services was the only safe outside contact they had. However, other women indicated they no longer practiced their religion, because giving it up eliminated a point of conflict with their batterer. Still others gave up their religion in disillusionment, feeling that a just and merciful God would not have let them suffer so. Others reported losing faith after having unsuccessfully sought help from a religious or spiritual leader.

Some women told stories in which their religious adviser suggested they pray for guidance, become better women, and go home and help their husbands "become more spiritual and find the Lord." Needless to say, these women did not have time to wait for their husbands to "find the Lord" while they continued to receive brutal beatings. Other women joyfully told of humane religious advisers who understood their problems and helped them break out of their disastrous relationships.

MYTH NO. 7: BATTERED WOMEN ARE UNEDUCATED AND HAVE FEW JOB SKILLS.

The education level of the women interviewed ranged from fifth grade through completion of professional and doctoral degrees. They were homemakers, teachers, real estate agents, lawyers, psychologists, nurses, physicians, businesswomen, politicians, and successful corporation executives. Some did well at their jobs and some performed poorly. Although many were successful career women, they stated they would give up their careers if it would eliminate the battering in their relationships. Most had tried changing jobs or staying home without any effect on their husbands' behavior. Those women who chose to be homemakers tried heroically to keep their lives from falling apart: they struggled to make financial ends meet, kept family chaos at a minimum, and tried to smooth life for their batterer. Most of them sought status in their home lives rather than in their careers. Thus, their self-esteem was dependent on their ability to be good wives and homemakers and was not well integrated with their successful professional activities.

MYTH NO. 8: BATTERERS ARE VIOLENT IN ALL THEIR RELATIONSHIPS.

Based on the women in my study, I estimate that only about 20 percent of battered women live with men who are violent not only to them but also to anyone else who gets in their way. Unfortunately, this violent group of men has been the most studied. They tend to be poorer and to live outside the mainstream of society's norms. They often have fewer resources or skills with which to cope with the world. Most street crime is committed by such men. They also have the most contact with society's institutions and seem always to be in trouble with the police. They often subsist on welfare payments; their children have behavioral and learning problems in school; they use hospital clinics. Courts send them to treatment facilities in lieu of jail sentences. Because so much of our resources is spent in dealing with these people, it often seems that they are representative of all of the violence in our culture. When it comes to battered women, this is simply not true. Most men who batter their wives are generally not violent in other aspects of their lives.

MYTH NO. 9: BATTERERS ARE UNSUCCESSFUL AND LACK RESOURCES TO COPE WITH THE WORLD.

It has been suggested that men who feel less capable than their women resort to violence. Contrary findings were reported in England, where physicians, service professionals, and police had the highest incidence of wife beating. Most of the professionally successful volunteers in this study have similarly successful husbands. Among the affluent batters were physicians, attorneys, public officials, corporation executives, scientists, college professors, and salesmen. Many of these men donated a good deal of time and energy to community activities. Often they would be unable to maintain their high productivity level were it not for the support of their wives. In one town, the mayor's wife, whose layers of make-up concealed the serious bruises he had inflicted upon her, regularly assisted him with all his official duties. In some cases, previously successful men lost their effectiveness because of alcohol or emotional problems. Many men were reported as erratic in performance by the women. As a group, however, the batterers in this sample would be indistinguishable from any other group of men in terms of capability.

MYTH NO. 10: DRINKING CAUSES BATTERING BEHAVIOR.

Over half the battered women in this sample indicated a relationship between alcohol use and battering. Many tended to blame the battering incidents on their men's drinking. Upon further questioning, however, it became clear that the men beat them whether or not they had been drinking. But some association between drinking and battering cannot be denied. Exactly what it is is still not known. It does seem reasonable, however, to suggest that in many cases alcohol is blamed as the precipitating factor, whereas it is only a component in the battering relationship. But it is psychologically easier for the battered woman to blame the violence on the batterer's drunkenness. Often the men in this study drank as a way of calming their anxieties. Drinking seemed to give them a sense of power. Many of the women felt that if they could only get their men to stop drinking, the battering would cease. Unfortunately, it just did not happen.

The most violent physical abuse *was* suffered by women whose men were consistent drinkers. Much work still needs to be done on the association between drinking and battering. I strongly suspect that there are specific blood chemistry changes that occur under a generalized stress reaction such as battering. Furthermore, these may be the same chemicals that are found in the blood of alcoholics. It is entirely possible that fundamental changes in brain chemistry cause both cycles. It is hoped that as our scientific technology becomes more precise, we will be able to measure these chemical changes with more accuracy.

MYTH NO. 11: BATTERERS ARE PSYCHOPATHIC PERSONALITIES.

If batterers could be considered antisocial and psychopathic personalities, then individual psychopathology could be used to differentiate batterers from normal men. Unfortunately, it is not that simple. The batterers in this sample were reported to have many kinds of personality disturbances other than just being psychopathic. One trait they *do* have in common with diagnosed psychopaths is their extraordinary ability to use charm as a manipulative technique.

The women interviewed all described their batterers as having a dual personality, much like Dr. Jekyll and Mr. Hyde. The batterer can be either very, very good or very, very horrid. Furthermore, he can swing back and forth between the two characters with the smoothness of a con artist. But, unlike the psychopath, the batterer feels a sense of guilt and shame at his uncontrollable actions. If he were able to cease his violence, he would.

MYTH NO. 12: POLICE CAN PROTECT THE BATTERED WOMEN.

The women in this study manifestly do not believe this to be true. Only 10 percent ever called the police for help. Of these, most stated that the police were ineffective: when the police left, the assault was renewed with added vigor.

Sociologist Murray Straus, in his studies on violence in the family, labeled such assaults a crime and declared that were the violence to occur in any setting other than the home, it would warrant prosecution. He cites studies indicating that somewhere between 25 and 67 percent of all homicides occur within the family in all societies.

A recently completed study in Kansas City and Detroit indicates that in 80 percent of all homicides in those cities, the police had intervened from one to five times previously. Thus, homicide between man and woman is not a "crime of passion," but rather the end result of unchecked, long-standing violence.

MYTH NO. 13: THE BATTERER IS NOT A LOVING PARTNER.

This myth has spawned others, most particularly that of the masochistic wife. Women have been accused of loving the batterers' brutality rather than their kindness because it has been difficult for society to comprehend the loving behavior of batterers. But batterers are often described by their victims as fun-loving little boys when they are not being coercive. They are playful, attentive, sensitive, exciting, and affectionate to their women. The cycle theory of battering described later on explains how the batterers' loving behavior keeps these women in the battering relationship.

MYTH NO. 14: A WIFE BATTERER ALSO BEATS HIS CHILDREN.

This myth has some foundation in fact. In my sample, approximately one third of the batterers beat their children. These men were also suspected of seductive sexual behavior toward their daughters. In another third of the cases, battered women beat their children. Although the children of the final third were not physically abused, they suffered a more insidious form of child abuse because of living in a home where the fathers battered the mothers. Those women in my sample who had seen their fathers beat their mothers report psychological scars which never healed. Children whom I encountered while doing this study seemed to be undergoing similar traumas. The National Center for Child Abuse and Neglect has reported a higher percentage of men in battering relationships who also beat their children than those who do not. Their data show that when there is concurrent child abuse in these families, 70 percent is committed by the violent man.

MYTH NO. 15: ONCE A BATTERED WOMAN, ALWAYS A BATTERED WOMAN.

This myth is the reason why many people have not encouraged women to leave their battering relationships. They think she will only seek out another violent man. Though several of the women in this sample had a series of violent relationships, this pattern did not hold true for most of those interviewed. While they wanted another intimate relationship with a man, they were extremely careful not to choose another violent one. There was a low rate of remarriage for older women who had left battering relationships. Most of them had left a marriage by going against the advice of their families and friends. They preferred being single rather than trying to make the male-female relationship work again. Women who had received some beneficial intervention rarely remarried another batterer.

MYTH NO. 16: ONCE A BATTERER, ALWAYS A BATTERER.

If the psychosocial-learning theory of violent behavior is accurate, then batterers can be taught to relearn their aggressive responses. Assertion rather than aggression, negotiation rather than coercion, is the goal. My theoretical perspective, then, indicates that this myth of once a batterer, always a batterer is just that. The data have not yet been analyzed to prove it false.

MYTH NO. 17: LONG-STANDING BATTERING RELATIONSHIPS CAN CHANGE FOR THE BETTER.

Although everyone who believes in the positive nature of behavior change wants to believe this myth, my research has not shown it to be true. Relationships that have been maintained by the man having power over the woman are stubbornly resistant to an equal power-sharing arrangement. Thus, even with the best help available, these relationships do not become battering free. At best, the violent assaults are reduced in frequency and severity. Unassisted, they simply escalate to homicidal and suicidal proportions. The best hope for such couples is to terminate the relationship. There is a better chance that with another partner they can reorder the power structure and as equals can live in a nonviolent relationship.

MYTH NO. 18: BATTERED WOMEN DESERVE TO GET BEATEN.

The myth that battered women provoke their beatings by pushing their men beyond the breaking point is a popular one. Everyone can recount a story where the woman seemed to deserve what she got: she was too bossy, too insulting, too sloppy, too uppity, too angry, too obnoxious, too provocative, or too something else. In a culture where everyone takes sides between winners and losers, women who continuously get beaten are thought to deserve it. It is assumed that if only they would change their behavior, the batterer could regain his self-control. The stories of the women in this study indicate that batterers lose self-control because of their own internal reasons, not because of what the women did or did not do. Furthermore, philosophically this myth robs the men of responsibility for their own actions. No one could deserve the kind of brutality reported in these pages.

MYTH NO. 19: BATTERED WOMEN CAN ALWAYS LEAVE HOME.

In a society where women are culturally indoctrinated to believe that love and marriage are their true fulfillment, nothing is lost by pretending that they are free to leave home whenever the violence becomes too great. In truth, battered women do not have the freedom to leave after being assaulted. Their psychological inability to do so is described in detail in the next chapter. Part II deals with the stark realities of having no place to go and no means of survival. A battered woman is not free to end her victimization without assistance.

MYTH NO. 20: BATTERERS WILL CEASE THEIR VIOLENCE "WHEN WE GET MARRIED."

A small number of women in this sample reported violence in their premarital relationships. They thought that their men would cease their abuse once they were married, because the men would then feel more secure and more confident of the women's exclusive love for them. In every case, the expected marital bliss did not happen. Rather, the batterer's suspiciousness and possessiveness increased along with his escalating rate of violence.

MYTH NO. 21: CHILDREN NEED THEIR FATHER EVEN IF HE IS VIOLENT—OR, "I'M ONLY STAYING FOR THE SAKE OF THE CHILDREN."

This myth shatters faster than some of the others when confronted with the data on the high number of children who are physically and sexually abused in homes where there is such domestic violence. There is no doubt that the ideal family includes both a mother and a father for their children. However, children of abusive parents, compared with children of single parents, all say they would choose to live with just one parent. The enormous relief in living with a single parent expressed by children who formerly lived in violent homes is universal. In this sample, young children from homes where the father beat the mother had severe emotional and educational problems. The women in this sample remained with their batterers long after the children left home, putting to rest the myth that they were staying because it was better for the children. They remained because of the symbiotic bonds of love established over a period of time in such relationships. Who, then, are the battered women?

COMMON CHARACTERISTICS OF BATTERED WOMEN

As indicated earlier, the battered women interviewed for this book were a mixed group, representing all ages, races, religions (including no religion), educational levels, cultures, and socioeconomic groups. The youngest was seventeen years old, and the oldest was seventy-six years old. The shortest battering relationship was two months and the longest lasted fifty-three years, when the batterer died from natural causes. The battered woman in this study commonly:

1. Has low self-esteem.
2. Believes all the myths about battering relationships.
3. Is a traditionalist about the home, strongly believes in family unity and the prescribed feminine sex-role stereotype.
4. Accepts responsibility for the batterer's actions.
5. Suffers from guilt, yet denies the terror and anger she feels.
6. Presents a passive face to the world but has the strength to manipulate her environment enough to prevent further violence and being killed.
7. Has severe stress reactions, with psychophysiological complaints.
8. Uses sex as a way to establish intimacy.
9. Believes that no one will be able to help her resolve her predicament except herself.

Although a few of the women were unmarried and not living with their batterers, most either lived with their batterers or had been legally married to them. Many women reported living with their batterers prior to marriage without experiencing abuse. Abuse usually began in the first six months of marriage. Some women had no children; several had seven or more; a few were interviewed during pregnancy. For many, this was their first marriage; for others, it was their second, third, and, in one case, her fifth. While some of the women were still living with the batterers, others had left the relationship prior to participating in this study. A number of the women began the process of terminating a battering relationship while the interviewers were still in contact with them. Several of the women interviewed were referred while in the hospital recuperating from injuries inflicted by the batterer. To the best of my knowledge, none of the women has died. Four killed their husbands and several others were arrested for assault on their men. The women who talked with us lived in urban environments, in suburbia, and in isolated rural areas. There seemed to be a high concentration of women living in areas which afford anonymity. Many Metropolitan Denver women lived in the foothills of the mountains, where they were isolated, especially in winter.

Low Self-Esteem

Because of their lowered sense of self-esteem, these women typically underestimated their abilities to do anything. They doubted their competence and underplayed any successes they had. Those battered women with activities outside the home evaluated their outside performance and skills more realistically than they could their wifely duties. They were in constant doubt about their abilities as housekeepers, cooks, or lovers. Thus, the man's constant criticism of them in these areas adversely affected their judgment. Women in general have not learned how to integrate their home lives and outside lives as men do. They tend to evaluate their performances at home and outside the home according to separate criteria. Battered women tend to be traditionalists about home performance, since that is the basis of their self-esteem. Activities outside the home simply do not figure in their evaluation of how they feel about themselves. Thus, when things are not going well at home, the battered woman considers herself a failure. She has internalized all the cultural myths and stereotypes and assumes the guilt for the batterer's behavior. She agrees with society's belief that the batterer would change his behavior if only she could change her behavior. If she has lived with him for a while, she is aware that although she can often manipulate him to some degree, she has, in truth, little control over his behavior. This makes her feel even more of a failure. Most of the women interviewed eventually got around to saying that they were still not completely sure that there was not something they could have done differently that might have made the batterer cease his abusive behavior.

Traditionalists

The traditionalist orientation of the battered woman is evident in her view of the woman's role in marriage. First, she readily accepts the notion that "a woman's proper place is in the home." No matter how important her career might be to her, she is ready to give it up if it will make the batterer happy. Often she does just that, resulting in economic hardship to the family. Even those who believe that women have a right to a career suspect that that very career might be causing the batterer's difficulties. Those women who cannot give up working feel guilty. Although many of the women work because the family needs the money, they also state that the time spent on the job provides a brief respite from the batterer's domination. But the batterer's need to possess his woman totally often causes her to lose or leave her job. The batterer batters her with a litany of suspicions about her supposed behavior on the job. Usually, he is jealous of her work relationships, especially those with other men.

Battered women who work often turn their money over to

their husbands. Even those women who provide the family's financial stability feel their income belongs to their husband. Ultimately, she gives the man the right to make the final decisions as to how the family income is spent. The battered woman views the man as the head of the family, even though often she is the one actually keeping the family together; she makes the decisions concerning financial matters and the children's welfare; and she maintains the house and often a job as well. She goes out of her way to make sure that her man feels he is the head of the home. Some of the women interviewed revealed elaborate deceptions they resorted to to put aside some money—money they saved secretly in order to leave the marriage. Often they did not follow through, but their nest egg helped them cope. Others left the relationship when they had enough money.

Keepers of the Peace

Another behavior common among battered women is the attempt to control other people and events in the environment to keep the batterer from losing his temper. The woman believes that if she can control all the factors in his life, she can keep him from becoming angry. She makes herself responsible for creating a safe environment for everyone. One woman interviewed spent an enormous amount of time talking about her efforts to control her mother, his mother, and their children so that none of them would upset her husband. She found that if she kept all these people in check through some interesting manipulations, life was pleasant in their home. The moment someone got out of line, her man began his beatings.

Severe Stress Reaction

The battered women in this sample were hard workers who lived under constant stress and fear. This had physical and psychological effects on them. Although most battered women report being able to withstand enormous amounts of pain during a battering incident, at other times they are often seen by their doctors for a variety of minor physiological ailments. Battered women often complain of fatigue, backaches, headaches, general restlessness, and inability to sleep. Psychological complaints are, frequently, depression, anxiety, and general suspiciousness. Being suspicious and secretive often helps a battered woman to avoid further beatings. Many battered women go to great lengths to find a few moments of privacy from their very intrusive battering husbands. They will often hide things from their men that they fear might precipitate another battering incident.

Childhood Violence and Sex-Role Stereotyping

I was curious to learn whether or not the women who lived in battering relationships with their husbands had also lived in battering relationships with their parents. Although this was true in a small number of cases, many more women reported that their first exposure to violent men was their husbands. Their fathers were described as traditionalists who treated their daughters like fragile dolls. The daughters were expected to be pretty and ladylike and to grow up to marry nice young men who would care for them as their fathers had. Doted upon as little girls, these women, in their fathers' eyes, could do no wrong. Such pampering and sex-role stereotyping unfortunately taught them that they were incompetent to take care of themselves and had to be dependent on men.

COMMON CHARACTERISTICS OF MEN WHO BATTER

Who are the batterers?
The batterers described were also a mixed group. They

represented all ages, races, religions (including no religion), educational levels, cultures, and socioeconomic groups. The youngest was described as sixteen years old and the oldest was seventy-six. They were unrecognizable to the uninformed observer and not distinguished by demographic data.

The batterer, according to the women in this sample, commonly:

1. Has low self-esteem.
2. Believes all the myths about battering relationships.
3. Is a traditionalist believing in male supremacy and the stereotyped masculine sex role in the family.
4. Blames others for his actions.
5. Is pathologically jealous.
6. Presents a dual personality.
7. Has severe stress reactions, during which he uses drinking and wife battering to cope.
8. Frequently uses sex as an act of aggression to enhance self-esteem in view of waning virility. May be bisexual.
9. Does not believe his violent behavior should have negative consequences.

The first three characteristics of the batterers are strikingly similar to those of the battered women. Batterers typically deny that they have a problem, although they are aware of it; and they become enraged if their women should reveal the true situation. These men do not want to discuss the problem, and attempts to learn more about batterers have not been successful. When these men do agree to be interviewed, often as a favor to their women during their contrite and loving phase, they cannot describe the details of an acute battering incident. They evade questions or claim not to remember very much of what did occur. Thus, the knowledge we have of these men comes from the battered women themselves and our few, meager observations.

Researchers Eisenberg and Micklow found 90 percent of

the batterers in their study had been in the military. Twenty-five percent received dishonorable discharges. I did not systematically collect such data for this sample, but subjectively it appears that a similarly high percentage were also in the military. Del Martin, feminist author of *Battered Wives,* suggests a correlation between the military as a "school for violence" and subsequent battering behavior in males.

Overkill

There is always an element of overkill in the batterer's behavior. For example, he reports he does not set out to hurt his woman; rather, he sets out to "teach her a lesson." He may begin by slapping her once, twice, three times; before he knows it, he has slapped her ten or twelve times, with punches and kicks as well. Even when the woman is badly injured, the batterer often uncontrollably continues his brutal attack. The same is true for his generosity. During his loving periods, he showers the woman with affection, attention, and gifts. Rather than buying his woman a small bottle of perfume, one batterer bought her a three-ounce bottle. In another instance, the woman asked for a pocket calculator to help her to keep their checkbook balanced. The batterer bought her a calculator capable of performing mathematical computations neither of them understood. Several women complained of their husbands' extravagance, stating that they had to work longer and harder to pay off the charge accounts. This quality of overdoing things tends to be a standard characteristic of battering relationships.

Excessive Possessiveness and Jealousy

Another staple characteristic is the batterer's possessiveness, jealousy, and intrusiveness. In order for him to feel secure, he must become overinvolved in the woman's life. In some instances, he may take her to work, to lunch, and bring her home at the end of the working day. In others, when he goes to work, he may require her to bring him coffee, lunch, his checkbook, and generally to account for every moment of her time. In one extreme case, the batterer escorted his wife to the door of the ladies' room in any public facility they visited. Despite this constant surveillance of her every activity, the batterer is still suspicious of his woman's possible relationships with other men and women.

A frequent subject for the batterer's verbal abuse is his suspicion that the battered woman is having an affair or affairs. Most of the women interviewed had not had other sexual liaisons. If they did engage in affairs, they were generally of very short duration and represented an attempt to alleviate some of their loneliness and stress. Most battered women do not expect another relationship to be any better than the one they are suffering through. If they had any such hopes, they probably would have left the batterer in search of a new Prince Charming long ago.

Childhood Violence and Sex-Role Stereotyping

Although battered women typically do not come from violent homes, batterers frequently do. Many of the batterers saw their fathers beat their mothers; others were themselves beaten. In those homes where overt violence was not reported, a general lack of respect for women and children was evident. These men often experienced emotional deprivation. These reports support the notion of the generational cycle theory that is so popular in our child abuse literature today. Children who were abused or witnessed abuse are more likely to grow up to be tomorrow's abusers.

Batterers' Relationship with Their Mothers

The women also reported that their batterers have unusual relationships with their mothers. It is often characterized as an ambivalent love-hate relationship. The batterer's mother seems to have a good deal of control over his behavior; yet he will often abuse her, too. In fact, many women report that acute battering incidents are triggered by a visit to the batterer's mother. Often their rages are reminiscent of infantile temper tantrums designed by angry little boys to provoke their mommies. Included in this study are several reports from women being battered by young sons. In one such case, a twenty-one-year-old college honor student beat his sixty-five-year-old mother several times a week. When the mother was ill or simply unavailable to him because of previous batterings, he would beat his twenty-year-old girl friend.

Much more research is needed before we can reach any definite conclusions about the relationship between the batterer and his mother. Psychology has done much damage by casting mothers in a negative light as being responsible for the emotional ills of their children. Still, we must look carefully at the role of the batterer's mother in this problem. Also, we must look at the role of the batterer's father and the father-son relationship. The information that we have collected can serve as a beginning to formulate new questions that need to be answered.

Mental Status of Batterers

Psychological distress symptoms were often reported in batterers, particularly prior to an acute battering incident. Alcohol and other drugs were often said to calm his nervousness. Although many of the men seemed to have a need for alcohol, few of them were reported addicted to drugs. Those who were had become addicted to hard drugs while in the military, usually in Vietnam.

Personality distortions were frequently mentioned by the women. They said the batterers had a history of being loners and were socially involved with others only on a superficial level. They were constantly accomplishing feats that others might not be able to. They loved to impress their women. For example, one man took his future bride into a furniture store and handed the salesperson two thousand dollars in cash for a bedroom set she admired. This sort of behavior tended to reinforce their women's viewing them as possessing extraordinary abilities.

The men are further described as being extremely sensitive to nuances in other people's behavior. Their attention to minimal cues from others gives them the ability to predict reactions faster than most of us can. Thus, they are helping their women to deal with others in their world when they share their usually accurate predictions of others' behavior. When these men decompensate under stress, their sensitivity becomes paranoid in nature. When they are comfortable, however, the women appreciate and benefit from this protective behavior, since battered women tend to be overly gullible and trusting of others. Much of this seemingly self-protective behavior becomes homicidal and suicidal when the batterer's violence escalates beyond his control.

Brain Diseases

Many of the battered women felt their husbands' violent behavior approximated some kind of brain seizure and that there might be a relationship between neurological disorders and violence. The most common disorder discussed was psychomotor epilepsy. This is a disorder of the brain manifested by sudden, unexplained outbursts of movement. Persons who suffer from such brain disorder often do not remember their episodes, especially if they result in violence. Sometimes an aura or feeling of an impending attack is identifiable but usually precipitation is unknown. Medication is often useful in controlling onset and frequency of attacks, although a cure is most times impossible.

Neurologists are studying the relationship of such brain diseases and violence. It is interesting, though, that seemingly only men, and not women, are so afflicted with such a physical disorder.

Another disease mentioned that may cause violent outbursts was hypoglycemia. This disease is characterized by low blood-sugar levels that cause starvation among body cells. The brain cells become irritable more rapidly than the rest of the body, and such irritability, it is theorized, can trigger violent outbursts. One woman reported that if she sensed a rising tension, she was able to avoid an acute battering incident by feeding her hypoglycemic husband. Although minor battering incidents still occurred, explosions disappeared. This improvement had been stable over the six months prior to her interview and followed a three-year battering history. I wonder how much her nurturing behavior of feeding him also helped to alleviate his explosiveness.

Further support for the theory of neurological or blood chemistry changes in batterers is found in the geriatric population. Some older women report dramatic changes in their husbands' behavior as they age. Senility or hardening of the arteries can cause previously nonviolent men to begin to abuse their wives. One sixty-eight-year-old woman told of her seventy-year-old husband's attacking her with his cane. Other stories indicate the cruel fate that can befall women who have devoted their lives to pleasing their husbands only to find that aging brings on organic brain syndromes that can impel them to violent behavior.

In conclusion, battered women and batterers come from all walks of life. This sample has indicated that they cannot be distinguished by demographic description or stereotypes. They do have some personality characteristics in common, but it is not known how much the victim/offender roles produce such personalities or whether they sought each other out first. Rather than concentrating on the study of individual personality, it appears that the study of the interrelatedness of the sociological and psychological factors may be the way to a solution.

2

Psychosocial Theory of Learned Helplessness

INTRODUCTION

While social scientists have long been concerned with the nature of violence among different societies, violence among family members has not attracted much attention, despite the fact that most people live in some kind of family structure. The family has been viewed traditionally as an oasis of calm in an otherwise violent world. In recent years, however, it has become increasingly apparent that the family, especially the nuclear family, is not at all the expected tranquil refuge. On the contrary, it is frequently a fertile ground for often lethal aggression.

Prior research on family violence has tended to be clinically oriented and to focus on the pathology of the individuals involved, primarily the intrapsychic conflicts of the man and the woman. The research I have been conducting since 1975 suggests this approach is inadequate for understanding the battered woman problem. Sociologists Straus, Steinmetz, and Gelles found that at least 28 percent of all family members experience violence in their marriages. When the incidence rate reaches this level, we are dealing not with a problem of individual psychology but with a serious social disorder. A combination of sociological and psychological variables better explains the battered woman syndrome.

The sociological variables have been well documented by others. Del Martin, in her book *Battered Wives,* presents detailed evidence on how a sexist society facilitates, if not actually encourages, the beating of women. Her research indicates, as does mine, that these women do not remain in the relationship because they basically like being beaten. They have difficulty leaving because of complex psychosocial reasons. Many stay because of economic, legal, and social dependence. Others are afraid to leave because they have no safe place to go. Police, courts, hospitals, and social service agencies do not offer them adequate protection. Psychologists tend to counsel them to keep the family together at any cost, which often turns out to be their mental health and sometimes their lives. Both the batterer and the battered woman fear they cannot survive alone, and so continue to maintain a bizarre symbiotic relationship from which they cannot extricate themselves.

In this chapter, a psychological rationale will be developed to explain why the battered woman becomes a victim in the first place and how the process of victimization is perpetuated to the point of psychological paralysis. This psychological rationale is in the social-learning theory called "learned helplessness."

Does a man's superior physical strength, and society's message that a woman belongs to a man like property, influence a woman's self-perception? Have women learned to believe that they are powerless against men as the learned helplessness theory suggests?

Through research on animals, and more recently with humans, psychologists are attempting to understand how people's perception of their control over events in their lives contributes to the way they think and feel about themselves and their ability to act. A brief examination of some principles of learning theory provides a framework for understanding how the battered woman thinks and feels about herself and her situation.

RESPONSE-OUTCOME

Most plants and animals have little voluntary control over what happens to them in their environment. Much of the time they merely react to events that happen. For example, if you place a plant on a windowsill, its leaves and stem will grow toward the light. The way in which it grows has nothing to do with whether or not the plant can change the direction from which the light comes; thus its movements do not change the relationship between the response and the outcome. Growing toward the light is not a voluntary response; the plant will grow that way regardless. Such behavior cannot be changed or modified. However, since human beings are not plants, we make many voluntary responses which can be changed or modified, depending upon the outcome. If a voluntary response makes a difference in what happens, or operates on the environment in a successful way, we will tend to repeat that voluntary response. This is the principle of reinforcement. If we expect that a response we make is going to produce a certain outcome, and our expectations are met when we make that response, we then feel that we have had control over that situation. To check whether or not we have actually had some control over a particular situation, we choose to make the same response the next time, and if that outcome happens again, we verify our ability to control it. We can then choose *not* to make the response and the outcome does *not* happen. Human beings thus can decide whether or not to make that voluntary response again, depending upon whether or not they want their expectations met. This gives us a certain amount of power or control over our lives. If, on the other hand, we expect certain things to occur when we make a certain response, and they do not, we will often look for explanations as to *why* such expectations did not take place. If we cannot find any logical explanations, after a time we assume we have no control over the outcome. In this way, we learn what kinds of things in our environment we can control and what kinds of things are beyond our control.

LOSS OF VOLUNTARY CONTROL

Laboratory experiments have shown that if an organism experiences situations which cannot be controlled, then the motivation to try to respond to such events when they are repeated will be impaired. Even if later on the organism is able to make appropriate responses which do control events, the organism will have trouble believing that the responses are under its control and that they really do work. Furthermore, the organism will have difficulty in learning how to repeat those responses. This results in an apparent disturbance in the organism's emotional and physical well-being. Both depression and anxiety seem to be the characteristics of such an organism's behavior.

LEARNED HELPLESSNESS

The area of research concerned with early-response reinforcement and subsequent passive behavior is called learned helplessness. Experimental psychologist Martin Seligman hypothesized that dogs subjected to noncontingent negative reinforcement could learn that their voluntary behavior had no effect on controlling what happened to them. If such an aversive stimulus was repeated, the dog's motivation to respond would be lessened.

Seligman and his researchers placed dogs in cages and administered electrical shocks at random and varied intervals. These dogs quickly learned that no matter what response they made, they could not control the shock. At first, the dogs attempted to escape through various voluntary movements. When nothing they did stopped the shocks, the dogs ceased any further voluntary activity and became compliant, passive, and submissive. When the researchers attempted to change this procedure and teach the dogs that they could escape by crossing to the other side of the cage, the dogs still would not respond. In fact, even when the door was left open and the dogs were shown the way out, they remained passive, refused to leave, and did not avoid the shock. It took repeated dragging of the dogs to the exit to teach them how to respond voluntarily again. The earlier in life that the dogs received such treatment, the longer it took to overcome the effects of this so-called learned helplessness. However, once they did learn that they could make the voluntary response, their helplessness disappeared.

Similar experiments have been performed on other species, including cats, fish, rodents, birds, and primates and humans, with the same kind of results. Some animals learned to be helpless at a faster rate and became more helpless across a greater number of situations. For some, the learning was discriminate and only occurred in one situation. For others, the sense of powerlessness generalized to all behavior.

An experiment demonstrating the generalization of learned helplessness phenomenon occurred in rats. Newborn rats were held in the experimenter's hand until all voluntary escape movements ceased. They were then released. This procedure was repeated several more times. The rats were then placed in a vat of water. Within thirty minutes, the rats subjected to the learned helplessness treatment drowned. Many did not even attempt to swim, and sank to the bottom of the vat immediately. Untreated rats could swim up to sixty hours before drowning. The sense of powerlessness was generalized from squirming in order to escape handholding to swimming in order to escape death. Since the rats were all physically capable of learning to swim to stay alive, it was the psychological effect of learned helplessness which was theorized to explain the rats' behavior.

The learned helplessness theory has three basic components: information about what will happen; thinking or cognitive representation about what will happen (learning, expectation, belief, perception); and behavior toward what does happen. It is the second or cognitive representation component where the faulty expectation that response and outcome are independent occurs. This is the point at which cognitive, motivational, and emotional disturbances originate. It is important to realize that the expectation may or may not be accurate. Thus, if the person does have control over response-outcome variables but believes she/he doesn't, the person responds with the learned helplessness phenomenon. If such a person believes that she/he does have control over a response-outcome contingency, even if she/he doesn't, the behavior is not affected. Therefore, the actual nature of controllability is not as important as the belief, expectation, or cognitive set. Some people will persevere longer than others in attempting to exert control; however, they will give up when they really believe the situation is hopeless. Witness the patient who loses the "will to live" and dies when she/he could have lived. The patient believes that nothing can save her/him, whether or not a cure is in reality feasible.

Once we believe we cannot control what happens to us, it is difficult to believe we can ever influence it, even if later we experience a favorable outcome. This concept is important for understanding why battered women do not attempt to free themselves from a battering relationship. Once the women are operating from a belief of helplessness, the perception becomes reality and they become passive, submissive, "helpless." They allow things that appear to them to be out of their control actually to get out of their control. When one listens to descriptions of battering incidents from battered women, it often seems as if these women were not actually as helpless as they perceived themselves to be. However, their behavior was determined by their negative cognitive set, or their perceptions of what they could or could not do, not by what actually existed. The battered women's behavior appears similar to Seligman's dogs, rats, and people.

In addition to the way they perceive or think about what happens, people also differ in how they explain normal occurrences. Different people have different predispositions to believing in the causations of events. For example, some people believe that most of the events that occur in their life are caused by factors outside themselves. We call these people "externalizers." Deeply religious people fall into this category, as do people who believe in strictly following rigid rules and regulations. People who believe that they have a lot of influence over what happens in their life are called "internalizers." It has been found that externalizers tend to become victims of learned helplessness more easily than internalizers. Research remains to be done to discover whether battered women can be classified as externalizers.

As in the experiment with rats, feelings of helplessness among humans tend to spread from one specific aversive situation to another. A battered woman therefore does not have to learn that she cannot escape one man's battering, but rather that she cannot escape men's overall coercion.

Helplessness also has a debilitating effect on human problem solving. Experiments with college students show that while the damage is not irreversible, it does alter one's motivation to initiate problem-solving actions. Thus, learning ability is hampered and the repertoire of responses from which people can choose is narrowed. In this way, battered women become blind to their options. People who feel helpless really believe that they have no influence over the success or failure of events that concern them. Women who have learned to expect battering as a way of life have learned that they cannot influence its occurrence.

The time sequence experienced by battering victims seems to be parallel to the time sequence experienced by victims of a major traumatic disaster. It has been shown that many people who experience a disaster immediately volunteer their time and energy in order to attempt to combat their feelings of helplessness. Some become Red Cross helpers over a large area; others become volunteers in the immediate vicinity. The feeling of being able to do something generally helps the volunteer as much as it helps the victim. This phenomenon is also seen in self-help groups such as Alcoholics Anonymous and Reach for Recovery. The general reaction to major traumas such as hurricanes, earthquakes, airplane crashes, or catastrophic fires is a feeling of powerlessness. However, unless such trauma is repeated, these feelings will usually dissipate over time. On the other hand, if there are repeated traumas within a short period of time, then people become immune, passive, and convinced that they cannot do anything to help themselves. Witness the results in concentration camps. A chronic feeling of powerlessness takes over which does not dissipate. The response of victims of repeated disasters is similar to battered women's perception of powerlessness. It is also probable that helplessness is learned on a relative continuum. There may be different levels of learned helplessness that a woman learns from an interaction of traditional female-role standards and individual personality development. The male-female dyadic relationship may be a specific area affected by this interactive developmental process. Battered women seem to be most afflicted with feelings of helplessness in their relationships with men. Women with responsible jobs and careers resort to traditional female-role stereotyped behavior with their men, even though such behavior is not present in other areas of their lives.

Thus, in applying the learned helplessness concept to battered women, the process of how the battered woman becomes victimized grows clearer. Repeated batterings, like electrical shocks, diminish the woman's motivation to respond. She becomes passive. Secondly, her cognitive ability to perceive success is changed. She does not believe her response will result in a favorable outcome, whether or not it might. Next, having generalized her helplessness, the battered woman does not believe anything she does will alter any outcome, not just the specific situation that has occurred. She says, "No matter what I do, I have no influence." She cannot think of alternatives. She says, "I am incapable and too stupid to learn how to change things." Finally, her sense of emotional well-being becomes precarious. She is more prone to depression and anxiety.

Are battered women "clinically" depressed? Many of the new cognitive theories in psychology define clinical depression as a state in which a person holds an exaggerated belief that whatever he or she does, it will not be good enough. Such people also believe that their inadequacies preclude them from controlling their lives effectively. A person who believes that she is helpless to control a situation also may believe that she is not capable enough to do so. The small number of women I have interviewed do not provide the basis for any scientific conclusions about depression; however, it does appear that much of their behavior is designed to ward off depression. For example, many of them attempted to exert a degree of control over their batterings. Although they accepted the batterings as inevitable, they tried to control the time and place. This small measure of control seemed to be an effort not to feel totally helpless. For example, when a woman begins to nag at a man after she knows he has had a hard day at work, she can justify her belief that she really deserved the battering she anticipated all along because she started it. Although she appears to be masochistically setting up her own victimization, such behavior may well be a desperate attempt to exercise some control over her life.

Another point we observed relative to depression concerned anxiety levels of battered women. When these women discussed living under the threat and fear of battering, there was less anxiety than we expected. In fact, in many cases it seemed that living with the batterer produced less anxiety than living apart from him. Why? She often feels that she has the hope of some control if she is with him. Another explanation is that a fear response motivates a search for alternate ways of responding that will avoid or control the threat. Anxiety is, in essence, a call to danger. Physiologically the autonomic nervous system sends out hormones that are designed to cope with the immediate stress. Once this stress is under control, anxiety returns to a normal level. Or higher levels of hormones are constantly emitted in order to live under such pervasive stress. This reaction will also occur when certain threats are considered uncontrollable. What also happens in this situation is that anxiety does not return to a normal level; rather, it decreases and depression takes over.

HOW BATTERED WOMEN BECOME VICTIMIZED

There seems to be little doubt that feelings of powerlessness by both men and women contribute to the cause and maintenance of violent behavior. However, although many men do indeed feel powerless in relation to their control over their lives, it is my contention that the very fact of being a woman, more specifically a married woman, automatically creates a situation of powerlessness. This is one of the detrimental effects of sex-role stereotyping.

Women are systematically taught that their personal worth, survival, and autonomy do not depend on effective and creative responses to life situations, but rather on their physical beauty and appeal to men. They learn that they have no direct control over the circumstances of their lives. Early in their lives, little girls learn from their parents and society that they are to be more passive than boys. Having systematically trained to be second best, women begin marriage with a psychological disadvantage. Marriage in our patriarchal society does not offer equal power to men and women. The notion that marriage laws protect women is questionable when statistics reveal the mental health problems and criminal behavior married women suffer from. On the contrary, the law seems to perpetuate the historical notion of male supremacy. In most states a husband cannot be found guilty of raping his wife. The husband still has the legal right to decide where the family will live, restricting the woman's freedom of movement. Power in marriage also is related to economic and social status. Since men more often than women hold higher-paying jobs with more status, their occupational prestige gives them decision-making powers they can use to engage in physical and psychological one-up*man*ship. Finally, most men are also superior in physical strength, another source of masculine power and confidence.

Cultural conditions, marriage laws, economic realities, physical inferiority—all these teach women that they have no direct control over the circumstances of their lives. Although they are not subjected to electrical shocks as the dogs in the experiments were, they are subjected to both parental and institutional conditioning that restricts their alternatives and shelters them from the consequences of any disapproved alternatives. Perhaps battered women, like the dogs who learn that their behavior is unrelated to their subsequent welfare, have lost their ability to respond effectively.

CONSEQUENCES OF LEARNED HELPLESSNESS

One result of learned helplessness can be depression, as discussed previously. Another result seems to be a change in the battered woman's perception of the consequences of violence. Living constantly with fear seems to produce an imperviousness to the seriousness of violence and death.

There is an unusually high incidence of guns, knives, and other weaponry reported in the battering attacks. I am constantly amazed that more people are not accidentally killed during these incidents. The women interviewed declared that they did not fear death, although they also did not really believe they would die, either. Those women interviewed who murdered their husbands all stated they had no idea they had killed them until the police informed them. One woman fought furiously with police when they took her to the homicide precinct for booking. She felt her husband would recover from the severe bullet wounds that had been inflicted. Several men reported surprise that their rage had inflicted any pain or injuries to the women. Both the men and the women involved in this violence repeatedly reassured other people that they wouldn't really hurt each other. As we begin to see more battered women, we also realize the high probability that as the violence escalates, they will eventually be killed by or kill their men.

STOPPING LEARNED HELPLESSNESS

If battering behavior is maintained by perceptions of helplessness, can this syndrome be stopped? Turning back to the animal studies, we see that the dogs could only be taught to overcome their passivity by being dragged repeatedly out of the punishing situation and shown how to avoid the shock. Just as the dogs have helped us understand why battered women do not leave their violent situations voluntarily, perhaps they can also suggest ways the women can reverse being battered. A first step would seem to be to persuade the battered woman to leave the battering relationship or persuade the batterer to leave. This "dragging" may require help from outside, such as the dogs received from the researchers. The safe houses for battered women are very effective here. Secondly, battered women need to be taught to change their failure expectancy to reverse a negative cognitive set. They need to understand what success is, to raise their motivation and aspiration levels, to be able to initiate new and more effective responses, so they can learn to control their own lives. Self-esteem and feelings of competence are extremely important in protecting against feelings of helplessness and depression. Women must be able to believe that their behavior will affect what happens to them. Counseling or psychotherapy can teach women to control their own lives and to be able to erase that kind of victim potential.

Battering behavior must cease. We cannot afford the toll it takes in our society. A thorough study of some of the particulars occurring in battering relationships may lead us to effective methods to reverse this tragic process. By examining in this book some of the techniques the batterers use, how they victimize women and cause further psychological destruction, I hope to improve the understanding of the nature of battering.

3

The Cycle Theory of Violence

Battered women are not constantly being abused, nor is their abuse inflicted at totally random times. One of the most striking discoveries in the interviews was of a definite battering cycle that these women experience. Understanding this cycle is very important if we are to learn how to stop or prevent battering incidents. This cycle also helps explain how battered women become victimized, how they fall into learned helplessness behavior, and why they do not attempt to escape.

The battering cycle appears to have three distinct phases, which vary in both time and intensity for the same couple and between different couples. These are: the tension-building phase; the explosion or acute battering incident; and the calm, loving respite. So far, I have been unable to estimate how long a couple will remain in any one phase, nor can I predict how long a couple will take to complete a cycle. There is evidence that situational events can influence the timing. The examination of some relationships that have lasted twenty or more years indicates that several different cycle patterns can occur. These patterns tend to correspond to different stages of life.

There is also some evidence that certain treatment interventions are more successful if they occur at one phase rather than at another.

PHASE ONE—THE TENSION-BUILDING STAGE

During this time, minor battering incidents occur. The woman may handle these incidents in a variety of ways. She usually attempts to calm the batterer through the use of techniques that have proved previously successful. She may become nurturing, compliant, and may anticipate his every whim; or she may stay out of his way. She lets the batterer know that she accepts his abusiveness as legitimately directed toward her. It is not that she believes she should be abused; rather, she believes that what she does will prevent his anger from escalating. If she does her job well, then the incident will be over; if he explodes, then she assumes the guilt. In essence, she has become his accomplice by accepting some of the responsibility for his abusive behavior. She is not interested in the reality of the situation, because she is desperately attempting to prevent him from hurting her more. In order for her to sustain this role, she must not permit herself to get angry with the batterer. She resorts to a very common psychological defense—called, of course, "denial" by psychologists. She denies to herself that she is angry at being unjustly hurt psychologically or physically. She rationalizes that perhaps she did deserve the abuse, often identifying with the batterer's faulty reasoning. When he throws the dinner she prepared across the kitchen floor, she reasons that maybe she did overcook it, accidentally. As she cleans up his mess, she may think that he was a bit extreme in his reaction, but she is usually so grateful that it was a relatively minor incident that she resolves not to be angry with him. She knows that the incident could have been worse. He could have thrown the dinner directly at her. Thus, however bad these isolated incidents may be, battered women tend to minimize them with the knowledge that the batterer is capable of doing much more. She may also blame a particular situation for the man's outburst. Perhaps he had trouble at work or was drinking too much and did not know what he was doing. If each isolated incident can be blamed on outside factors and not on the batterer, it is easier for her to deny her anger. If external factors were responsible for the batterer's abusiveness, she thinks there is nothing she can do to change the situation. If she waits it out, she reasons, the situation will change and bring an improvement in his behavior toward her. This reasoning unfortunately does not bring an improvement, only a postponement of the second phase of the cycle, the acute battering incident.

Women who have been battered over a period of time know that these minor battering incidents will only escalate. However, using the same psychological defense, they deny this knowledge to help themselves cope. They also deny their terror of the inevitable second phase by making themselves believe they have some control over the batterer's behavior. During the initial stages of this first phase, they indeed do have some limited control. As the tension builds, however, the control is rapidly lost. Each time a minor battering incident occurs, there are residual tension-building effects. The battered woman's anger steadily increases, even though she may not recognize it or express it, and any control she may have over the situation diminishes. The batterer, spurred on by her apparent passive acceptance of his abusive behavior, does not try to control himself. Society's *laissez faire* attitude also reinforces his belief in his right to discipline his woman. He is aware that his behavior is inappropriate, even if he does not acknowledge it. Most batterers are only violent in their own homes. They understand all too well that such behavior would not be tolerated in public. Knowing his behavior is wrong creates the further fear in him that she may become so disgusted with him that she will leave. He thus becomes more oppressive, jealous, and possessive in the hope that his brutality will keep her captive. Historically, this behavior has been successful. It is only recently, with society's increased attention to and concern with her situation, that the battered woman has begun to find a way out.

The battered woman's attempts to cope with the minor battering incidents of the tension-building phase are the best she can do. Most women in a sexist society experience similar battering incidents. The difference between most women and battered women is that the battered woman is more prone to the learned helplessness syndrome; she has learned that she is powerless to prevent the rest of the cycle from occurring. Many couples are adept at keeping this first phase at a constant level for long periods of time. Both partners want to avoid the acute battering incident. An external situation will often upset this delicate balance. Many battered women recognize this and go to great lengths to control as many external factors as possible in order to prevent further battering incidents. As already mentioned, they work hard to manipulate the behavior of other family members toward the batterer. They cover up for him, make excuses for his rude behavior, and often alienate loved ones who could help them. Some women drive away their parents, sisters, brothers, and often children because they fear they might upset the batterer and then be harmed themselves. They recognize that the batterer is capable of inflicting further harm. He often threatens such brutality to the woman during verbal harassment periods. One woman reported that the first phase lasted for longer and longer periods as her children grew older. Once the children were out of the home, phase one could last for several years before an acute battering incident would occur. Ten years had passed without an acute battering incident when one of the couple's children was killed in an accident. Her husband expressed his grief by beating her so severely that she was hospitalized for several months. At the time of her interview, five years had passed since that acute battering incident. Minor battering incidents were occurring constantly, and they clearly were in the first phase of the battering cycle. It was probable that they could remain in this phase until another external event caused escalation into the second phase.

As the batterer and the battered woman sense the escalating tension during this first phase, it becomes more difficult for their coping techniques to work. Each becomes more frantic. The man increases his possessive smothering and brutality. His attempts at psychological humiliation become more barbed, his verbal harangues longer and more hostile. Minor battering incidents become more frequent, and the resulting anger lasts for longer periods of time. The battered woman is now unable to restore the equilibrium as she could earlier in this phase. She is less able to defend herself against the pain and hurt. The psychological torture is reportedly the most difficult to handle. Exhausted from the constant stress, she usually withdraws more from the batterer, fearing she will inadvertently set off an explosion. He begins to move more oppressively toward her as he observes her withdrawal. He begins to look for expressions of her anger, sensing it even though she may still deny it or think she is successfully hiding it. Every move she makes is subject to misinterpretation. He hovers around her, barely giving her room to breathe on her own. Tension between the two becomes unbearable.

PHASE TWO—THE ACUTE BATTERING INCIDENT

There is a point toward the end of the tension-building phase where the process ceases to respond to any controls. Once the point of inevitability is reached, the next phase, the acute battering incident, will take place. Phase two is characterized by the uncontrollable discharge of the tensions that have built up during phase one. This lack of control and its major destructiveness distinguish the acute battering incident from the minor battering incidents in phase one. This is not to say that those incidents that occurred in phase one are not serious and do not constitute unlawful assault, but it is both the seriousness with which phase-two incidents are viewed by the couple and its uncontrolled nature that mark the distinction between the phases.

During phase two, the batterer fully accepts the fact that his rage is out of control, as does the battered woman. In phase one, his battering behavior had usually been consciously measured by the batterer as he meted it out. In phase two, although he may start out by justifying his behavior to himself, the batterer ends up not understanding what happened. His rage is so great that it blinds his control over his behavior. He starts out wanting to teach the woman a lesson, not intending to inflict any particular injury on her, and stops when he feels she has learned her lesson. By this time, however, she has generally been very severely beaten. When batterers describe acute battering incidents, they concentrate on justifying their behavior. Often they recite a great many petty annoyances that occurred during phase one. Sometimes they blame drinking or overwork. The trigger for moving into phase two is rarely the battered woman's behavior; rather, it is usually an external event or the internal state of the man.

The battered woman occasionally does provoke a phase-two incident. When this occurs, the couple usually has been involved in battering behavior for a long period of time. The woman often senses that the period of inevitability is very close, and she cannot tolerate her terror, her anger, or anxiety any longer. She also knows from experience that the third phase of calm will follow the acute battering incident. She would prefer to get the second phase over with rather than to continue in fear of it, so she provokes the batterer into an explosion. She then has control over when and why the incident occurs, rather than being at his total mercy. The battered woman often does not realize she is provoking the incident, although a few do.

The second phase of the cycle is briefer than the first and the third phases. Usually it lasts from two to twenty-four hours, although some women have reported a steady reign of terror for a week or more.

From the women's reports of the events leading up to the battering, it has been impossible to predict the kind of violence that will occur during this acute stage. Even the women who moved from phase one to phase two while our interviews were in progress were unable to give us clues to predicting the violent phase-two incident. Lack of predictability and lack of control both characterize phase two.

Anticipation of what might occur causes severe psychological stress for the battered woman: she becomes anxious, depressed, and complains of other psychophysiological symptoms. Sleepless nights, loss of appetite, or their opposites, overeating, oversleeping, and constant fatigue, are frequently reported during this time. Many women suffer from severe tension headaches, stomach ailments, high blood pressure, allergic skin reactions, and heart palpitations. In the case of one woman we interviewed, her physical ailments temporarily averted a phase-two acute battering incident. When she was hospitalized for severe back pains, her husband became attentive and loving, engaging in behavior similar to the third phase of the cycle. However, as soon as she returned home from the hospital, the brutality resumed.

The information available describing acute battering incidents comes from the battered woman. The few batterers interviewed have been unable to describe much about what happens to them during the second phase. And people have not been present to observe the battering incidents. It has been suggested that, in fact, the presence of another person (other than their offspring) drastically alters the nature of the violence between the couple, and might indeed prevent an acute battering incident. It seems reasonable to conclude that the men know their behavior is inappropriate, because they keep battering such a private affair. According to reports from the battered women, only the batterers can end the second phase. The woman's only option is to find a safe place to hide. Why he stops is also unclear. He may simply have become exhausted and emotionally depleted. It is not uncommon for the batterer to wake the woman out of a deep sleep to begin his assault. If she answers his verbal harangue, he becomes angrier with what she says. If she remains quiet, her withdrawal enrages him. She gets the beating no matter what her response is. In fact, the woman's screaming and moaning may excite him further, as may her attempts to defend herself. Many women have their arms twisted and broken when they raise them to ward off blows. Severe injuries also occur if they fall or are pushed against objects in the room. The violence has an element of overkill to it, and the man cannot stop even if the woman is severely injured.

Distortion of time seems to play an important part in battered women's attempts to control what happens to them. The battered woman relates that during an acute battering incident, she usually functions fairly well. That does not mean she fends off her attacker, but rather, while he is raging, she is able to prevent inciting him further. Generally she realizes that his battering behavior is out of control and that he will not respond to reason. In most instances, she does not resist; she tries to remain calm and wait out the storm. She does not feel the pain as much as she feels psychologically trapped and unable to flee the situation. This feeling is usually accompanied by a firm belief that if she does anything to try to resist, her attacker will only become more violent. There is also a sense of distance from the actual attack. Some women say that it was as though they could stand back and watch their disembodied selves being thrown against a wall or down a flight of stairs. The dissociation is coupled with a sense of disbelief that the incident is really happening to them. An enormous amount of detail is remembered about the attack, suggesting an equally enormous amount of concentration on the actual movements that are occurring. Perhaps this helps the women to stay alive. Extreme instances of psychological cruelty are also related. Battered women can give verbatim reports of what the batterers have said to them. It is much more difficult for the women to remember what they themselves did during the attack. The one feeling that consistently comes across is the futility of trying to escape.

When the acute attack is over, it is usually followed by initial shock, denial, and disbelief that it has really happened. Both the batterers and their victims find ways of rationalizing the seriousness of such attacks. If there has been physical violence, the battered woman will often minimize her injuries. For example, a woman whose husband tried to choke her with a metal chain reported that she was grateful that she only had marks around her neck, rather than cuts from the chain breaking the skin. The fact that she could have been choked to death was skirted by her saying, "Gee, it didn't even break the skin." When the women report verbal humiliation, they also find it easy to pass off the potential hurt that they receive. For example, a woman may say, "He only said that because he was angry. If he had been his normal self, he wouldn't have said it."

Most battered women do not seek help during this period immediately following the attack unless they are so badly injured that immediate medical attention is called for. While hospital emergency rooms do not keep statistics on the number of these women they treat, most emergency room and intensive care personnel have many stories of battered women. It is with great disbelief that they also relate that once these women recover, they return home to the men who inflicted the injuries.

A good many of the reactions battered women report are similar to those of catastrophe victims. Disaster victims generally suffer emotional collapse twenty-two to forty-eight hours after a catastrophe. Their symptoms include listlessness, depression, and feelings of helplessness. Battered women evidence similar behavior. They tend to remain isolated for at least the first twenty-four hours, and it may be several days before they seek help. Mental health workers report that their clients frequently do not call them immediately after a battering incident, but rather several days later. The same pattern occurs in seeking medical attention for nonemergency physical injuries. It is not uncommon for a woman with a broken rib to wait several days before she seeks medical attention. This delayed-action syndrome also prevails when battered women seek help from lawyers or any other source. As yet, we don't know whether women would be quicker in seeking help from shelters if they were more widely available. Perhaps they believe if they do not tell anyone about their battering, they can pretend it really did not happen.

Women who have been battered state that they feel no one can protect them from their men's violence. They frequently comment that they feel their batterers are beyond the grasp of the law.

The police are usually called during phase two—if they are called at all. Of the women interviewed, only 10 percent had ever called the police. Many of them stated that they do not call the police because they do not feel the police can deal effectively with the batterers. Statistics confirm this assumption. In Kansas City in 1976, a study found that over 80 percent of all women murdered by their men had called for police help one to five times prior to being killed.

The police themselves attest to the difficulty of interrupting a phase-two acute battering incident. They have been trained to counsel the victim and the batterer, to calm them down, and then to leave them alone. Many women report police attempts to dissuade them from filing charges. While counseling techniques might be useful during other phases of the battering cycle, they are not during phase two; in fact, most women report that violence increases after the police leave. It is critical that helpers deal with the self-propelling, uncontrolled nature of phase-two violence when they intervene. Police training programs fail both to point out and to understand the tenacity of the batterer's behavior. Most police are not trained in ways to diffuse such anger. Studies by Morton Bard, a New York City psychologist who works with the police, have shown that when police officers are properly trained to deal with violent family situations, mortality rates go down.

Police also complain of being attacked by the women themselves if they attempt to intervene during a phase-two incident. They become understandably indignant when the very person they set out to help turns on them. They interpret her behavior as complicity with her husband's violence. What they fail to understand is that the battered woman knows that when the police leave she will be left alone with the batterer again, and she is terrified of being further abused. When she attacks the police, she is trying to demonstrate her loyalty to her batterer, hoping to avert further beating. Battered women state that if they were certain the police would remove their husbands from their homes and not permit them to return, they would not attack the police. But battered women understand all too well the ineffectiveness of the police in dealing with the batterer. Perhaps that is why so few ever call for them.

PHASE THREE—KINDNESS AND CONTRITE LOVING BEHAVIOR

The ending of phase two and movement into the third phase of the battering cycle is welcomed by both parties. Just as brutality is associated with phase two, the third phase is characterized by extremely loving, kind, and contrite behavior by the batterer. He knows he has gone too far, and he tries to make it up to her. It is during this phase that the battered woman's victimization becomes complete.

The third phase follows immediately on the second and brings with it an unusual period of calm. The tension built up in phase one and released in phase two is gone. In this phase, the batterer constantly behaves in a charming and loving manner. He is usually sorry for his actions in the previous phases, and he conveys his contriteness to the battered woman. He begs her forgiveness and promises her that he will never do it again. His behavior is described as typical of a little boy who has done something wrong, the child caught with his hand in the cookie jar. He confesses when caught in the act and then cries for forgiveness. The batterer truly believes he will never again hurt the woman he loves; he believes he can control himself from now on. He also believes he has taught her such a lesson that she will never again behave in such a manner, and so he will not be tempted to beat her. He manages to convince everyone concerned that this time he really means it. He will take action in order to demonstrate his sincerity. He will give up drinking, dating other women, visiting his mother, or whatever else affects his internal anxiety state.

It is at the beginning of this phase, immediately following the acute battering incident, that I have usually encountered battered women. This is when they are most likely to flee. Some of the women who volunteered to participate in the interviews got in touch with me immediately after their hospitalization for injuries received during the acute battering incident. But as they progressed from the end of phase two into phase three of the battering cycle, the change in those women whom I visited daily in the hospital was dramatic. Within a few days, they went from being lonely, angry, frightened, and hurt to being happy, confident, and loving. Initially, they had realistically assessed their situations. They accepted their inability to control the batterers' behavior. They were experiencing anger and terror, which helped motivate them to consider making major changes in their lives.

These women were thoroughly convinced of their desire to stop being victims, until the batterer arrived. I always knew when a woman's husband had made contact with her by the profusion of flowers, candy, cards, and other gifts in her hospital room. By the second day, the telephone calls or visits intensified, as did his pleas to be forgiven and promises never to do it again. He usually engaged others in his fierce battle to hold on to her. His mother, father, sisters, brothers, aunts, uncles, friends, and anyone else he could commandeer would call and plead his case to her. They all worked on her guilt: she was his only hope; without her, he would be destroyed. What would happen to the children if she took their father away from them? The emotionally crippling role models that the batterer and the battered woman provided those children did not seem to matter. Although everyone acknowledged the batterer to be at fault, the battered woman was held responsible for the consequences of any punishment he received. Since most battered women adhere to traditional values about the permanency of love and marriage, they are easy prey for the guilt attendant on breaking up a home, even if it is not a very happy one. They have been taught that marriage is forever, and they believe it. The battered woman also gets the message that the batterer needs help, the implication being that if she stays with him, he will get that help. During this intense campaign to persuade her to remain with her batterer, everyone really believes these rationalizations. The truth is, however, that the chances of the batterer's seeking help are minimal if she stays with him. We have found that the most common time a batterer seeks help is *after* the woman has left him and he thinks psychotherapy or other help will enable him to get her back.

Other battered women often recount stories similar to those experienced by the hospitalized woman. Their reward for accepting the abusive violence is a period of calm and kindness. For some women, however, this period is not always happy. One woman said she dreaded this phase, because her man attempted to make her feel better and himself less guilty by buying extravagant gifts that they could not afford. If she attempted to return the gifts, he rapidly became abusive again. If she kept them, she worried about how they would pay for them. And it was she who had to work extra hours to earn the money to pay for them or else face repossession proceedings. Thus, she had no real respite; she also suffered during phase three.

The battered woman wants to believe that she will no longer have to suffer abuse. The batterer's reasonableness supports her belief that he really can change, as does his loving behavior during this phase. She convinces herself that he can do what he says he wants to do. It is during this phase that the woman gets a glimpse of her original dream of how wonderful love is. His behavior is her reinforcement for staying in the relationship. Even women who have long ago left a battering relationship will recollect with fondness the sincerity and love they felt during this period. The traditional notion that two people who love each other surmount overwhelming odds against them prevails. The battered woman chooses to believe that the behavior she sees during phase three signifies what her man is really like. She identifies the good man with the man she loves. He is now everything she ever wanted in a man. He is seen as strong, dependable, as well as loving. If only they could help him, this is the way he would be all the time. There is no way of knowing whether that is true or not; however, it is interesting that these women choose to believe that the contrite behavior is more indicative of the real person than the battering behavior. Helpers of battered women become exasperated at this point, since the women will usually drop charges, back down on separation or divorce, and generally try to patch things up until the next acute incident. It is also during this time that the battered woman realizes how frail and insecure her batterer really is. Included in his entreaties are threats that he will destroy his life if she does not forgive him. He reminds her how much he needs her and asserts that something awful will happen to him if she leaves him. Suicide is not an idle threat. Almost 10 percent of the men who battered the women in this sample killed themselves after their women left them. Battered women sense their men's desperation, loneliness, and alienation from the rest of society. They see themselves as the bridge to their men's emotional well-being. Nearly half the women interviewed reported that their husbands' sanity deteriorated after they left them. At least a quarter of them stated that they felt their own mental health was seriously threatened by a separation.

The couple who live in such a violent relationship become a symbiotic pair—each so dependent on the other that when one attempts to leave, both lives become drastically affected. It is during phase three, when the loving-kindness is most intense, that this symbiotic bonding really takes hold. Both fool each other and themselves into believing that together they can battle the world. The sense of overdependence and overreliance upon each other is obvious in each phase of the cycle. The bonding aspects of it, however, are laid down during phase three.

Since almost all of the rewards of being married or coupled occur during phase three for the battered woman, this is the time when it is most difficult for her to make a decision to end the relationship. Unfortunately, it is also the time during which helpers usually see her. When she resists leaving the relationship and pleads that she really loves him, she bases her reference to the current loving phase-three behavior rather than the more painful phase-one or phase-two behavior. She hopes that if the other two cycles can be eliminated, the battering behavior will cease and her idealized relationship will remain. If she has been through several cycles already, the knowledge that she has traded her psychological and physical safety for this temporary dream state adds to her self-hatred and embarrassment. Her self-image withers as she copes with the awareness that she is selling herself for brief periods of phase-three behavior. She becomes an accomplice to her own battering. The women interviewed consistently admitted, although somewhat shamefacedly, that they loved their men dearly during this phase. The effect of their men's generosity, dependability, helpfulness, and genuine interest cannot be minimized.

The exact length of time that phase three lasts has not yet been determined. It does seem to be longer than phase two but shorter than phase one. However, in some cases it seems difficult to find evidence of this phase lasting more than a brief moment. There does not seem to be any distinct end to this phase, either. Most women report that before they know it, the calm, loving behavior gives way to little battering incidents again. The phase-one tension building recurs, a new cycle of battering behavior begins. However, some women have become very adroit at keeping this loving phase going for a long period of time. When this is then followed by an intense period of phase-one behavior, these women often lose control of their suppressed rage and seriously injure their men. Three of the women in this sample shot and killed their husbands and one stabbed him to death. Many others have lashed back with knives and other lethal weapons. In each case, retaliation took place after several short intense cycles of battering, followed by longer periods of calm. The death occurred after phase-one behavior began again. The women involved seemed to feel that they just could not cope with any further assaults. None of them stated she intended to kill her man; each said she only wanted to stop him from hurting her more.

PART II

Coercive Techniques in Battering Relationships

Introduction

Many women I have encountered throughout the country often timidly ask if I can tell them how to prevent or stop their being battered. "Give me suggestions," they plead. "How can I recognize whether or not my man will beat me up?" is another question. This research has not given me the answers to those questions. The best I can do is outline some of the common techniques used by men to batter women. These are both psychological and physical in nature. Although I am sure that I cannot have heard all of the different ways to humiliate and abuse a woman, in the next five chapters I have detailed some of the more representative coercive techniques that men have used in battering relationships.

Defining what constitutes battering behavior is difficult for many people, including battered women themselves. Everyone understands the kind of violence that begets broken bones and bleeding wounds. The confusion begins when the violence produces less acute and less visible results. Frequently women will ask, "Am I a battered woman if my husband only hits me once in a while?" "If he only threatens to hurt me and then takes away my car keys for punishment, am I being battered?" "If he calls me once an hour every day to ask me how I am, am I battered?" These women usually start out saying, "I have a friend who probably could be considered a battered woman, but I'm just not sure. I don't know if she's ever been seriously injured. Her man sure does treat her mean, though."

What is the definition of a life-threatening incident? While it is true that little incidents add up and can explode into an acute battering episode without much provocation at any time, many people reserve the battering label only for those incidents resulting in serious bodily harm. For me, the process of abuse is important to analyze, too. The slow emotional torture which produces invisible scars is as abusive as the quick, sharp physical blows. No one in my study reported receiving physical abuse without also telling of having experienced psychological harassment. The resulting psychological terror creates a stress reaction which produces all kinds of physical and psychological problems, including suicide. Knowing about a lot of different kinds of examples of battering incidents can assist us in ascertaining whether or not true battering is involved.

Few of the battered women I interviewed were sure whether to classify themselves as battered. Most would begin to describe an incident, then hesitate, seeking confirmation that they were in fact describing a battering incident. Others were reluctant to talk about anything other than serious physical abuse that required medical attention. Despite strong probing techniques, these women were reluctant to classify such violent episodes as battering behavior. They were sure they were assaulted and sure of their injuries, both psychological and physical, but they were uncertain whether or not to apply the label "battered woman" to themselves. Some wished to avoid the stigma associated with this label. Others simply denied the reality. Most feared accepting the hopelessness it meant for their relationship. For many, the myth of the stereotyped bedraggled battered woman was inconsistent with their own self-image. This denial is similar to that observed in alcoholics who believe all alcoholics have to be skid-row bums and that average people are by definition not alcoholics. Batterers and battered women have similar difficulty recognizing and accepting when they are in trouble. Clarifying the kind of coercive techniques used in battering relationships should help clear up some of this confusion and make self-identification easier for battered women and batterers.

After completing about twenty interviews, it became clear to me that the battering histories of the women had some striking similarities. The stories became so repetitious that I found myself filling in their omissions. The women began to react to me as if I had supernatural powers. How could anyone guess what they had gone to great lengths to keep hidden? As you read through the next four chapters, you also will undoubtedly be able to identify some of these similarities:

1. *Initial surprise.* Most of the women stated that they were taken unaware by the violence demonstrated by their men. They could not have predicted that these men would have been so violent until after the initial incident occurred. Then, using hindsight, they could identify characteristics which led up to the actual acute battering incident. There was a layer of gentleness, however, that masked the brutal potential.

2. *Unpredictability of acute battering incidents.* Despite the number of times a battered woman went through the cycle of violence, she still could not predict exactly when an acute battering incident would occur. She was also unable to predict how serious the violence would be during such an incident. Unless she was engaged in and was aware of her own provocation, acute battering incidents were controlled by the men.

3. *Overwhelming jealousy.* Batterers were jealous of other men, women friends, family, children, grandchildren, and jobs. As the batterer's jealousy increased, so did his

possessiveness about the battered woman and his intrusiveness into her life.

4. *Unusual sexuality.* Battered women all reported unusual kinds of sexual behavior that their batterers expected in their relationships. For some, this sexuality would be considered bizarre. Others included seductive and overtly incestuous relationships with their daughters. Yet despite this, they commonly discussed the sensitivity and sensuality these men expressed toward them when they were not being brutal.

5. *Lucid recall of the details of acute battering incidents.* Battered women were always able to recall the details of such violent incidents. They remembered every word spoken and every blow delivered. Although they were able to discuss these lurid details with others, most people could not bear to listen to their stories, which only deepened their shame and need for concealment.

6. *Concealment.* Although these women vividly recalled battering experiences, they frequently denied and concealed this information to protect their batterers. So they knew exactly what happened and could repeat it, but also denied their men's responsibility. When no one wanted to listen to them and they needed to deny what was happening, a cloak of conspiracy developed.

7. *Drinking.* Many of the battered women reported that their men had difficulties in controlling alcoholic intake. It appeared from their descriptions that their men were addicted to alcohol no matter what quantity they drank. Although a clear relationship was not found, excessive drinking was a common experience most women reported.

8. *Extreme psychological abuse.* Almost all battered women reported severe verbal harassment and criticism by the batterers. These women were constantly accused of bungling behavior. The men were adept at finding the battered women's weak spots and using them for their own purposes. They were reported to use brainwashing tech-

niques in their psychological harassment. In these power struggles, the women always lost.

9. *Family threats.* As an important coercive technique, batterers threatened to harm the families or close friends of the battered women. Most of them believed that he was capable of carrying out his threats.

10. *Extraordinary terror through the use of guns and knives.* Batterers reportedly would frighten their women with terrorizing descriptions of how they would torture them. They often backed up these descriptions through the use of guns, knives, and other weapons in their abusiveness.

11. *Omnipotence.* Battered women believe that batterers can accomplish things others cannot do. Both positive and negative kinds of tasks are included in this category. The batterer creates a sense of omnipotence through his extraordinary sensitivity to people, and the battered woman believes in his omnipotence. At the same time, she believes the contrary—that he is fragile and can fall apart at any moment.

12. *Awareness of death potential.* Battered women all stated that they were aware their batterers could kill them. They knew the threats of violence were not idle and that the batterers were capable of killing the women and/or themselves.

The next set of interviews took on the flavor of a detective story once I became aware of the striking similarities in the battering histories of the women interviewed. I proceeded to ask more detailed questions to corroborate the cycle theory I was beginning to formulate. When I became more persistent in my questioning, less obviously recognizable battering incidents were recalled. These incidents may have been different in intensity, frequency, or the specific technique used by the batterer; nevertheless, they were coercive and assaultive. Once these incidents were defined as battering incidents, the women began to remember others. Given some guidelines as to what constituted coercive techniques, they could both recall and complete battering histories.

In order to insure that I was not biasing these interviews by asking leading questions, I stopped doing the interviews myself. I trained several other interviewers without sharing any of my theoretical considerations, especially the cycle theory. Though part of their training was to listen to the tape recordings of some previous interviews, no mention was made of the possibility of similar experiences among the women. The points of correspondence in this group's stories to those of the previous two groups interviewed were striking. The results of the other interviewers were the same as mine. The coercive techniques, although unique for each individual, were still remarkably similar.

Despite the recent publicity about the horrible physical abuse of battered women, their suffering cannot be overestimated. Although in my study the physical harm from the abuse could be minor or major, the impact of the damage was still the same. There was the same ineffectiveness of self-defense, and the same futility of contact with helpers. Relatives, doctors, police, counselors, and others were unable to help the battered women get out of their predicament. Many women became confused as to whether their behavior was ineffective self-defense or simply provocative in nature. When detailed battering histories were obtained, what looked to be verbal provocation on the woman's part turned out to be an attempt to defend herself against further brutality. The women dealt with injuries in typical post-injury behavior styles. Most of them engaged in concealment, denial, assumption of the man's guilt as their own—all of which led to a further loss of their own self-esteem.

As this research progressed, I began to share my findings with different groups around this country and in England. I asked others working with battered women to see if the cycle theory applied and also about the similarities which clearly identified groups of battered women. After every speech I made, women would come up to me and share their personal experiences. Again the battering stories were similar, although the details were varied. Many stated that they had never before thought of themselves as battered women.

The purpose then, in the next few chapters, is to help identify coercive techniques so that battering behavior can be more clearly defined, labeled, and recognized by batterers and battered women. The techniques which seem to be the most similar and relevant are physical, sexual, economic, familial, and social. I have chosen to devote a chapter to each of them, fully recognizing that there may be overlaps between all of them in any one particular case. The women who were interviewed have all given their permission to have their ugly stories told. They do so in the hope that others will recognize coercive techniques and prevent their future occurrence.

4

Physical Abuse

Despite the publicity recent television documentaries, newspaper articles, and magazine feature stories have focused on the bleeding and bruised victims of battering, the extraordinary physical abuse that battered women suffer cannot be overestimated. Some incidents are more gruesome or more degrading than others, but all of them are terrifying. Most of the worst incidents in this study occurred during the second phase of the battering cycle, although some occurred during phase one when tension was building. Most of the abuse was caused by the men, although in some instances the women inflicted injury on the men. These assaultive women were generally defending themselves.

Not only are men physically stronger than women, but also they are trained from early childhood how to fight. Women do not have this strength or training, so they are at an immediate disadvantage in a physical struggle. Even those women who had some form of self-defense training were unable to use their knowledge successfully to fend off a physical attack from their men. Although many of the men in the cases studied were much larger than the women they assaulted, not all of them were. The stereotype of the six-foot-four football player beating up the five-foot-two, hundred-pound woman generally held true, as did a second major type: the small, thin, shy, but explosive man.

The abuse reported by the women in this study ranged from minor to major physical assaults. Some examples of the former were: a slap in the face, a smack on the rear end, a pinch on the cheek or arm, a playful punch, and hair pulling. If these behaviors occurred regularly, without respect for the woman's well-being, they were considered battering behavior. In many cases, these minor attacks quickly escalated into major physical assaults. Having struck a woman a first time seemed to make it easier for the man to do it again. It is as if a taboo is broken and the behavior, once unleashed, becomes uncontrollable.

Major physical assaults included: slaps and punches to the face and head; kicking, stomping, and punching all over the body; choking to the point of consciousness loss; pushing and throwing across a room, down the stairs, or against objects; severe shaking; arms twisted or broken; burns from irons, cigarettes, and scalding liquids; injuries from thrown objects; forced shaving of pubic hair; forced violent sexual acts; stabbing and mutilation with a variety of objects, including knives and hatchets; and gunshot wounds. The most common physical injuries reported are those inflicted by the man's hands and feet to the head, face, back, and rib areas. Broken ribs and broken arms, resulting from the woman's raising her arm to defend herself, are the most common broken bones.

Several women in this sample have suffered broken necks and backs, one after the man stomped on her back, others after being flung against objects in the room. One woman suffered the loss of a kidney and severe injury to her second kidney when she was thrown against a kitchen stove. Others suffered serious internal bleeding and bruises. Swollen eyes and noses, lost teeth, and concussions were all reported.

Surgery was required in a large number of cases. Women were often knocked unconscious by these blows. Many others were choked nearly unconscious.

Most women hide after these brutal beatings. Their ability to withstand intense pain without seeking immediate medical attention is remarkable; frequently they will not seek medical help for several days. Doctors who have examined women immediately after such brutal beatings often comment on their ability to minimize and withstand severe pain.

It usually takes physical abuse before a woman will admit to herself that she is being battered. Even the most extreme form of psychological terror is excused. Thus, most of the women in the sample were physically abused before they volunteered to participate. Yet, as stated earlier, almost all of the women were quite surprised when the first acute battering incident occurred. The few who lived in relationships where they had never experienced physical abuse were aware that the threat and potential for physical battering were always present.

Here are some representative stories from the women interviewed. Rochelle was forty-one years old when she married. Although she had dated other men prior to meeting George, there had been no one special in her life for a number of years. When she met George, he was in the process of going through a divorce from his first wife. The wife had left him and taken the children, and George was feeling sad and alone. They met at the office, and George endeared himself to Rochelle by performing little chores that made her work easier. They dated for several months before being married.

> I wasn't really looking for anyone specifically. George would see me putting equipment in boxes and would help me. You know, he was one of those employees that was just being nice. Then he called me and told me exactly what his situation was at that point. He was going through a divorce, and I told him to wait until that was over. Then we dated for quite a while. I was never suspicious that *that* might happen! I didn't even know things like that *did* happen, because I'd never seen it in my

home or in my friends' homes. As I look back on it now, I can
see indications that this could have been a problem, but didn't
interpret it as being one. For example, he would, like, walk out
on situations, not facing them, the problems, just saying things
weren't wrong when they were. He ignored problems. I have
more education than he does, and I tried to talk to him about
this as a problem. I think it really is. I think he feels inferior in
everything except for his brute strength. He really isn't. He has
a good mind. The circumstances of his life are such that he
didn't really have the opportunity to go to college. He could
have done it, 'cause he's certainly very bright.

The first incident happened very soon after we were married,
like in a couple of weeks. My dad is in an association, and he
wanted us all to be at the national convention. We knew before
we ever got married that I was going to go to that. It was about
three weeks after we got married. He beat me so badly that I
could hardly walk. A month after we were married, I got a
broken arm and broken veins. I didn't do anything about those,
but they hurt for long enough that I should have. One of the
worst times was when he shoved me out of bed on my head. I
had a crack and some bruises, which I guess could really be
serious. I went to the hospital that time, because I knew then
that there was something seriously wrong.

I wasn't really able to understand what brought those attacks
on. He got angry and then he would start yelling at me, and I'd
tend to defend myself. He accused me of having ulterior
motives for trying to irritate him. I try not to, but I don't think
two people can live together without irritating each other
sometimes. He certainly irritates me! I tried talking back to
him, and answering back, and defending myself. I used to feel
somewhat guilty when I got cross. I don't anymore, because I
don't think I'm at fault. At least I don't provoke it knowingly. I
feel so sorry for him. He's never really had a chance in life.

Lorraine's battering occurred in her second marriage. Her
first marriage, when she was a pregnant sixteen-year-old, was
to a high school principal in a small town. They had four more
children, and Lorraine spent seventeen of those twenty married years rearing the five children. She then went to school to
study to become a medical technician. After she had been
working for two years, her husband left her for another
woman. There had never been a battering incident in this

relationship. Lorraine was alone for one and a half years until she met and married Dick. Unlike George (Rochelle's husband in the preceding story), Lorraine's husband was more educated than she. He had a college degree and graduate credits in creative writing.

I would have described Dick as one of the most exciting men I've ever met. At the time I met him, I lived in and owned a very large old house, which had a couple of apartment areas in it. I was renting these areas in order to make enough money to support the children and myself. Dick answered an ad in the newspaper, and rented my basement apartment. He was like someone from another world, having traveled and lived in Mexico and Europe. His career as a free-lance writer and photographer, being his own boss, was so completely different from my first husband's career, being a high school principal at the beck and call of the entire public. This intrigued me.

I guess he first got my attention by offering to help me do a lot of work around the house. He enjoyed doing handyman things as a relaxation. We first really got acquainted when we did a lot of work on his basement apartment. Within three months, we were living together. He drank most of his adult life, from about seventeen on, and he was drinking fairly heavily when I met him. Even before I actually moved in with him, he was abusive to me.

The first incident—I remember my complete astonishment—occurred when he was not able to pay me the rent on time. He began drinking one evening and ended up screaming at me and knocking me against the wall and throwing a chair at me. I think I was just so completely dumfounded at the things going on that I thought this must just be a once-in-a-lifetime sort of thing. I sort of brushed it off, believe it or not, and went on with my eyes wide open and my heart, too, unfortunately, into the relationship.

We lived together eleven months before we got married, and he was abusive during that whole time. I knew exactly what I was getting in for, and I'm still puzzled by the fact that I wanted to marry him. . . .

Barbara became a battered woman sometime within the first six months of her marriage to Ed. Already in her fifties, having been widowed several years before meeting Ed, she was especially vulnerable. Ed was charming, vibrant, and made her feel young again. Although they did not have a sexual relationship prior to being married, Barbara is certain that Ed's sensuality is what really attracted her to him. Once they were married, their sexual relationship became a delight and a joy for her. He taught Barbara that she had feelings she never knew existed. Those first few months were described by her as completely idyllic. Since her previous husband's estate left her sufficient money to live very comfortably, work was not an issue for either of them for several months.

Ed and I did everything together during the first few months of our marriage. It seemed so wonderful, so flattering, to wake up in the morning with him next to me. We went shopping together and spent day after day just enjoying each other's company. Ed went everywhere with me, and I went everywhere with him. I still did not understand that the closeness we were experiencing was so abnormal.

Our first fight occurred around my children. My children occasionally complained that when I went to visit them and played with my grandchildren, Ed would make them feel uncomfortable because he didn't have anything to do. One day Ed and I had planned to spend the day together when my daughter called and asked if I would baby-sit for my three-year-old granddaughter. I had always helped my daughter and loved to baby-sit for this child. Ed seemed to like her also; but for some reason, on this day, he was simply too irritable to even want to be a part of their lives. I suggested that perhaps he might want to use the day doing something alone and that I would go to my daughter's house to take care of the baby. Ed became enraged. He began to scream and yell that I didn't love him, that I only loved my children and grandchildren. He then began to tell me how worthless and helpless he felt because he had nothing to do, nothing that was in his life. I protested and said, "Maybe you would like to come with me," thinking that if he came, he might feel more a part of the family. He just became further enraged. I couldn't understand it. My daughter, son-in-law, and granddaughter had always treated him kindly, but he didn't see that. He began to scream and yell and pound on me with his fists. He threw me against the wall and shouted that he would never let me leave, that I had to stay with him and could not go. I became hysterical and told him that I would do as I saw fit. I said my daughter was expecting me and I was going to go. Ed then became even further enraged and began beating on me even harder. I was amazed and couldn't believe what was happening.

I decided that perhaps if we began a little business together, Ed would not feel so left out of things. I really could understand how he might be jealous of my former husband and my children, but I really could not believe that he would act so brutal because of it. I guess I really didn't want to deal with the fact that Ed might have some emotional disturbance. I loved him so much. He brought such joy to my life. I just could not face the fact that I might lose him.

Denise was twenty-three and Jerry was twenty-five when they met. He seemed to be very kind, gentle, and understanding during their courtship.

I couldn't comprehend that Jerry's father beat his mother. I'd never encountered that before in my life. I just felt that something wasn't right. I didn't question it an awful lot, but he did mention that he would never do that, that he thought it was terrible, it really upset him, it was a miserable childhood, stuff like that. He never disclosed too much about how he was treated as a child, but I found out from his mother and sister, probably after we were married, that he was treated pretty miserably. I know for sure that he was abused psychologically, but I'm really not sure about the hitting, if he was hit a lot or not. I don't think they ever actually came out and said that. Psychologically, he was really torn apart more than his mother.

After we got married, every little thing would set him right off. It seemed he needed extra special loving at all times, and I kept throwing hurdles because I wasn't doing that. Evidently, that was causing him to be very upset. I always got the impression that I wasn't loving enough, giving enough, that there was something defective in my character as far as giving love. That's basically the message he gave to me.

There was physical abuse right away. He would slap me a lot, and I would fight back. Sometimes I didn't, because I thought if I didn't, it might cure him. I never started the fights, I mean physically. I just wasn't inclined to strike out at anybody, ever. Then I tried striking back. I thought that might do it, that if I really fought back, he would straighten out; but that didn't solve it either. I think it made it worse.

I really saw red. I mean, when he hit me, it was like putting a cape in front of a bull. I could hardly see straight, just amazed. I just wanted to kill him. A couple of times, I got to the point where I would pull a knife on him. I don't think I ever would have stabbed him, but I just came darn close to it. I felt like ... oh, I just had to.

In the beginning, I couldn't tell anyone what was happening; yet it was terrorizing me. I had one girl friend I told about it, and it turned out she was being slapped, too. She could sympathize with me, but it was something that I couldn't and wouldn't talk to anyone else about. Every time I went to my parents, I wouldn't tell them. My brothers and sisters ... I wouldn't tell anyone. It was very, very embarrassing to me. To them, he was still this gentle, kind, charming man.

Madeline met Joe while she was still married to her first husband. Although he wasn't the first man that she had dated while she was married, there was something about Joe that Madeline was attracted to from the very beginning. Like many of the other women, she describes her man as having an excitement and vibrance that other men often lack. Her marriage of ten years had left her feeling as though her life was meaningless. After dating Joe for several months, Madeline decided to leave her husband. She had been under psychiatric care for depression at that time, and her husband persuaded her to leave their two young daughters with him until she was on her feet again. He and his attorney also persuaded her to sign some papers, and in doing so she unknowingly signed away her rights for custody of the children once the divorce was final. She did want her daughters back, but her husband was transferred overseas by the military, and she did not see them again for several years. Joe became her entire world, and as soon as her divorce was final, she married him.

Thirty minutes after we got married, Joe wasn't speaking to me. I never understood why he became so angry. "Angry" may not be the word for it, because he did not seem to be angry. He just stopped speaking with me. I didn't understand what was happening. I was so happy and he was so withdrawn. We went to our motel and he wanted to make love. Our lovemaking turned into a brutal session. He was so violent. There was no tenderness, no loving care. I got dressed, ran out of the motel, and just wandered around for a while. I didn't know what to do. I made up my mind that if he didn't want to be married that I would leave him alone, so I went back to the motel to split the money and the clothes. Joe was very apologetic. He said he didn't know why he was behaving that way, and he promised that it wouldn't happen again. We went on to Idaho, where we were going to live. During our trip, one day he would be kind and loving and the next he would start abusing me and accusing me of acting like a pig. I felt so sorry for him. He was so charming, so talented, but so insecure. It was tough for him to give love.

For about six months, things were pretty consistent. At the end of six months, I couldn't stand his name-calling. I walked in after work one day, and he started accusing me of flirting and dressing too sexy. I called him a liar and slapped his face. He gave me a black eye. After that, I never hit him again. The battles only got worse.

Although Brenda knew that Ira had been violent toward his first wife, she believed all his stories about how his wife drove him crazy. She sided with Ira, and although she disapproved of violence, there was no doubt in her mind that this woman had deserved being battered. Within two months after they were married, however, Ira was beating her as well.

The first time Ira ever showed violence toward me was when his mother had come to visit us. We all went to see a movie together, and came back to our house. While I was fixing dinner for us, Ira and his mother were sitting at the table, and the three of us were talking about the movie we just saw. I didn't like what his mother said about one of the characters. I didn't agree with her, and I told her I thought she was wrong. Her interpretation of what had happened was different from mine. Ira became enraged. He threw the glass of water he was drinking at me. He then went to wipe me off, as I was dripping wet. As he was wiping me with a towel, he started slapping my face. His mother sat there without saying a word. I fled the room, absolutely shocked. It didn't happen again for another few months. And again, the next time was over a fight about his mother. Sometimes I think Ira really wasn't hitting me. He was really hitting his mother.

In these examples, it is clear that all the women were surprised when their husbands or lovers began to beat them. Even when their men had been involved in violence before and they knew about it, these women felt it couldn't happen to them. In many instances, the women felt that they could somehow take care of the men, treat them better, and soothe the hurt and pain that they felt their men had gone through. Almost all the men were described as having grown up in brutal homes. Many of them had endured a great deal of emotional deprivation, but many were also physically abused as children, and many saw their fathers beating their mothers. This was not so for the women. Only a few of them had come from violent homes and been abused as children; most had not.

Lorraine's reaction to the violence that she was living with (case 2) is fairly typical for most of the women interviewed. During the interview, Lorraine stated:

> ... I knew exactly what I was getting in for, and I am still puzzled by the fact that I wanted to marry him. There were two kinds of abuse, or maybe even three types. There was the verbal abuse of just dirty name-calling and accusing things. There was the complete tear-down of my ego or personality, and then there was the third kind, the physical, the actual hitting or sitting on top of me and screaming at me ... and hitting me. So there were really three kinds of abuse, and sometimes they were all coupled together, which was a pretty bad scene. It all sort of runs together in my mind when I try to go back and sort out if it was progressive or if it was just always there.
>
> The angry feelings were there each time. They started coming out early in our relationship. By then, I knew enough of his background and his childhood and upbringing that I could understand where a lot of the bad feelings were coming from. I thought I could help him learn to deal with that or change them or accept them.
>
> I was working in the city, and we were living in the mountains at the time, so I commuted several days a week.

Many times I would come home at 6:30 or 7:00 in the evening and he would already be drunk. It would start the minute I walked into the house. He would just be crazy angry over some little incident. I would come home, and the kids would be waiting outside for me, telling me, "Don't go in, Mother, he's drunk and crazy again, just don't go in the house." That got old pretty quick, not even being able to enter my own house because he was already haywire. It became the pattern. The kids and I would have to go away and stash ourselves with various friends or spend the night at a motel just to get away from the house. It was costing quite a bit of money. I tried to be better, being good, being quiet, being very solicitous, being sexually attractive, being not sexually attractive, keeping the kids quiet, sending the kids away, but it never did any good.

The violence was almost always connected with his drinking. The children and I learned that we could tell the instant he changed from the man we really respected and loved into the monster we couldn't deal with, or make any sense with, and learned to fear. I tried drinking a lot of beer myself, so he would have less. I got beat up one night for that, for drinking his beer. I can really only remember a couple of times, when he was attempting not to drink, that I said or did the right thing and it worked out, but those were very few times. I was never able to stop it once it got started. I felt that he deliberately beat me so that I would have to be dependent upon him.

I have never seen him what they call "chemical-free," as far as drinking. There was one six-week period that he didn't drink. Otherwise, it was maybe three or four days at the most that he would go without getting drunk, so I can't accurately compare what he might have been like without it. I suspect very strongly that the rage and frustration and things that were inside of him were inside there all the time and that the drinking was just allowing him to get them out.

Although in Lorraine's case drinking played an important part in the battering behavior, many battered women had partners who did not drink. Most of them learned to recognize the warning signs of an acute battering incident; however, they were unable to prevent it from happening. Most of them knew that if the batterer did not beat them one day, he would the next; they therefore submitted just to get the beating over with. Despite the overwhelming violence that was being inflicted on them, most of the women interviewed were able to describe the assault in clear detail. Lorraine describes the following assault:

The night my arm was so badly damaged, Dick and I had a horrible fight. I was sitting in the bathroom on the stool, and he came in and started choking me. The toilet was situated in the bathroom, and it was out in a little alcove. I was totally trapped. He choked me to the point I knew I was going unconscious. I did what I consider the last-ditch thing to do as far as protection. We were both nude. When I could feel myself fainting, I reached out and I grabbed him by the balls and just twisted them. He let go of me. I ran toward the bathroom door. He reached out and grabbed my right arm and twisted it behind my back to the point where my hand was clear up between my shoulder blades, almost up to my neck. There were a lot of other blows that night, on the shoulder and the back and around my head.

He used an open hand or the side of his hand, like a karate-type thing. I didn't even realize that my arm was injured that bad until I went to the doctor a couple of days afterward and had him count my bruises. My woman counselor told me that if I ever got physically abused again I should get it documented. The doctor didn't find anything that was terribly, terribly bad, but I began to have trouble with real severe backaches and then my arm just wouldn't work. My hand muscles wouldn't work, especially when I was working at the office. My arm would be just horribly tired and I couldn't move it anymore. I called the doctor and he said, "Well, it should go away in a day or two; if it doesn't, call me." In a day or two, it was worse, so I called him. The doctor asked me if there was any point in the fight where I had tried to fend him off. I just looked at him and said, "Oh, my God!" I knew what had happened, and I described the arm-twisting thing. What had happened was that the tendons had been torn loose at the elbow, and the connection was inadequate to make the muscles work in my arm. It wasn't that painful, or I would have known or thought about it ahead of time; it's just that it wouldn't work. The doctor told me that I should quit work for two weeks, and put it in a sling, and that probably it would be O.K. It was my working arm and you can't work without a good arm as a medical technician, so I quit work the next day. It never did heal. I finally had to have surgery. It was thirteen months after it happened that I was finally taken off disability.

I knew the doctor well enough. He knew what was going on in my life all along. I'd even talked Dick into having a complete physical in May, before we got married in August, on the theory that if he was an alcoholic or if there was something really wrong, the doctor would have been able to pick it up, which he was unable to do. Dick is very intelligent. He knows how to work things around. But anyhow, I was not afraid to tell my doctor anything that was going on. He never really did get very adamant about me getting out of the situation. If I would ask him about it, he would avoid saying things. Finally, he said things such as Dick may be an alcoholic, or that Dick had a personality disorder that would be difficult for me to live with, and this sort of thing. But he never really advised me about getting out of the marriage. At one point, when I was very discouraged with my physical health and my mental health, I asked my doctor what he thought. . . . "You know," I said. "What do you really think of me? Will I ever be well and whole and in good health again?" And he said, "Well, I think you're standing up remarkably well under everything you're going through, as it is, and I think if you ever get your personal life straightened out to where it's halfway normal, that you will regain your health." And then he gave me tranquilizers to help me cope with the situation.

Alice was not married to her batterer. She had been dating him for several months. As a forty-one-year-old single physician, it wasn't easy for Alice to find men to date. Most of the men that she was attracted to were married or unavailable. The single men she met just were not up to her standards, or they had their own troubles, with children to support. About sixty pounds overweight, Alice also felt physically unattractive. She felt that most men would not like her because of her appearance, her intelligence, and her commitment to her profession. When she met Mike, her whole world brightened. They became intimate very early in their relationship. Alice described all of the excitement and wonder of a woman in love.

I first met Alice when she was hospitalized after a battering incident. When I walked into her room, she was lying in bed with tubes all over her, looking very forlorn and frightened. As we began to talk, her depression turned to overt anger against her attacker. She related the details of the assault as follows:

Mike and I had been dating for about four months. He was the greatest thing that had come into my life. I hadn't been with a man for so many years, I had forgotten what it was like, how much fun it was to be in love, how happy it was to have someone make you smile, and someone you could smile with. I guess I was so busy being in love that I didn't see some of the little incidents that were happening. I guess maybe if I would have opened my eyes, what happened the other night wouldn't have happened. I just don't know. I just don't understand it all.

Mike had come over at about four in the afternoon, and we were going out to dinner and then to a game. I was excited. I had never been to a hockey game. Mike was going to explain everything that happened for me, so that I would understand what was going on. We were supposed to go with a couple of his friends. I had a patient, and I didn't get home until close to 4:30. Mike was pacing up and down the floor when I walked in. I apologized for being late and told him that I was sorry but I could not leave this patient. We had had little incidents before, but this was the first time I really began to be fearful. Mike's face started to get red, and I looked in his eyes and I became frightened. His eyes just looked like they belonged to someone else. His whole body began to change. It became more rigid, and he started to yell at me. At first, his abusiveness was really only putting me down for only caring about my patients and not caring about him. When I protested and tried to calm him down, he only seemed to get angrier. Before I knew it, he was shaking me and slapping me, as well as screaming at me. I screamed back at him to stop, but he wouldn't listen. In fact, he reminded me of patients I have had who have gone into psychomotor seizures. At that point, I started pushing away from him and attempted to flee, but he caught me and started swinging me around in the kitchen. All of a sudden, he took me and flung me across the room, and I felt myself crashing into the stove. That was the last thing I knew. I fell on the floor, and I could feel somebody stomping and kicking me as I lay there. I sort of felt like I was drifting in and out of consciousness.

I don't know how long I lay there on the floor; but when I woke up, Mike was gone. The house was dark. The pain was so bad I could barely move. I knew that I had to have been seriously injured. From the pain, I thought maybe I had some internal bruises. Thank God there's a phone in the kitchen. I crawled and barely made it to the phone. I pulled on the cord so that I could knock it down to the floor, because I could not stand. I called my partner and just told him that I was physically injured. I didn't tell him what happened to me but just told him to send an ambulance. The next thing I knew, I was here in this hospital bed. I don't know what happened. I don't know how I got here. All I know is what they had told me the next morning.

Apparently, when Mike pushed me into the stove and maybe when he was stomping on me with his feet, my kidneys were damaged. As soon as they got me to the hospital, they could barely find my pulse, and they knew there was internal bleeding. They rushed me into the emergency surgery and had to remove one kidney. My second kidney was badly damaged, but they think they can save it. I don't know what happened. I don't know how it got so bad. It just seems like it's all one great big nightmare. I just don't know what I'll do. How can anyone so kind and gentle like Mike, that I could love so much and who could love me so much, do this to me? I just don't understand.

Alice's tragic story did not end there. She asked me to come back the next day to talk some more. When I walked into her hospital room the next day, I was amazed. What had been a bare, plain hospital room had turned into a greenhouse. There were flowers and boxes of candy everywhere. Alice, who had been lying very critically ill and depressed the day before, was now sitting in bed talking on the telephone in much more cheerful spirits. We sat and talked for a while but never really got a good conversation going. Every ten or fifteen minutes, the telephone interrupted us. Mike, or one of Mike's friends, or somebody in Mike's family, was trying to persuade Alice that she should not leave him, that she should forgive him. Alice looked at me after one such interruption and said, "I just don't know what to do. I love him and he loves me. I can't give him up, can I? At my age? Looking the way I do? Who else would want me?"

Alice and I talked some more, and I agreed to come back the following day. When I got off the elevator the next day, the flowers had reached the nurses' station. This time when I walked into the room, Alice was sitting up. It was hard to believe that this was the same woman who had been so defeated and injured only two days earlier. She was bubbly and excited. She told me how delighted she was that she and Mike were going off on this wonderful cruise as soon as she got out of the hospital. When I asked her how she felt about being in the hospital because of Mike's brutality, she said:

> I'm really not sure how the whole incident happened. Perhaps it was my fault. Mike says he really didn't throw me against the stove. He just pushed at me and I fell and hit the stove. I really believe him. He couldn't have wanted to hurt me as badly as I was hurt. It really must have been an accident.

Mike's and Alice's experience is not unusual. Many of the battered women interviewed reported that over a period of time they began to deny the reality of the acute battering incidents. It seemed as though they could not continue to think that their men, who said they loved them, could be as brutal as these incidents revealed. In many ways, the denial served as a survival technique for those women who went back to live with their batterers. I interviewed several other women in the hospital whose stories were similar to Alice's. The first day after the acute battering incident, they remembered every detail clearly, and often with a lot of anger at their batterers. However, after the batterer began his phase-three loving and kind behavior, each of them became very certain that the incident had not occurred as she originally remembered it, but rather as he told her it had occurred. She also began to assume much of the blame for the incident.

Within an acute battering incident, it is often difficult to sort out how much provocation and guilt belongs to the battered woman and how much is due to her distortion of reality. Perhaps assuming a lot of the guilt for the incident makes battered women feel as though they have more control. Many of them talk about being physically abused after a round of verbal abuse in which they actively participate. Others assume blame because they introduced weapons, although the men were the ones actually to use them. The reverse has also occurred. I have testified in several murder trials in which the man brought out the weapon but the woman used it on him before he had a chance to use it on her. This is one such instance where the woman eventually did kill the man:

> We were making a trip back to Minnesota. When we got to his mother's house, I knew it was a mistake to have come. His mother started picking on me for all the things I did wrong with the baby. Nothing I did was right. David wouldn't protect me. He never stood up for me with his mother. She was always right and everything I did was wrong. Even though he knew that his mother didn't like me and I didn't like her very much, he still made us stay at his mother's house. I could feel animosity within every room of that house.
>
> After two days of the visit, we were sitting out on the porch and we were talking about somebody in the family behind her back. I couldn't stand it anymore because I knew they did that to me, too, so I just said very quietly that people in a family have to stick together, that they can't go against one another, that it just isn't fair and it isn't right. All of a sudden, David stood up and said, "You talk too much; you just talk too much, lady." He pulled me off the chair. He grabbed me and I fell flat on the floor. I couldn't say anything. I think the wind was knocked out of me. He put one of his feet on my hip or my stomach and the other knee on my neck, and I could just feel myself passing out. He stuck his face straight at mine, and said again, "You talk too much, Joanna." And that was the last thing I could remember for a few minutes. I think he got up off of me and walked into the house. When I came to, lying on the floor, his mother was just sitting there. She turned to me and said, "You do talk too much. You heard what your husband said, you just talk too much." She got up and walked away. I couldn't believe it. The first thing I thought was, how could she sit there and let him do that to me? He could have killed me. I

might have died. It didn't seem to matter to his mother, and I guess it didn't seem to matter much to him either.

We never talked about that incident. The next day, I was supposed to go visit my parents, so I took the baby and went, and he stayed with his mother. Several days later, I got a phone call from him, saying I needed to sign some papers to sell our house. He told me that I could just fly down, sign the papers, and then go right back and finish my vacation. I agreed to go, even though I still hadn't healed from the last beating. When I got off the plane, he met me and he was very kind and very loving. I didn't bring up the other incident. I was afraid to spoil his good mood. We went to the house, and he got out the papers. I sat down in the kitchen, looked at him, and said, "What if I don't sign them?" He gave me a look and I looked in his eyes, and I knew I shouldn't have said that. He just said, very quietly, "You *will* sign the papers." And he ran into the bedroom. He came out with a gun and he put it to my head. He said again, "You *will* sign these papers." I was so surprised and stunned, I couldn't believe what was happening. I really was kind of teasing him, but maybe some of that was me being angry with him for having hurt me earlier at his mother's house. I really wasn't that angry with him for making me sign, because I knew I was going to sign. That's why I came back in the first place. Why did he need to do it? Why did he need to get a gun? Why couldn't he have just asked me to sign those papers again? I think I knew then that he was going to kill me. I knew he could do it. From that time on, there was never any doubt that one of us would die.

Valerie lived in a home where her father beat her mother, so she was not a stranger to this kind of violence. She had also been in two previous relationships where men had beaten her. In each case, she had left the batterer. She had previously been married, but her husband never physically abused her. Valerie had been living with Ken for only a couple of weeks when the violence began, and she was not sure whether it was her fault or Ken's. During the interview, she said, "How come I always seem to end up with men who beat on me?"

Valerie had been in therapy for a couple of months when she first met Ken. She was beginning to become more independent and able to take charge of her life. She met Ken when she went to the bank and opened her first checking account. Ken worked for the bank as an officer, and had Valerie fill out the appropriate papers. He was so charming and helpful that she immediately decided she wanted to begin a relationship with him. She flirted, and he flirted, and soon they were dating on a regular basis. As Valerie was becoming stronger and more independent, she tried some of her new assertiveness with Ken, but he reacted in a very negative way. It was as though he were threatened by her new-found strength. Little fights began to grow into larger ones, until several acute battering incidents occurred.

I can remember lying on the kitchen floor, sore and hurting all over my body. No one was around. I remember just lying there and thinking, Oh, no, not again, I can't believe it's really happening. Oh, my God! . . . What's going to be? Even him! I thought he was so nice and so different from the other men. Why did he do it? Could it have been me? As my head started to clear a bit, I tried to sit up and found I had this excruciating pain. It wouldn't go away. I finally managed to get to my feet and walked through the other rooms of the house. When I got to our bedroom, I saw Ken sitting on the bed sobbing. I don't remember exactly what I was thinking then. I think a little bit of anger at him for doing it, at me for whatever I did, but also feeling sorry for him again. And I wondered, Are all men like this? Is this what it's all about? I never saw anything different. Every man that I had ever had a relationship with always let me down in the end. I walked over to him and put my hand on his shoulder, and he looked up at me and grabbed me, and the two of us just cried together.

I don't know what caused that fight, and I don't know what's caused the fights since. Sometimes I think they're all my fault when I yell and scream at him, or when I assert myself and say that I really want to do something independently. It seems to be too much for him to stand. Two days after that fight, I still hurt. I couldn't believe how bad my body still hurt, but I ignored it. I went to work and we didn't talk about it. By the third day, I knew something awful was wrong. Instead of getting better, it was getting worse, but I pretended that if I ignored it, it would go away. Finally, four days afterward, I made Ken take me to the emergency room. The doctor was nice, but he really didn't understand. He took Ken and me into the room and he examined me. And when he touched my chest, I knew that I must have broken some bones. Sure enough, the X-rays showed that I had three broken ribs. The doctor looked at both Ken and me and asked me how I had gotten them. "I was climbing up to the kitchen cabinet to get a bowl down," I said very quickly, "and I fell and hurt myself." "Where were you?" the doctor asked Ken, who turned to him and said, "I was in the other room. I don't know what happened." I felt like I wanted to die at that point. I don't know whether the doctor believed us or not. I don't think he did, but he didn't ask any more questions. All he had to do was take me into another room and ask me, when Ken wasn't there, and I would have told him what happened. I guess I was angry enough and disappointed enough and I was scared. This time he had really done it. He had broken three ribs. But he didn't ask, and Ken and I went home that time.

Donna was sure that she goaded her husband into beating her for each battering incident that occurred. The one that was most descriptive of the way the batterings went in Donna's life is as follows:

I couldn't stand it anymore. I knew Paul had been working very hard. He had this account, and he had to get the work out for them or he might lose the account. I knew if he lost that account, that would be it. His job would be all over. This was one of the biggest accounts that the firm had, and it was up to Paul to keep the customers happy. I had been alone night after night after night and I couldn't stand it anymore. I needed some companionship. Paul's tantrums and his weird behavior had made it so I couldn't keep any friends, so I had no one to turn to.

When he walked in that night at eleven o'clock, the dinner was cold and soggy. I just pounced on him. I started screaming and throwing things. I know I shouldn't have done it. I know I should have kept my temper, but I couldn't stand it anymore. I was just so alone. I thought, Maybe he'll notice me. How can I make him notice me? I threw a glass and it hit his head and then went onto the wall and shattered. I then shoved a chair and caught him in the knee. That was more than he could stand. He gave me a punch in the jaw and I went flying across the room, banging into the china closet in the dining room. At that point, all of the glasses started to smash. When I heard the noise, I was furious. I lunged back at him and he started shaking me. He then started slapping and punching me. All I can remember is being punched and slapped and hit and glasses breaking.

I know it was my fault. I should never have started it up with him, but I couldn't stand the loneliness. I had to make him listen to me. I had to make him look at me. I had to make him pay attention to me.

In all these last incidents, it is difficult to sort out how much the battered woman entered into her own victimization. In Donna's case, it is clear that there was a good deal of provocation. There is no doubt that she began to assault Paul physically before he assaulted her. However, it is also clear from the rest of her story that Paul had been battering her by ignoring her and by working late, in order to move up the corporate ladder, for the entire five years of their marriage; although this one incident alone might have been Donna's provocation, it could have been retaliatory, too. In other cases, the provocation is not quite clear. Did Joanna really talk too much? If she did, did she deserve to be battered into unconsciousness or threatened with a gun at her head? Because Ken was not the first man to batter Valerie, can we make the assumption that she was doing something to cause that kind of physical assault? I think not. Anger built up in the initial phase is often released by the woman during the acute battering incident. This anger may initiate an incident or be evidenced as self-defense.

Both Rochelle and Lorraine had their arms broken and severely damaged because they raised them in order to defend themselves. All of the women interviewed claimed that there was a time when they fought back during an acute battering incident but that it was to no avail. It tended to enrage their batterer rather than deter him. Much of the woman's anger was self-defense. She fought back in order not to feel like a totally helpless, passive victim.

Women who have lived with their batterers for many years

have learned a variety of coping styles that can often prevent abuse from escalating. It must be emphasized, however, that these coping styles do not prevent the abuse from occurring, but they do keep the women alive.

Kathy used a marriage counselor in an attempt to lessen the violence in her relationship with her husband. She thought that if she showed John she really cared about him and she really wanted their marriage to work out, some of the violence would be stopped. Unfortunately, the exact opposite occurred.

After the last session at the marriage counselor, John felt that I really was going to leave him. It seemed that even when I would save up all of my angry feelings to bring with us to the counselor's office, John couldn't handle them even there. The marriage counselor seemed to be more on John's side than mine, but I thought that was O.K. I really thought that if I could at least tell him all of these things that John was doing to me, he would tell John to stop, and John would listen to him then. But he didn't believe me. Each time I told him something that John did, that man would say to me, "What did you do to cause it?" We had gone for counseling about three or four times when this happened. I wasn't sure I was going to go back. I really felt that the counselor wasn't believing anything I was saying. John could be so charming, you know.

John was very jealous of my boss. I *did* enjoy going to work, and I *did* enjoy that man. Honestly, I would have done anything for him, but I wasn't in love with him the same way I was in love with John. He was my boss. He was married. There really was nothing between us. John couldn't stand my loyalty to him.

Well, John and I got into this big fight. Before you knew it, he was screaming and yelling at me and accusing me of sleeping with my boss. I tried to explain to him that there was no way that I could be having an affair with my boss. We just weren't alone often enough for it to happen, besides which John used to drive me to work in the morning and walk me up to my office until I sat down at my desk. He'd come pick me up at lunchtime and take me to lunch, and then he'd come to pick me up at exactly five o'clock, and I couldn't be late. If my boss needed me to do something extra for him and stay for a few minutes, John would have an absolute raging fit. This one night, my boss really had some emergency dictation that had to go out that night, and I was stuck in the office. John came up and was pacing and pacing and pacing, and I was in tears by the time I finally got the material typed and sent out.

We went out to eat to a restaurant. Just my luck, there was a fellow in the restaurant whom I knew from high school. I hadn't seen him for years and years, but he recognized me and smiled and came over and said hello. Well, that was it. I thought John was going to have a stroke right then and there. He just gave me one of those looks and didn't say a word until this guy left.

I was feeling so tense and so upset that my stomach started in on me. At that point I had to go to the bathroom. I was so afraid that John was going to think that I was leaving him to go see this other guy again that I asked him to walk me to the bathroom. This was something I would do often when I felt that he was getting out of control or that he was going to accuse me for hours later of making eye contact with someone. In fact, I used to walk with my eyes looking down at my feet so that I didn't make eye contact with a guy. Well, I asked John to walk me to the bathroom, which he did, and he waited for me outside the door while I threw up everything I had just eaten. I have this nervous-stomach condition, and I just couldn't keep food down when I was feeling that way. He walked me back to the table, paid the bill, and we left.

All the way home, it was silent. I was afraid to say a word. I was afraid I would set him off. He didn't say anything to me either. We went into the house and we sat down and John said to me, "I think you better leave, Kathy . . . I really think so. I don't think this is working out and I really think that I'm going to hurt you again." I couldn't believe what he was saying. It was the first time ever in the ten years we were married that he ever acknowledged that he might have had some idea that he was going to hurt me before it started. I told him, "O.K., I really think I should leave now . . . just so you don't hurt me," and I started packing my things.

He helped me pack some of the stuff up, and we loaded the car together. He said he was going to take me to help me find a place. I really was feeling good, like maybe I finally had it under control. I went down to the car with another load of clothes. When I came upstairs again, I looked for my purse, and it was missing. I started getting a little suspicious that maybe John wasn't really telling the truth, that maybe he really wasn't going to let me leave. My heart started pounding, but I went ahead, and I started looking for my purse. I couldn't find it anywhere.

All of a sudden it hit me that he *wasn't* going to let me leave. I heard him clicking his guns. I really got scared then. I knew he was going to kill me. There just was no doubt in my mind.

I always had planned that maybe I would have to run, so I hid an ignition key underneath the car mat in the car. I ran out of the house and didn't even stop to take my glasses or my shoes. I just ran and ran and ran. John heard me as the door slammed and started yelling after me, but I just kept running all the way down the stairs. I didn't even stop for the elevator for fear that he would run after me. I ran down those four flights of stairs and got into that car, locked all of the doors, and drove off.

Kathy was a lot luckier than Janet. Janet had been married about twenty years. She had learned to predict when the first tension-building phase was about to escalate into an acute battering incident; yet she was sure that Lewis, her husband, would beat her no matter what she did. Janet had left Lewis several times, and each time he came after her and persuaded her to return. He often threatened to kill her, to kill himself, or to kill them both. Janet knew that he was capable of carrying out his threats.

The house was strangely quiet. Somehow, I just knew that tonight was going to be the night. It didn't matter what I did. I thought that perhaps I could stave it off. Maybe if I tried just a little bit harder, it would all work out. I cooked stew, one of his favorite dinners, and I set the table with his favorite tablecloth. I even put out some pretty candlesticks that he had bought me as a gift after one of the times that he had beaten me badly. I decided that I would wear something that he really enjoyed. I wasn't sure that I wanted to have sex with him, so I didn't do it too sexy. I just did it kind of pretty, a dress that he had bought me after another fight. It is interesting, isn't it, that I always picked the things that he gave me afterward. I knew that it made him feel good to see me using them, but I have to tell you that sometimes I didn't even want to have anything to do with them.

Sure enough, when Lew came in, I could tell that he had a couple of drinks with the guys after work. I decided not to say anything that might infuriate him even more. I went in and greeted him, gave him a big hello, a big hug and kiss, usually things that he liked. I told him what I had made for dinner and suggested that maybe he wanted to relax a little before we ate. He snapped back at me, "No, I'm hungry . . . I want food right now. Now, I want my food." I agreed to give it to him and suggested that he wash up and sit down, that I'd have dinner on the table in a few minutes.

I went into the kitchen and started serving out the dinner, and I heard Lew sit down at the table. All of a sudden, I heard a crashing sound on the floor and footsteps as he came running into the kitchen. I knew there was trouble ahead. "Why the hell did you put the goddamn candlesticks on the table?" he screamed. "What's the matter with you? You're so stupid. Don't you know that we save those only for good occasions? What's so good about tonight? Why do you always do things like that? Now your damned tablecloth is ruined. Why is it that you have to ruin everything? Don't you like anything that I give you? Can't you keep anything right? You're so stupid. You just can't do anything right." And on and on he went. I put my hands over my ears because I couldn't stand listening to it anymore. Immediately tears started welling in my eyes. I tried again to smooth things over, but it just didn't work.

"I'm sorry," I said to him, as I usually do when I see him getting so out of hand. "Please sit down and let's eat dinner, and I'll take care of it afterwards." He said, "O.K., just get the food on the table. I'm hungry." I finished serving out the stew and brought the two plates in, trying hard to conceal my horror when I saw what a complete mess the table was. I don't know how he did it. I still don't understand what happened. Maybe he tripped. Maybe he did it on purpose. I just don't know.

We sat down and started eating, the whole while Lew screaming at me that the food was lousy and that I was a lousy cook. I tried hard not to answer him back, even though I was getting angrier and angrier. I thought to myself, Why do I put up with all this stuff? Why do I have to stay? The kids are gone now. What's in it for me? Finally, I couldn't take any more. I turned to him and said, "If you don't shut up, I'm leaving."

Lew lunged at me and grabbed me, holding me with his left hand, pushing the plate of stew in my face with his right hand. The scalding pain was more than I could bear. I screamed and screamed. He slapped me, kicked me, and pulled my hair until I just didn't know what was happening anymore. I started to run, and he grabbed me and ripped my dress as I was running. I didn't know what to do. I ran into our bedroom, instantly realizing I had made a mistake. I knew he'd follow me there and beat me more.

I quickly made it to our bathroom and locked the door and prayed that he wouldn't break the lock again, as he had done in previous fights. I was lucky this time. The shouting and screaming stopped. The banging on the door went away. I just sat down on the floor, just thinking and staring into space. I didn't know what to do.

A few minutes after hearing it quiet down, I got up and washed my face off. I put cold water where he had thrown the food, hoping that nothing was going to swell and that I wouldn't get any burn blisters. I cleaned myself off, and I put on a bathrobe. I slowly opened the door and came out to see what had happened. Lewis was lying there. It looked like he had passed out on our bed. I tiptoed very quietly into the dining room and cleaned up the mess, tears streaming down my face, realizing that no matter what I did, Lewis wasn't going to change. The beatings weren't going to get better.

It must have taken me about an hour to clean up everything. Just as I was finishing, I heard Lew starting to get up. I knew things were still bad, that he wasn't finished yet, the way he was slamming and yelling for me. I decided, without really thinking, that I'd better get out of the house. I quietly closed the door, took my pocketbook, and started walking.

I didn't know where to go. Lewis had sold my car a couple of weeks earlier, saying that I didn't really need it. I didn't have the keys to his car. I thought maybe I should go to my mother, who lived on the other side of town, but there was no way that I could get transportation there. Lewis had threatened that if I ever went to my mother's, he would kill her, too. He used to describe just exactly how he would do it.

Going nowhere in particular, I passed the police station, and thought to myself, Why not? I walked into the station, told the policeman that I wanted to go to my mother's house. He looked at me and said, "But you're wearing a bathrobe. Why don't you let me take you home? I'll take you back to your place. Where do you live?" I said, "No, no, no. You can't take me back to my place. There's somebody there—a prowler, I think. That's why I don't want to go back to my place." I was thinking that if he took me back to the apartment, Lew would take out the gun and kill him, and he'd kill me. I couldn't let this happen. I couldn't let this poor innocent policeman get involved. I said, "No, please just take me to my mother. I'm too frightened to go home."

I guess I must have been a good enough actress, and I guess I must have looked pretty weird in my bathrobe. My eyes were probably red and swollen from crying, and I didn't look too good from the beating I had gotten earlier. I guess the bruises weren't too bad, because he never asked me about any bruises or how I got them. In fact, he never even asked me if I was married or not, and I thought everybody in town knew that I was. Anyhow, he took me to my mother's house. When we got there, I asked him to walk me inside, because it dawned on me that maybe Lew had gotten there first and was inside waiting for me. We woke up my mother and it was obvious that Lewis had not been there. My mother was frightened because she knew what had been going on between Lewis and me. She said, "Janet, Janet, what's the matter?" I said, "Nothing, Mom," figuring I'd tell her after the policeman left. I motioned to her to be quiet, which she did. Bless my mother, I don't know what I would do without her. She's just been so wonderful through it all.

The policeman left, and then I was in a real bind. Lewis had said that he had my mother's whole house bugged. I really believe that he did. He showed me the master channel that he had that could pick up all the conversations and he showed me the little wafer-thin electronic devices. He told me he had them on my phone at work and at my mother's house, so he would always know everything that I was saying. I said to my mother, "I don't want to tell you anything in here. Come sit on the porch, and I'll tell you everything that happened out there." My mother, not understanding, but still willing to go along with me, agreed because she saw that I was pretty hysterical.

We were sitting on the porch and I was telling her the whole story and who should drive up but Lew in his car. I knew it. We weren't sure what to do. We tried running into the house but it was too late. Lew grabbed me and told my mother that I was sleeping with other men, that I was really a dirty slut, that he was really sorry for what had happened, that it would never happen again. He was going to be really big-hearted and take me back.

My mother looked at me and said, "Janet, is that true?" I

didn't know what to do. I realized that if I said yes to her, Lewis would leave me alone. I said, "Yeah, Ma, it really is true." She said, "Oh, Janet, don't you realize how bad things are? Go back with him. Stop running around. Maybe then he won't beat you." I thought to myself, She doesn't understand either, and it's my fault. I just don't let her understand. I knew someday when I told her the truth, she would really understand.

Well, I went back with Lewis, and that wasn't enough for him. He beat me so badly that night that the next morning I had to go to the doctor. I explained to the doctor that I had fallen, and that that's where I had gotten my injuries. I didn't tell him the truth. I just couldn't. If I did, Lew would only beat me again.

Most of these women sought help from somebody, but they never felt free enough to tell them the truth about what was happening. Even Janet, who felt her mother was supportive, couldn't tell her the truth. In many cases, batterers threatened violence against the woman's parents, children, friends, co-workers, or other people in their support system. These women believed that their men could and would commit such acts of violence. Sometimes they took the beating rather than allow someone else to be harmed.

In most cases, the women understood that the men would fight them until death. Often there was a fine line drawn between whether the batterer would kill the woman or himself. Batterers who used guns or other weapons to threaten women would often turn them on themselves. In some cases, these desperate women used the weapons against the men. Four women in my research sample killed their batterers. Many more were found guilty of assault. The life-or-death nature of acute battering incidents is terrifying. The violence and rage exhibited have no limits or control. Death is often a relief from such terror and pain for both the woman and the man.

Most of the women interviewed said that physical violence became more acute during pregnancy and their child's infancy. Men who are dependent upon their women logically become frustrated when the woman begins to pay attention to dependent infants instead of to them. I suspect that is probably one of the reasons why violence increases during pregnancy. All of a sudden, the man is forced to share his woman with another person. In some cases, the women said that they thought their men were attempting to prevent another human being that might have the same bad genes as himself from being born into the world. More often, it was a simple case of prenatal child abuse.

Much of the mutilation that occurs during pregnancy is sexual in nature. Women have suffered mutilated vaginas, nipples sliced off, and repeated blows to their protruding stomachs. There is no way of knowing how many infants have been born deformed because of such abuse. Medications are often prescribed for pregnant women to calm the anxieties caused by their battering relationships. Such medications can also cause deformity in infants. However, the medication may be all that stands between the women and insanity.

Other forms of physical abuse, which are indirectly visited upon the women, are all the psychosomatic ailments. Working in a rural medical center, Elaine Hilberman, a psychiatrist at the University of North Carolina Medical School, and her staff have seen many women with psychophysiological ailments that were due to battering. They come in with backaches, headaches, stomach ailments, respiratory problems, eczema and other skin rashes, hypertension, and other disorders caused by stress and anxiety. This same phenomenon has been observed by social worker Karil Klingbeil at Seattle's Harborview Medical Center, and psychologist Vickie Boyd at the Group Health Organization in Seattle. I have included the interviews done with women who have had psychophysiological problems in the chapter on psychological coercion, but I mention them here because they cause real physical damage to the woman's body. The kind of generalized stress reaction that battered women live under day after day is an insidious form of physical abuse.

5

Sexual Abuse

When I first conceived this book, I did not plan to include a chapter on sexual abuse, since I wanted to avoid the sensationalism which might result from describing sexual behavior in a violent relationship. I also felt that many other authors had devoted entire books to exposing the degradation of rape and understanding its psychology. I could hardly do justice to this problem in one chapter, nor did I want to describe sexual battering totally in the context of rape, although there are many similarities between rape and sexual battering. In America, the subject of rape had been closely studied before the broader context of all violence against women was given any attention. On the other hand, the English studied battered women before they studied rape. Only today are the studies of all forms of violence against women being integrated. Therefore, I changed my mind and decided to include this chapter on sexual abuse in an effort to contribute to the expanded field of studies of violence against women.

Psychologists have placed sexual abuse on a continuum. The University of Colorado psychologist Dr. Margie Leidig, who has been conducting research on women's experiences with sexual abuse, includes in her study the following as noxious events: (1) obscene telephone calls; (2) Peeping Toms; (3) exhibitionism; (4) little rapes, such as sexual cat-calling on the street and unwanted sexual comments regarding women's bodies; (5) body grabbing; (6) rapes; (7) sexual abuse of girl children; and (8) seduction and rape by a person in the helping professions. Leidig's preliminary research indicates that between 80 and 90 percent of women in a university sample have experienced at least two of the eight. Leidig's work has also examined the similarities between sexual violence and violence against women in general. Not surprisingly, she found an anti-woman bias in both. These forms of violence are seriously underreported tip-of-the-iceberg phenomena. Another area of similarity is the blaming-the-victim phenomenon which occurs with both rape victims and battered women.

Despite the similarities between rape and battering, there are also significant differences that occur when sex between a couple is on a repetitive basis. The most obvious one is that sexual activity between the couple can be very enjoyable at certain times, especially during phase three or the loving phase of the battering cycle. It is during the tension-building phase and the acute battering phase that sexual abuse most frequently takes place. Marjory Fields, the New York City attorney specializing in domestic violence, states that if all the marital rapes were added to the official rape rate, the resulting figure would be overwhelming. Most of the women interviewed in this study felt they had been raped by their batterers. Their sexual relations with these partners brought both pleasure and pain, each at a different and often unpredictable time.

Battered women have trouble foretelling when sex will be pleasurable. Because of the batterer's unpredictable nature, they keep hoping the pleasure will occur each time. Behavioral psychologists call this intermittent reinforcement. Experiments have shown that it is most difficult to stop behavior that has been intermittently reinforced, especially on a random and variable schedule. This is exactly the condition of the battered woman's sexual relationship with her partner. It contributes to her victimization in that the loving behavior is the reinforcer, which keeps her hoping that the next time will be better. If the reinforcement theory is taken into consideration, the battered women who describe positive sexual experiences with their batterers become understandable.

Joan and Peter met when she was twenty-eight years old. They were both artists. Peter was highly successful, selling his work both commercially and in studios. Very often, Joan was the one who had the ideas for commercial layouts; however, when the work was in her name, it didn't sell. If it was in Peter's name, it brought fantastic prices. When Joan described their sexual relations, her eyes twinkled.

> Peter was just the greatest lover I'd ever had. He was kind, gentle, and just, oh, so good. Somehow he always knew just what to do to pleasure me. I never experienced such highs with anyone else. I really didn't know I was capable of it. I used to lie in bed and tease him about how he could make more money with his sexual ability than as an artist. Maybe that was part of it. Maybe some of the creativity he had with his art rubbed off in our sexual behavior. All I can say is it didn't matter what he did or how he did it, any place he touched me, I felt like an electric light was going off. All those silly movies you see when you're a kid and all those books that you read about bells ringing and about true love and how he just had to look at me or touch me and I would be afire—all that really was true with Peter and me. It was a real kinship we had together. But when Peter's mood changed, he could be the most vicious and violent man. I soon learned to be fearful until I knew which Peter would be with me.

Emily met Ned when he was a service station attendant.

> The first day I drove my car into Ned's filling station, I knew that he was someone special. Life had been boring for me. My husband was out of town all the time. I really had nothing to do. I felt as though life was just passing me by. With Ned, it was different. He would come up to my window and smile that cute little-boy smile of his and just kind of flirt, you know. It

started out that way, just a whole lot of harmless flirting. Then all of a sudden one day, I just couldn't believe it, he looked at me and I looked at him, and it was as if we both knew it was right. We made plans to meet, and we began sleeping with each other. Sex was just so good, I couldn't believe it. It was none of the routine monotony that was going on in my marriage. With Ned, it was for real. It was just the way I wanted it to be. In my wildest fantasies, it couldn't have been better, until I made him angry with something unimportant that I did, and he began to beat me.

Judith is an orthodox Jewish woman who met her batterer at a youth group for Jewish teen-agers.

Meyer was the youth leader at the community center. He was tall, had dark wavy hair, and was so good-looking that all of us girls used to just drool over him whenever we would go to the center. He was kind of a flirt, but at the time I thought he was just trying to be nice to us girls.

One night I went down to the center with some of my friends, but it was pretty quiet there that night. Meyer came over to me and said he wanted to talk to me alone. When I look back on it, I really think he was making eyes and flirting with me before, but at that time I wasn't really old enough to really understand it. I mean, we kids as teen-agers were just so protected. We really didn't understand sexual messages at that time. Anyhow, Meyer asked me if I would come into his office, that he had something to show me, and I told my friends I'd be right back and I went. He was just being so nice. We went into his office, and he started talking to me, and getting kind of close to me, and I kind of liked it. It was a warm, good feeling and I liked Meyer. I trusted him and he was real gentle. At that time he wasn't brutal at all. All of a sudden, I turned around and I found myself with our faces almost meeting. He looked at me, and I looked at him, and we started kissing. That was all that happened that night, but we both agreed that there was something special between us. We also agreed not to tell anybody about it, because it just seemed wrong. He was the youth director, and I was just one of the kids who went there. We would make up excuses, and they believed me. They didn't know anything was going on. Meyer and I started sleeping together a couple of times. It was nice. It was warm; it was good, but I had a lot of trouble and so did he, because our Jewish traditions said that you shouldn't do that without being married. Before you knew it, Meyer and I decided that we'd better get married so that we could legitimize the good sexual feelings that we had about one another. It's hard to remember those good times, since they've been so poisoned by Meyer's unpredictable cruelty toward me. Yet he is still all right working at the youth center.

Karen met Mal when she was a nursing student and he was an intern at the same hospital.

One of the reasons that I had gone to nursing school was that I really hoped that I was going to meet a nice, handsome doctor and get married. I had been told that since I was a little girl, and I thought it made sense. When I first met Mal, I was working in the recovery room. It was tough work, because you always had to be alert and watch the patients very carefully. Mal was helping out in this one particular surgery with a patient who we didn't think was going to make it. The man's heart had stopped several times while he was being operated on, and we were watching him very closely in the recovery room. Mal kept coming in to check the patient more often than most interns would. The first thing that hit me was his overwhelming concern for this man. When I think back on it, it was kind of like some of his overwhelming concern was for me, too. Well, despite Mal's concern and despite my concern, the man didn't make it. He died. After about three hours of really trying hard to work on him, it really shook us both up. It was the first patient that had ever died that I had been working with so closely, and I started crying. Mal, who also knew I was really upset about it, put his arms around me and tried to comfort me, as I was almost hysterical. I couldn't be comforted. I think back on that now, and I wonder at my own innocence then. At that time, however, it was just the worst thing that had ever happened to me, and I didn't know how to handle it. Mal suggested to the nurse on duty that he take me home. She agreed, and I eagerly went with him. On our way out of the hospital into the parking lot, I was sobbing and Mal had his arm so protectively around me. It just seemed very natural when we got into the car that he turned to me and I turned to him, and all of a sudden we were embracing one another. We didn't leave the parking lot for several hours. It was late at night and quite deserted, and Mal and I began making love in the back seat of the car. I don't know how it happened. I think I was all caught up in the emotions of what had just happened that evening. I think back sometimes on that night, and remember how beautiful and how tender and how wonderful sex with Mal really was.

Good sex often turns into assaultive behavior after a while, as in this story.

The sex that Craig and I had was very definitely one of the biggest motivations for me to stay married to him. He was so exciting, so alive, and sex was so good together that it really was the reason I didn't want to leave. When he would touch me, the whole world seemed aglow. I like sex. I'm a very sexual and sensual woman. Craig knew that, and I think he knew that that was the way to really keep me with him. We had sex all the time. It wouldn't be unusual to start out by going to bed early in the evening and make love, and then fall asleep and wake up later on and make love again, and maybe two or three more times before we got out of bed the next morning. This would go on almost every day in the beginning of our relationship. I loved it, and I guess I loved Craig, too, for being such a willing wonderful sexual partner. But then it changed. He wasn't as available and I never knew what to expect.

Another major difference between sexual behavior in a battering relationship and rape is that the former begins with a touch of consensual illicitness, while rape never does. Most of the battered women interviewed had sexual relationships with their partners prior to marriage. Many of the women met their lovers when they were young and had trouble distinguishing between loving behavior and sex. But many of the older women also had sex prior to marriage. Although the data are not definitive, it appears that many young women became pregnant and then married. For those of them who came from abusive homes, marriage seemed like the perfect escape. In most of these cases, there was a great deal of embarrassment about engaging in sex without knowing the partner very well, yet also a great deal of pleasure from the sense of intimacy they gained from the relationship. For various reasons, these women were looking for an intimate loving relationship, and sexual intimacy was interpreted as being the same thing. Many of them stated ashamedly that they had initially enjoyed their lover's possessiveness as proof of his love. Its crippling oppressiveness did not become apparent to them until later.

Debbie had been married to Henry for three years when she met Stan, her batterer. Debbie and Stan were both high school teachers. Although her husband, Henry, had never physically battered Debbie, his abuse could be classified as social isolation.

I would be alone night after night while Henry was out drinking and running around. I knew that if I didn't get out of this marriage, I was going to go crazy. I never had friends, and I could not go anywhere or do anything. One afternoon I was sitting at my desk at school when Stan came into my room. We both teach English, and we were getting our classes together so we could all see a movie. He was just so different from Henry. He was kind and gentle. Anyway, he seemed to be that way at the time. We finished making the plans that we needed to, and Stan asked me to go out for a drink with him afterward. I thought to myself, Well, Henry won't be home; why not? And so I agreed to go. We were sitting in the bar listening to some good music and really talking to each other. I think that's what really attracted me the most to Stan, that we really could talk together. Henry and I hadn't had a decent conversation, at least one that wasn't filled with angry words, for a long time. We also hadn't had sex in months; and frankly I think I was just a little bit horny. After a couple of drinks, Stan really started looking very sexy and very attractive to me. I don't know whether he put the moves on me, or I put the moves on him. I guess it really doesn't matter much. All I know is that we went back to Stan's apartment and we made love. It was not the best, but not the worst either. Let me tell you, for a woman who was as horny as I was, it was absolutely great. I really felt like someone cared about me. I don't know whether there was that much excitement because I was still married and sleeping with Stan, but our affair continued during my whole separation and divorce from Henry. There were times when I was really so guilty about it, I would look at Henry and think, You poor man. Look what I'm doing to you. I would forget that it had been two years of Henry's never being home and my being alone. Somehow, though, my having an affair with Stan just made me forget all about that. Stan didn't begin beating me until after my divorce was final. I've never understood why.

Janey was a successful forty-two-year-old attorney when she first met Larry. Although she had been married for a short time and divorced fifteen years earlier, she had had few relationships with men. Then Larry came into her life.

It was the greatest thing that had happened to me in a long time. Can you imagine what an unattractive, intelligent woman who thought herself asexual for so many years feels when a man finally pays attention to her? I know it sounds dumb now, but I didn't think of myself as a woman. I thought of myself as a lawyer. You had to be tough and aggressive to get ahead in my business. You didn't have time for nonsense like sex, but when Larry came along, all of a sudden it wasn't nonsense. I found myself being the feminine sweet little thing that my own self-image never said I was, and I have to tell you, I loved it. When Larry would smile at me with that charming smile, when he would touch me with those magic fingers, my whole body seemed alive. I tell you, when I would reach orgasm with Larry, it would be better than winning a case in the courtroom. Now how do you like that for a successful lawyer? I'm embarrassed to say it because it took me so long and so hard to get to where I am professionally, and I'd never give up my profession. I know that now, but there was a little bit of time with Larry that I really thought I could. That's how powerful sex was between us, and it would have to have been the sex, because there really wasn't much else that was good in that relationship.

Sexual jealousy is almost universally present in the battering relationship. The batterer consistently accuses the woman of having sexual affairs with other men and sometimes with women friends. The unreasonableness of the accusation is evident when there is great confusion between appropriate and inappropriate suspects. Anyone who is kind to the battered woman becomes a target of the batterer's sexual jealousy. This includes her father, brother, boss, male co-workers, next-door neighbor, supermarket clerk, bartender, hairdresser, milkman, and so on. In some cases, any man who glances at the woman in public becomes a potential target. Often this irrational jealousy spills over onto her women friends, and she is also accused of having lesbian affairs. No wonder battered women isolate themselves from other people, especially those for whom they really care.

Battered women are often told that they are being sexually provocative to other men. They are accused of dressing too sexily, frequently after the batterers have insisted that they buy or wear the particular outfits in question. Their make-up is wrong; their dress is too short; their slacks are too tight; they smile too invitingly; they talk too much—all, says the batterer, because they secretly want to have an affair with someone else. On the contrary, the women interviewed stated that the last thing they wanted was an affair with another man. Most had enough trouble with their own men, and they could not imagine coping with two of them. Many did not see other men as different from their batterers. If another man was kind, they suspected he was just in his loving, charming phase. They suspected that he, too, could become abusive over something real or imagined that they might do.

Occasionally, some women reported that they did indeed have sex with another man. Usually it happened only once or twice. Those women with an outside sexual liaison were embarrassed and guilty about it. A few women admitted they felt that they frightened potential lovers away by being so much in need of love. Several said potential lovers were frightened away by the possibility of violence. Most reported they would not take the chance of putting another man in danger of being harmed by their batterer. For some women, another man's love became the way to free themselves from their batterer. However, this last was a rarity among the women in my sample.

Most of the women interviewed had traditional sexual values. They believed sex without marriage was wrong, and they believed in fidelity though their behavior did not always conform to these values. Those who reported enjoying sex felt slightly embarrassed about admitting it. They did not condone premarital and extramarital sex, even though almost all had practiced one or the other. The batterer could thus use accusations of infidelity as a psychological weapon to induce guilt, even when he did not know for sure that the woman had been unfaithful. Guilt was a particularly powerful psychological weapon in those instances where the woman had been unfaithful to a previous husband. Such guilt could then impair her judgment in recognizing the batterer's irrational jealousy.

Wendy was caught in this interaction between her own guilt and her batterer's jealousy. She met Bob while she was still married to her first husband, and started an affair with him. As her relationship with Bob strengthened, her marriage began falling apart. Her marriage had probably been deteriorating all along, but her affair with Bob was the precipitating factor in her obtaining a divorce. Bob was extraordinarily jealous and possessive.

> He used to drive me to work in the morning, pick me up at noon so we could have lunch together, and then pick me up at five o'clock so that we would go home together. I couldn't have any friends at work except those I could talk to between the jobs I had to do during the day. I never could have lunch with a friend or go out for a drink after work. Bob was always there. At first I liked it. It gave me a feeling of security. After a while, however, it really started to grate on my nerves because it restricted my freedom. One day when we were in a restaurant together, a good-looking man was sitting across the room. His eye caught mine. You know how it is when you make eye contact with someone. I smiled at him and he smiled at me. That was it. Nothing was ever said. Well, that was the cause that night for a battle you wouldn't believe. I was accused of sleeping with this man, and not only was I accused of having an affair with him, but Bob spent hours telling me in detail every single sexual act that we had done together. Can you imagine that? I couldn't believe it was really happening. I couldn't even protest sufficiently because it seemed so absurd to me, but it really wasn't absurd to Bob. He also believed I was having an affair with my boss, and he went so far as to call my boss's wife and tell her what he suspected. That poor man. I ended up quitting my job after that, even though everyone knew, including him, that there was no sexual affair going on. My boss was just the kindest, sweetest man. Besides which, he was in his sixties. If I were interested in having a sexual affair, it certainly wouldn't be with someone who was that much older than me. But it never seemed to matter to Bob who it was. One night, we

had a party and I invited all of our neighbors. It was Bob's idea. He wanted to meet them all. We had people going in and out of our house all night. I knew that I couldn't flirt with anybody, and I knew that I could be nice but not too nice to them. But it didn't matter. Toward the end of the evening, two men who shared an apartment together came in and we offered them some drinks. I went into the kitchen to get some ice and fix their drinks, and one of them came in with me to help me. We were only a few minutes, but when we came out, Bob started screaming and yelling at me that it took me too long, that I was really having oral sex with this guy in the kitchen. It was that kind of behavior, that kind of harassment, that always happened with Bob. Yet he was the one who insisted that I dress pretty, and that I wear sexy clothes. I thought his jealousy was cute at first, but after a while jealousy like that just had to be sick. I did think that as it got worse, and as Bob's drinking got worse, the jealousy became crazier and crazier.

The reported stories of sexual jealousy took on similar characteristics. In all cases, the batterer verbally harassed the woman with detailed fantasies of what form her sexual infidelities took. At the same time, he became more intrusive into her thoughts and actions, so that even if she did want to have an affair, she had no time for it. The man would even adapt his irrational thinking to account for any time problems by accusing the woman of short-term sexual behavior, such as oral sex that would take two or three minutes, rather than longer encounters. It is interesting that despite reports of their being such wonderful lovers, these men were often reported as having difficulty either achieving or maintaining an erection or being able to reach orgasm very rapidly. It is entirely possible that part of their sexual jealousy included projecting their own problems onto the woman. Many of these men were suspected of having sexual liaisons with other women, and in some cases it was confirmed. In others, they were actually having sexual affairs with men. Again, the possibility of projecting their own feelings onto the woman and ascribing them to her is a real question that needs to be answered by more research.

Another characteristic in the sexual relationships of the

battered women interviewed is the types of sexual behavior in which they engaged. They reported some of the most unusual, kinky sex that I have heard about in my ten years of clinical psychology practice. I find this behavior most curious in view of their generally traditional attitudes toward sexuality.

One common finding is that these women had very little knowledge of normal sexual behavior before they met their batterers. They typically grew up in families where discussion of sex was forbidden. Sex education was nonexistent. By puberty, they were aware of their sexual feelings but left it to their lovers to teach them what sex was all about. Many of the women became involved with one man early in their lives and did not have much experience prior to meeting their batterers. Although the men were reported to be more experienced in sexual intercourse, most of them knew little more than the women about the relationship between sex and love. Initially, sex was considered good and fulfilling by most of the battered women. As we have seen, many of them experienced joy and excitement in finding someone to love them. To them, sexual intimacy was the language of love. As the years progressed, however, the nature of the sexual relationships changed. Sex became kinkier, as though it needed more variety or stimulation to become exciting. Because these women were isolated from other women, they were not always aware of the bizarreness of their sexual relationship. The batterer attempted to provide the reality checks for his woman, and she had trouble distinguishing what was real for the rest of the world and what was real just for them. Nowhere is the isolation of the battered woman more poignant than in her sexual relationships. This is true especially in a world where sexual mores are changing. All the batterer has to do is call his woman a prude, and she then tries to please him by submitting to his new ideas. She does not want to think of herself as being old-fashioned. The battered woman often does not have the right to determine whether or not she is pleasured in their sexual interactions. The pleasure, most of the women state, is in pleasing their men. Sometimes sex is unpleasant for the woman. Sometimes it is exciting. Most often, it is a compromise in order to keep the violence under control.

There is a significantly frequent mention of animals, objects, third persons (usually other men), other couples, oral and anal sex, and unusual positions in sexual intercourse in battering relationships. There is real difficulty in distinguishing when such experiences were pleasurable and when they were coercive for the woman. I will let the women's own stories speak for themselves.

Millie met her husband at a school dance when she was fourteen and he was sixteen. She came from a home where there was lots of violence, and so did he. He was the first person who paid attention to her. He was kind and gentle and loving.

I liked boys and dated many of them, but it wasn't until Jeff came along that I really fell in love. He was so good to me. We did fun things, like sipping sodas at the drugstore. He wanted to share things with me and do things with me. Soon after we met, we started fooling around with kissing and petting and then having sexual relations. I was a virgin when I met him, and it really made me feel very grown up and excited to be having sex together. I felt, because we were having sex and because I had been a virgin, that we must marry. I also couldn't wait to escape from my home. My mother and father both discouraged my getting married. My father said I'd better not marry him. When I went crying to my mother, she said that my father was really just jealous of me and wanted me to stay home forever. I became pregnant. We did have some good times together, but I didn't marry him for love. I liked him, but mostly I felt that I had to marry him, being a virgin and all that. The fun things that we did together soon stopped after we were married. He only had an eighth-grade education, and he had to work hard in order to scrape by enough money so that we could live. He didn't really start to beat me until I started showing how pregnant I was, until my belly started swelling. Then it was like he was jealous of that baby, before he was even born. He was jealous of my babies even when he went into the Navy. He would come home and beat them and beat me. If the babies would be quiet, then sex would still be fun. But after he came out of the Navy, sex became real weird. Sometimes it was like it was in the beginning, but most of the time it just got worse and worse and worse.

I have to admit I was a willing partner, but then it got too much.

When Jeff came home from the Navy, he told me how he learned to please women in Thailand and Japan. Naturally, I was so glad to have him home with all of us and resume sexual relations again, I wanted to learn some of what he had learned. At first, he would tie me up about half the time. I did not like to be tied up and begged him not to do that. He promised he would not hurt me. The times that he didn't hurt me, it wasn't so bad, but I never knew what to expect. Of course, if you're tied up, you can't do anything about stopping it. Most of the time he would want me to suck his cock. Sometimes I liked doing it, but it got to the point where I had to do that all the time or he couldn't come. He would tie me up and force me to have intercourse with our family dog. The dog was a big German shepherd, and the first time he told me to do this, I thought I'd vomit. He would get on top of me, holding the dog, and he would like hump the dog, while the dog had its penis inside me. I used to cry sometimes. I didn't want to do it. I mean, the dog seemed like another child of mine. It was such a part of our family. But every time I would protest, I would get beaten and then tied up and then he'd force me to do it anyhow. I mean what can you do when your legs are spread apart? So after a while, I just used to close my eyes and make believe that it wasn't really the dog, that it was really him. After the dog would finish fucking me, then Jeff would get on top of me and mount me just like the dog did. I used to wonder how he could stick his cock in my vagina after the dog had just been in it. It just seemed so disgusting to me, but somehow that used to just turn him on and excite him. In fact, I think he used to get his hardest hard-ons then. He would get on top of me, and he would just stick it in and out and in and out and in and out until he finally would come. Sometimes it used to take him half an hour or more before he could finally come. It felt like he was just beating on me and beating on me. There was no enjoyment. But I let him do it, so I guess I was to blame, too. I used to wish sometimes that I had someone to ask if that was normal or not. Somehow, I just didn't think it was. But who can you ask? Who can you talk to? I was just a kid. I tried to tell one of my girl friends, and she looked at me like I was crazy, and said to me, "Oh, well, I guess it must be pretty exciting having a husband who traveled around the Far East. I guess people over there like it better than we do, don't they?" I guessed she was right, and I stopped asking after a while. Once he tore me up so badly that I had to go to my gynecologist and have stitches. I'm not sure what he did. I think he ripped the scar from when I had the babies. In any event, it sure was painful. He reopened those stitches by forcing me to have intercourse again before they were healed, and I had to go back again. I lied to my gynecologist, though. I didn't tell him the truth. How could I? He would have thought I was really crazy. I bet you do, too. I do, too, sometimes. How could I have let it happen? How could I have let it go on? What's worse, how could I have liked some of it?

Lois looked at least twenty years older than she was. She was scarred all over and appeared to be crippled. Many of the scars were on her face.

My husband did this to me, you know. If I didn't want to have sex with him. Even if I did, it didn't seem to matter. He would take out his knife and he would cut marks in my skin with it. He would tie me whenever we had sex to a bed or a chair or whatever. Sometimes he would force me to suck him and would stick his penis in my mouth all the time. Sometimes he would tie me and turn me around facing the other way and would have anal sex with me. He ripped my rectum so many times that the doctors in the emergency room used to laugh when I'd walk in. I think his favorite was when he would masturbate and I had to masturbate him at the same time with various objects. He would use whatever was around. Sometimes he was very creative. Once he found a cantaloupe that I was saving for dinner, and he cut a round hole in it just about the size of his penis, and then he would put his penis in and out of the cantaloupe, and he used to make me watch it. He would make me say things and scream things at the same time to get him even more excited. The time with the cantaloupe, after he came all over it, he wanted to cut it up, and then he wanted me to eat some. I just couldn't do it. I gagged and I vomited, which seemed to turn him on even more. He had to be weird. He would stick all kinds of things in my vagina, like the crucifix with the picture of Jesus on it. One time he took a whole bunch of St. Christopher medals to see how many he could get in at one time. That time he was jerking off at the same time, and then just when he was about to come, he would stick his penis right by my vagina and get his sperm all over. I remember one time crying because he took some goldfish I had just bought the children. He wanted to see what would happen if he took a goldfish and put it all the way into my vagina. I'll never forget the sensation of that goldfish flapping around. Then he took his penis and stuck it in my vagina afterward, and it was him and the goldfish. I just remember him and the goldfish, him and the goldfish, him and the goldfish. I can't remember all the times he'd stick, push, and stuff all those objects inside of me. Sometimes I used to get up when he'd untie me, and I'd go into the bathroom and douche to clean myself out. I'd feel so filthy and so degraded. Once he caught me doing it and decided that that was a new toy for him to use, so he would take the douche bag and fill it up with all kinds of liquids, stick them in me, and watch them come out. I got a bad infection from that, and my doctor told me to throw the bag away, which I did. I can't remember when we ever had sexual intercourse normally. I know we did at the beginning of our marriage but it sure changed later on.

Maggie told a chilling, Frankensteinish tale of horror.

One night when Jerry and I were home, Jerry was in a foul mood, and the telephone rang. It was a man whom I had met when Jerry and I were separated. He was the man with whom I had sex and then told Jerry about. We had only had sex one night, but this guy was a friend of a friend of mine and was just passing through town and didn't know that Jerry and I were back together. I answered the phone, and Jerry picked up the extension. When this guy said his name, Jerry recognized it. He got on the phone and said to the guy, "Why don't you come up?" He told him that we were living together again, but said he'd like to meet him, he'd heard some nice things about him. I tried to say some funny, strange things into the phone to warn this guy not to come up, but I couldn't do it very well. I was scared of Jerry's temper, and I could see he was on a dangerously short line.

This fellow came up and Jerry was just as charming as he could be. All three of us sat down in the living room and had drinks together. We were all laughing and joking, and Jerry excused himself to go to the bathroom. He came back with his gun, loaded. The other man turned white. I thought he was going to have a heart attack. He started mumbling and pleading with Jerry. It didn't matter what this man said, Jerry terrorized him with the gun in the way he knew so well and told him that he was going to kill him for degrading and violating his wife. I cried and pleaded, but that didn't do any good, so I stopped. I think I stopped before this other man did. I knew it wasn't going to help with Jerry. I knew it wouldn't do any good, and I was afraid to make it worse. I thought maybe if I kept quiet, Jerry wouldn't use the gun. Sometimes that helped.

At this point, Jerry decided that the only way that this man was going to live was if he and I fucked right in front of him. He made the man take off all of his clothes. The man was so scared that he actually wet his pants as he was doing it, and I thought to myself, the poor man, how terrible it must be for him. Isn't it kind of funny that I never thought about myself at that point? I knew that I wasn't in danger; it was this man who was. I was really kind of outside of it all, kind of like I was an observer, even though I was the one who was going to get fucked. When the man was totally undressed, Jerry gave him directions, exactly what he was supposed to do. He told him how to touch me, where to touch me. It was really weird. I guess part of the strange feeling was that Jerry knew my body so well; he knew just where I responded, and when he told this man how to touch me, he expected me to respond the same way I might have responded to him. It's funny, you know. After a while, the physical part just takes over, and I was able to respond without any trouble. I think I had less trouble than that man did.

Just as the man and I were about to reach orgasm, Jerry stopped us. He was really going to be in charge that night. At that moment, he started undressing, still holding the gun on both of us. He then turned to me and the man both and started telling us what to do to him. I had to suck his penis, and the man had to stick his penis in Jerry's anus. I couldn't believe it. The man was so frightened, it was obvious he had never done anything like that before. Somehow, I mean, raping a woman seemed preferable to this man than what Jerry was telling him he had to do to him. I looked at the guy and I said, "You better do it, because if you don't, he'll really kill you." I think the man knew it. I certainly did. Jerry held that gun in his hand that whole entire time. How that man was able to get an erection and perform sex on Jerry as well as on me, I still don't know, but he kept it up until Jerry finally came. It's funny, you know, it didn't matter what I did or the other man did at that point. Afterward, Jerry made that guy go back to me again. Then he went on me, and it was really the three of us engaged in sex for hours that night. Every time that other man would plead with Jerry to stop it, Jerry would pick up the gun again. At one point, Jerry started sucking the other man's penis and putting the gun in the guy's mouth at the same time. The mixture of violence and fear and sex was absolutely incredible. I don't think I'll ever forget it. After several hours, the guy was finally allowed to go free. Strange, isn't it? I can still hardly believe I participated in it. No one got physically hurt that night, but I know I'll never forget it, and I'll bet that other guy doesn't either.

There are many questions that still need to be answered about these unusual sexual practices. My research did not adequately cover the question of the women's sexual satisfaction. Many reported reaching orgasm, but I suspect that cannot be used as the only measure of the woman's sexual satisfaction. I have reported that battered women often dissociate their body feelings from their cognitive thinking processes. This helps them to bear all the physical pain that they must. The dissociation must also blunt their physical satisfaction in sex. In fact, the most successful techniques I have used in helping battered women to gain control of their lives are body awareness exercises. Regaining control of their bodies helps them regain control of their lives. Thus, I really cannot evaluate whether what battered women report as good sex would also be considered fulfilling by non-battered women.

Battered women seem to have more trouble with sensuality than with sexuality. Sensuality can be thought of as the loving and nurturing behavior that occurs with intimacy. Sensuality is not always sexual in nature, but it feels good emotionally. It usually involves touch, sight, hearing, and can include other senses as well. For example, fantasy and imagery can often evoke sensual feelings by remembrance of past stimulations. Sensual feelings are associated with sexual stimulation but can also occur by themselves. Battered women talk a lot about trying to experience sensuality more frequently than they actually do. In truth, their sexual contacts are often bereft of any sensuality.

Discussing sexual intimacy with anyone, even a researcher

or a doctor, is anxiety-producing for most people, and even more so for battered women. Nonetheless, I have persisted in trying to collect some information about sexuality, because I feel it can help us to understand the nature of the intimacy between people who live in violence. Love and violence do not go together in our minds; yet for violent couples they do. At first, it was difficult to understand how women would want to have sexual relations with men who harmed them. Yet once understanding of the loving periods is gained, it makes sense. The information that we have collected so far is just a beginning. We need to know more before conclusions can be drawn.

There is also a question of sexual satisfaction for the men. In relationships that have existed over a period of time, the batterer is reported as having difficulty achieving and maintaining an erection. An association exists between impotency and alcohol-related problems, which may be significant in umderstanding the batterer's sexual performance. We know that there is an association between drinking and battering, although it is probably not a cause-and-effect relationship. However, if a man is drinking and becomes more aggressive and wants to have sex, he may be impotent owing to the alcohol. Many of the men are described as being bisexual, and some have even maintained male lovers over a period of time. It is not known whether they batter their male lovers, too. The women, in addition to Maggie, who have reported participating in such a *ménage à trois* arrangement say that the other man is also battered. Those few who reported engaging in a foursome stated the other woman also was battered by her man.

More investigation is needed on how participation in unusual sexual practices can keep the battered woman from leaving her partner. There seem to be two different reasons why the battered woman does not leave. Most feel guilty and ashamed about what they are doing. They thus rationalize that their violent beatings are punishment for their alleged sins. Others believe that if they leave this marriage, they will never again find such sexual excitement. They may stay in the marriage until the brutality becomes more aversive than the reinforcement of sexual pleasure.

I feel that I cannot leave this issue without saying a few words about pornography. The women's movement has targeted pornography as an underlying cause of the rape culture in which we live. I strongly agree that the kinds of pornography that are so degrading to women also perpetuate this kind of sexual behavior. The nature of the relationship between pornography, sex, and violence needs better understanding. Pornography contributes to women's being seen only as sex objects. It reinforces the view that women are either whores or madonnas and confirms battered women in their belief that they must be bad and evil if they engage in or even like sex other than married sex in the missionary position. Pornography also facilitates fathers' seductive behavior toward their daughters, which leads to incest with girl children, a topic which will be covered in the chapter on family discord.

The violence and brutality in the sexual relationship between assaultive couples seem to escalate with time. As marital rape becomes more frequent, loving, tender sex becomes more rare. When brutality is at its height in other areas of the marriage, it seems as if more coercive techniques need to be used in order for sex to happen at all. Almost all of the women in this sample report being sexually abused by their men. The concept of marital rape is not acceptable under the law in most states, although most married women could describe instances where it occurred. Most men feel that their wives' sexual availability is guaranteed by the marriage license. Women who live with men are also under the same misapprehension that their sexuality is barter for economic support. It seems evident that sexual assaults occur both in and out of legal marriages. Brownmiller's hypothesis that women choose to be married to one man and endure sexual assaults from him rather than run the risk of being raped and assaulted by any number of men in their lives typifies how the women in this sample feel.

6

Economic Deprivation

Many people believe the cornerstone in the victimization of battered women is economic. Such diverse groups as feminists and police officers believe that if these women were economically independent, they would not remain in their battering relationships. Money, however, does not protect women from battering. The image of the battered woman as a middle-class or upper-class woman is difficult for most people to comprehend. "Why doesn't she leave?" is the perennial question. "She certainly has enough money to escape," say the critics. It is only when the interaction between the economic factors and the psychological bonds is understood that we begin to comprehend more fully the battered woman syndrome.

Financial stability is rarely experienced by a woman even if she is economically independent. Professional women, women who have inherited wealth, and businesswomen all feel that men control their money—not only housewives who in fact depend upon their men's income and generosity for support. Interestingly enough, the women who are most likely to leave a battering relationship are those supported by welfare payments. They know that if they follow the eligibility rules, the state will support them and their children. As degrading and humiliating as the welfare system might be, these women know they are not the victims of a boss (usually male), unjust and unenforceable alimony and child support laws, or the unemployment spiral.

Women are financially better off when they are married. Usually, husbands have better earning potential than their wives. Combining two incomes or the property of two people gives the woman more spending power. Men also benefit economically from marriage by increasing their spending power, especially if they can control the use of the money. Married men are paid higher salaries than women (married or not) and unmarried men for the same work. This discrepancy is usually justified by a married man's need to support his family, and it is indicative of the unjustness of our entire economic system.

Even so, it is still difficult to understand why wealthy women remain in violent marriages. Christina is a good example of how economics can trap someone who has her own professional career, yet is bound to a battering husband who earns over $150,000 per year.

I finally decided to leave him. I had had enough. Even though he became extraordinarily violent only once or twice a year, the psychological harassment and minor incidents became too much to bear. Though I was fearing another incident which I felt impending, I filed divorce papers. Within a short time, the Internal Revenue Service filed a claim with my attorney charging me $35,000 in taxes that represented my share of the income Russell was earning. Although I never saw most of that money, as far as the government was concerned, this is what I owed them. On my $18,000 salary per year, I simply couldn't afford it. So Russell and I decided to try to live together again. What a mistake. Before the year was out, I had almost killed him in defending myself from another brutal beating. Fortunately, a court hearing determined that my fair share of the back taxes was a much more reasonable sum of money.

American society reinforces marriage. Despite the fact that married women are more often depressed and mentally unhealthy than single women, they are encouraged to stay married for economic reasons even when they are battered. And they do stay married.

Economics can be used in two ways in a battering relationship. One way is to trap the woman in the relationship through her fear of becoming poor. The second way is to use money as a coercive weapon. It is this second area that I wish to emphasize. It occurs across all socioeconomic levels and is as powerful a technique among the poor as it is among those who have higher standards of living. The economic stability of battering couples is usually a trouble spot regardless of socioeconomic level.

Economic deprivation is a form of control that can be both psychological and physical in nature. Most of us know what it feels like not to have something because we do not have the money. The pain and hurt of such deprivation are real no matter what the income level, whether the deprivation is a new sofa for the living room, a new dress for a special occasion, a new car because the old one is simply unsuitable, or money to buy the children's clothes or groceries, or to pay a doctor's bill. Such deprivation is particularly painful when women serve as homemakers and do not have outside income of their own. These women know that the money they receive depends upon whether or not their husbands earn it. Even when the women have their own income, their money is usually not spent on themselves but is used to support their families.

The legal status of homemakers is still in question, and both men and women are not certain of their rights. Within this climate of uncertainty, the battered woman is especially vulnerable. Not only does she fear that her man will give her money inadequate for her needs, but she also fears that if she contributes to his unrest his earning power may be diminished. She fears a similar loss even if it has been her money that purchased necessities for their home. Another problem is that frequently the woman's name does not appear on the couple's joint property. This arrangement often exists in order to secure adequate financing credit. Although the credit laws have changed and are much more equitable toward women today, most joint property was purchased prior to the legal changes. Even now, women are still talked into signing over their property to their men.

Batterers often have a history of financial instability. Professional men may earn varying amounts of money, depending upon their mood, health, or circumstances. This variability occurs even when the woman has a separate source of income. In many cases, the woman eventually has to bail the batterer out of financial problems.

Frequently, the use of economics as a coercive tool results in the denial of the basic necessities of life. The men become angry with their women and refuse to give them money to pay for the rent or needed medicine. Women's fear of being cut off with no money for the basic necessities of life perpetuates this kind of psychological battering. Often women relate stories of having to deprive their children of clothing, medical attention, and food in order to please their batterers and avoid a beating. The use of money in the couple's relationship can be controlled unfairly in different ways, and often this control becomes coercive.

For example, the man may hand his pay to his wife, after removing the amount of money that he needs, and say, "Pay all the bills." What he does not take into consideration is that there may not be enough money left to meet all the expenses. This is true especially if the batterer has spent unreasonable sums of money on gifts during his phase-three contrite period. When she comes up short, the man gets angry and begins to batter and punish her. It is her responsibility, he reasons, to make sure that those bills are paid. If they are not, it is her fault. He gets his constant sum of money, and she gets the remainder. She may try to cut corners by putting cheaper meals on the table or by getting a job to supplement their income. He then becomes angry because she is serving him inferior food or because she is working, and "No wife of mine is going to work." He perceives himself as inadequate and fears that the entire world thinks so, too. This anger often escalates into physical abuse or verbal humiliation and other forms of coercion. If the batterer also has a drinking problem, the woman often has no choice about whether or not to manage the money. If she allowed him total control, he would spend it all on alcohol.

Another unfair economic arrangement that was reported in these interviews occurred when the man did not allot the woman an adequate amount of spending money. Here the man usually took the initiative and said he would take care of all bills. The woman thus had to ask him for any extra money to buy the things she needed or wanted. Not only did she have to go to him for money, in essence she also had to ask his permission to spend it. For example, she might ask him for money to buy a new coat, and he might reply, "But I bought you one last year. Isn't that good enough? What do you need another one for?" So she finds herself making excuses, pleading, and having to watch his moods to approach him at the right time. Her judgment on how to spend money is constantly in question. Often these women did not understand the inappropriateness of this behavior, although they thoroughly disliked it. Many of them had gone from their father's home to their husband's home, and having to justify the money they needed was an adolescent way of life they were used to. Furthermore, it took the responsibility of money management away from them, a burden that no one enjoys, especially when there is not enough money to go around. This economic arrangement is predicated on the belief that the man is the better manager of money. However, without the woman being aware of it, the man's mismanagement or overextension of credit can bring financial ruin on both of them. Many of the women interviewed told of how they lost homes, cars, and other possessions when their batterers secretly took out second mortgages and then could not meet their financial obligations. Another economic factor which affects battering relationships is the loss of a job. There is no doubt that as unemployment becomes more chronic for both men and women, the rate of violence between them appeared to rise.

Another coercive economic situation occurs when the man does not work and the woman's income must support them. Many of the older battered women interviewed found themselves in this position. When the men were younger, they were able to work at a steady job and bring in some income. As they grew older, however, they became less able to perform a job. For some, flaring tempers interfered with normal business relationships. For others, alcohol played havoc with their careers. These women generally had had steady jobs over the years. It was their money that kept the family unit economically stable.

In several cases, the battered women inherited money. In these relationships, the women never controlled the inheritance. At best, the inheritance was shared, but usually the money went to support the batterer.

Kate's story is typical of an older woman with an independent income who experienced economic coercion. She was in her late forties when her first husband died, leaving her a sufficient amount of money to live comfortably. Her children were grown and no longer needed her support. She met Pat ten years ago on one of the many trips she took to ease some of the loneliness and boredom in her life.

> When I met Pat, I was impressed with how charming and kind he really was to me. My husband had been dead for two years, and I was just starting to become interested in the possibility of having a relationship with another man. Right away I knew that Pat was a bit manipulative, but he was just so charming. I hate to say it now, but I think I was seduced rather easily. He knew I had money and I knew he had none. Our relationship started out that way. It sounds terrible when I say it, almost like a gigolo, but in a sense there were a lot of elements like that in our relationship.

We were traveling together, I forget which country, and Pat told me that he had run out of money. I was planning to go on a tour that day, and I thought how much fun it would be if we could share it together, so I told him that I had enough money and wouldn't mind treating him. At first Pat was a bit taken aback, or at least I thought he was, but then he agreed that he would enjoy the tour, too, so he went. After a couple of times of my picking up the check for dinner, my paying for traveling, and my paying for all the entertainment that we had, it began to get easier for Pat to accept and for me to give him money. I really didn't mind; and, in fact, things seemed to have much more meaning when we shared them together. It seemed like money was a small price to pay for that kind of companionship, especially when I missed it so much and was so lonely after the death of my husband.

The trouble really didn't start until Pat and I decided to get married. I thought it would be important for him to have something to do, so that we just didn't hang around the house together all day long. At my suggestion, we decided to look for a little business. We took about $100,000 out of my money, and we bought a little travel agency. It seemed so natural, since travel was what we loved to do the most together. It didn't take long before things started to go sour in the business. All of a sudden, Pat needed more money for this and more money for that. When I began to protest, he would get physically coercive. I didn't know what to do. I was torn between saving my original investment and the business and taking over the management of the business, which would only get me more bruises. I'm at a real important decision place now. Do I try to save this business by putting some more money into it, but maybe also risk my life? He has threatened me with his guns lately. Or do I leave him and walk out on that investment? I feel like I've been conned, but I still have enough money that if I'm careful, I'll be able to live for the rest of my life without having to depend on my children for financial support. That's why my first husband left me so much money. He didn't want me to have to depend on the children, although I know my son and daughter would be more than willing to support me rather than see me get hurt time after time with Pat.

Adelle was a woman in her early sixties. Separated for a year from her husband of over forty years, she was struggling with the question of whether or not to go ahead with the divorce. Adelle was a handicapped woman, one of the many who were interviewed in this sample. She suffered from severe crippling arthritis and was unable to work. She couldn't get disability payments from the state because of her difficulty in untangling bureaucratic red tape. We were able to assist her in obtaining disability payments, which helped her regain some of her self-esteem. Adelle began her story by telling of a lifetime of hard work.

> My parents were immigrants to this country, and they had to work very hard just to make sure we had enough food to eat and to pay our rent. None of us kids got very much in the way of material things. It was kind of a harsh life we lived, filled with hard work and religion and not very much fun, but we didn't expect to have any fun. We were really too busy just trying to survive.
>
> I met Lars when I was working on this estate. I was the maid there, and he was the handyman. I was always very plain, but it didn't matter to me. Lars wasn't really very handsome. He was a plain man, too, but there was something about him that I kind of liked. We didn't get married for about three years. I continued to work hard, and Lars worked, too. We saw each other outside of work maybe once or twice a week if we weren't too tired. Finally, we had scraped enough money together to get married. We were given a little apartment by the family that I worked for, a little garage apartment where they had room. I had always lived there while I worked and just went home on weekends. It had a tiny little bedroom and a little living room and just a little kitchen you couldn't do very much in. It was a pretty little place, though, and I tried hard to fix it up. I would work all day and then spend the evenings working in my little place. I don't mean to complain by telling you all this, just to tell you how hard it really was sometimes. Because we didn't have too many other expenses, I could save the little bit of money that I made and Lars's money.
>
> We were just ready to buy our own little house, and maybe think about starting a family, when my mother got sick. Daddy had died a few years before Lars and I got married, but Momma had always been a fairly well woman. When she got sick, there seemed to be no choice. We would have to move in with her. Lucky for us, we had the money saved, so we could

help pay off the rest of the mortgage on her house. Otherwise, she would have lost it.

I continued to work for a while. Then I just couldn't work and take care of Momma at the same time, so we decided we would start a family then. Lars was a good, kind man. He never abused me then, even though it was just too much for him after the babies started coming and Momma was getting sicker and sicker. Money just always seemed to be going out. We never seemed to have any. No matter how hard I saved, we had so little left over. I worked hard, though, and I was real proud. After Momma died, I changed some of the things in the house so it would be our house.

As my little girls grew up, Lars got better and better jobs. He went to school at night and he studied hard, and he got a job with a good company. Things really started looking better. We sold Momma's house, and we bought a new house. You know, out south where they were building all those new houses then. I loved that little house. I still do. I won't give it up for anything, even for those people down in the welfare department who tell me I have to sell my house if I want to get money from them now. They can't make me do it. Well, anyhow, Lars was working real hard, and then all of a sudden one day he had an accident on the job. He was going into one of the warehouses, and some big boxes fell down and hit him on the head. He was knocked unconscious, and for a while they didn't know if he was going to make it or not.

That was the beginning of all the rest of our troubles. He did recover, but the doctor said he had permanent brain damage. I don't know if it was true or not, because nothing else ever changed for Lars, except that that was when he started getting violent, and he started beating me. He had never touched me before then. He was a good man, Lars was, until that accident. That was about seven years ago. They kept him for another two years at that job, and then his boss called me one day and said to me, "You know, Adelle, I don't know where Lars is anymore. He doesn't come into work; and when he does, he doesn't do his work. I'm really sorry but I'm going to have to fire him. I feel terrible because I think it happened because of the accident. He never was like that before then. I just don't know, Adelle, but I can't keep him on anymore." Well, I thought it was real nice that his boss called me to tell me that, but I also think it was rotten, because I really think it was because of that accident that our whole lives became ruined. Anyhow, Lars got a lot of jobs after that. I can't keep track of them all. He couldn't keep any of them. He really couldn't work anymore. One time we even hired a lawyer to sue the company for causing his disability, but we couldn't do anything, because Lars had signed some papers that said that he didn't have any more claims against the company in order for them to pay him some disability when he was recovering.

The beatings started getting worse and worse until finally about a year ago. When I called the police, they took Lars away and put him in the hospital. The social worker in the hospital told me that I should not go back to live with him, that he was too violent, and that he really needed to be in the hospital in their special program for a while. I knew it was a mental hospital, and I really didn't want to put him there, but I had no choice. He might kill me. He's a strong man, my Lars. He never forgave me for doing that. He got out of the hospital after two months, and he came over to the house and he beat me so badly. While he was beating on me, he was telling me what an awful wife I was to lock him up in that horrible place. He beat me for all the pain that I caused him for staying in that place, and then he left and said he wasn't going to come back. I know he's not working. I know he's not doing anything, but I also know that his father died last year, and Lars is his only heir. I know he's going to get some money. It's the only money we've ever had in our whole life, and I want some so I can live, too. If he doesn't want to live with me, I understand that and that's all right. I'd rather live alone now, whatever years I have left, than to continue to live with him, but I want some of that money, and I don't know what to do. How can it happen that I could live a whole life with this man, work so hard, and then he comes into money and he gets to keep it all, and I don't get any of it? It just isn't fair. It just *isn't* fair and I don't know what to do. I can't work, and I just don't know what to do.

Loretta is another woman who was trapped economically in a battering relationship. She had been assaulted for years while her children were growing up. After ten years of battering, Loretta decided that she was going back to school.

One morning I woke up and decided this was it. I had just had enough. I was still sore from the beating I had suffered the night before, and I was exhausted from being up half the night while he was still harassing me. I don't know why that morning was any different from other mornings, but I decided that I had to make something of myself, or I'd be with him forever, or I'd be dead. Without thinking of what kinds of consequences there might be, I decided that I was going to enroll in school. I went to the phone and I called the medical technician school that one of my friends had gone to. I thought that was as good a career as any, and I knew it didn't take that long to get a degree. I enrolled in school that afternoon, and I loved it. It was my sanity. It took me almost two years to finish the program, and there were lots of beatings in between. But each one got a little easier to bear as I got closer to the day when I knew I could go out and earn money on my own. It was like my little secret. I knew that when I finished with school, I would also be finished with my marriage, and so it was.

Julia, on the other hand, was not as lucky as Loretta. She had a harder time attempting to assert her independence. Julia was the wife of a colleague of mine. Interviewing her and using her story have been very difficult for me. Enough of the facts have been changed so that she is unrecognizable, but her story is true, as is the double jeopardy that faces battered women married to mental health professionals. Julia's husband had been educated while Julia worked as a secretary. She was permitted to take several classes at night, but he was the psychologist. When Julia wanted to go back to school, he refused to pay for it. "You don't need a college degree," he told her. "You can continue working with me and that is all that is necessary. You're smarter than them anyhow. How can you possibly learn more than what I've already taught you?" Julia believed him when he said this, because she had been his silent partner for years. When he had term papers to write in school, Julia helped him. Not only did she type the papers, but she began editing them and making constructive comments where they were appropriate. He trusted her judgment, and soon she was ghostwriting his professional papers. They collaborated on most of the research work that he did. Julia said she did not need individual recognition. It was satisfying enough to see him gain such acclaim. When, however, the abusiveness he had used against her escalated and she could no longer tolerate the pain and suffering, she began to think of leaving the marriage. She even left him and lived on her own for a short period of time.

> All of a sudden, I felt as though my self-worth was gone. I couldn't get a job in psychology. I didn't have the credentials. I couldn't do the work that I was used to doing. He was my ticket into an exciting professional career. It didn't matter that my name wasn't on the work, until I really needed to get a job on my own; then I realized what a waste of time it had been all those years. No one would hire me. No one would give me the same respect that I got being his wife. It didn't matter that no one knew that I was doing the work, too, until I had nothing to put on my résumé when I went to look for a job. How could I be a secretary again when I had been doing all those other exciting things? It wasn't enough for me then. It still isn't enough for me.

In talking with Julia, I attempted to persuade her to go back to school and get her own degree. She was certainly competent enough to do it. She said, "I can't do it. It'll take too long. I just can't do it. No matter what you say, I don't need the degree. I don't need it and I don't want it. I just want to be able to do the work I can do without going to school. It just seems like such a waste of time."

I have concentrated on retelling many of the economically middle-class women's stories because most people believe that finances trap only the poor. Rarely have the middle-class women come forth. "If they can afford it, why don't they leave?" people ask. These women felt that they couldn't afford to leave. Money, in addition to psychological bonds, tied them to their batterers. It might be difficult to feel sorry for Christina, who needed to cut her spending power from over $150,000 down to $18,000 per year, when so many women must exist on less than $10,000. Yet Christina was faced with losing her home, friends, children's school, and other supports in her life, in addition to facing a heavy debt to pay her share of the back taxes. All because her husband was a batterer. In these cases, the women had no personal power over their economic status. The men did or didn't give them money, depending on their own whims. Sometimes more affluent women feel better about themselves for having succeeded in getting their husbands to provide well for them; most recognize that all that money can disappear in a very short period of time.

The use of economic deprivation as a coercive technique results in bargaining and trade-offs. Not only is the woman deprived economically, but also she is emotionally deprived as an adult. She has virtually no freedom. She is not permitted to learn how to manage money; or if she does, her abilities are discounted, and she is not allowed to make adult choices. Furthermore, when she realizes she wants something, she then has to learn a whole range of manipulative techniques in order to get it. Recent self-help books for women purport to teach them how to manipulate men to get material items or to gain love. These authors condone a woman's putting her thumb in her mouth, stamping her foot, and sulking like a little girl in order to get what she wants. In addition to being psychologically unhealthy, this kind of behavior perpetuates women's inability to ask directly for things they want. What happens in this kind of manipulative bargaining is that the woman is not trying to get her man's love, but rather to stop further economic deprivation, and she becomes angry at the song and dance she must perform in order for it to work. The thing that is wrong with both of these kinds of manipulations is that the women may accomplish their immediate ends, but in the long run they do not stop economic deprivation.

None of the stories that I have presented so far reflects extreme poverty and deprivation. It is not that they did not occur; they did. In story after story, women had barely enough money to survive. There were stories of women who were awarded inadequate amounts of alimony and child support by the court and who did not receive any of it. Stories of women denied child support because they refused to allow their battering husbands to exercise their visitation rights with the children they abused. Stories of women who, fearing for their lives, chose to give up child support payments rather than let their men know where they lived.

Terry was typical of these women. She came to Denver via the "feminist underground railroad." That is, she went to a battered women's shelter in a city near her hometown, and when the shelter staff heard her story, they sent her as far away from there as possible. In her case, her husband's previous behavior indicated he would probably kill her and her children rather than let them leave him. Thus, Terry and her three children came to a battered women's shelter in another part of the country, away from family or friends, with no money or familiar possessions to comfort them. To get her application through social services for money for her and her children took close to two months; registering the children in school became a major hassle; finding new housing took great skill; even obtaining a current driver's license was fraught with roadblocks. Without the help of advocates, Terry would probably not have been able to resettle and begin a new life. Economically she was destitute, and our institutional response to her was inadequate merely because she had previously lived elsewhere. When Terry decided she wanted to find a job, her troubles began anew. If she earned money, her medical benefits for the children would cease and she would not be eligible to use legal aid services. The mental health center would charge her for psychotherapy, and her new bills for the same services would leave her penniless again. Our welfare system is a "catch 22" for people who wish to improve themselves. But so is the job market for women.

Economic deprivation ceases to be a coercive technique only when women accept their right to economic freedom. Economic relationships between men and women need to be relationships of equality and parity rather than superiority and control. Both partners need to contribute to decision making and financial management. Each person must give the other person credit for work contributed in the relationship. It is quite simple for a batterer to keep his woman economically dependent upon him. In her book *Battered Wives,* Del Martin has described the injustices to women in the job market. Similar injustices occur for women who choose to stay home and be homemakers. Tradition has decreed that these women be excluded from their rights to all medical disability, pension, and other benefits that workers receive. Our capitalistic society, which needs to keep competition stable in order to thrive, historically has kept women out of the job market according to its needs.

The capriciousness with which society treats women as workers is indicated in Ellen's story. She was fifteen years old and pregnant when she got married in 1943. She and her husband had not lived together more than a few months when he was drafted into the Army. World War II was being fought, and all available men were taken. After those few months that she and her husband had together, Ellen was not really sure she ever wanted him to come home from the war.

I didn't understand it, but it wasn't more than the first week of our marriage when he started hitting me. By the time he left several months later, I was a mass of bruises. I feared for my unborn child, because he often would beat me right around the stomach and in the breasts. I wondered if I would be able to nurse my child, if the pain would ever stop long enough. It turned out that I didn't need to worry about that with the war and everything. I had to work, so I didn't have time to nurse anyhow. After my baby was born, I decided to get a job in the factory. There was a munitions factory out here, and all the women were encouraged to work. It's funny how they encouraged us by not only offering some decent salaries, but also by setting up a day-care center so that we could leave our babies there, close to work. I have to laugh now, when my daughter-in-law tells me how hard she's fighting for day care for my grandchildren. I had to laugh when President Nixon was saying how it was going to undermine the whole family structure of the country. It's so funny because during the war years they had day-care facilities set up all over for all of our babies. We weren't told how bad it was for children and family then, were we? Especially when our government needed our help, because if we didn't do the work, it wasn't going to get done.

Well, it was the first time that I was ever economically independent. I earned my own money, and I got a little allotment from the Army, and I was really feeling good about life. I dated a little bit, but nothing serious. I really wasn't interested in having any other relationship, and it was O.K. then not to have sex. Somehow, during the war years that was the right thing to do, you know, to kind of deprive yourself a little bit, so that you could feel some of the same kinds of pain that was going on for all the boys who were going over and getting killed. It was kind of our way of saying, "See, we really do care!" Well, I loved working, and I did well. I was promoted, and soon I was a foreman or forewoman, as they call it now. It really was good for me, and my little boy grew strong and healthy. His father didn't see him until he was back on furlough and the baby was two years old. The Army flew me to Hawaii, and I brought the baby with me. What a mistake! I thought his father would want to see him. Well, the baby couldn't treat this strange man as his father. He never knew him, and I had a hard time being a loving wife to this man who was only my husband for a few months, the memories of whom were fairly brutal. But I tried. Honestly, I really tried. I tried to be cheerful and happy. I mean, we were in Hawaii, too. After the years of hard work, and I had never been anyplace like that. It should have been exciting, but it wasn't. By the time his furlough was over, I was a nervous wreck, and so was my baby. We both couldn't wait to get back home, and I have a feeling my husband couldn't wait to get back into combat either. Well, it was really only about another year and a half or so that we were able to continue working in this factory, and then Ben came home. I really wanted to continue working. I thought that would be good for us. He had a hard time getting a job at first, and I wanted to keep little Benjie in the nursery. But the first thing they did was to shut down all of the nurseries. All of a sudden, when the country didn't need the women to work in the factories anymore, when the country wanted its men back to work in the factories, they shut down the child-care centers, so that we had no place to leave our children.

Well, I thought since Ben couldn't get a job, he should stay home and take care of Benjie, and I would stay working. So I wasn't one of the first women to give up the jobs, as I saw all of my friends dropping out of work one at a time. I got a lot of harassment for doing that. Other men and women all pointed their fingers at me and told me it was my fault that all these returning vets couldn't get jobs. My keeping my job made it so hard because they couldn't get jobs, and I should go back home and take care of my child because isn't that what you're supposed to do? Isn't that what a woman was supposed to do? I really was confused. They really did a job on my head at that time, plus things at home just weren't going as well as I thought they would. Ben couldn't stand little Benjie. He never loved him. I still, to this day, think he resents our son, Ben, because he wasn't there when he was born. His violence and his brutality would be taken out on his little boy. I would come home and my previously happy, joyful little boy became a sullen angry child, with bruises and welts all over his body. I remember crying one night to Ben, and pleading with him not to beat up on this little boy. How could he hate his own flesh and blood? I remember Ben saying to me, "Well, if you would have another baby, maybe I could love Benjie as much. Let's have another child." Fool that I was, I gave in. Oh, I'm not sorry now that I had both James and Greg. All three of my boys have been the greatest joy to me, but at the time, the last thing in the world I needed was another baby. Of course, becoming pregnant and having another baby meant that I had to give up my job, and that was the end of my economic independence and my freedom for the next few years.

It didn't take too long for Ben to find a job. It also became clear to me that I was bored at home. I loved working, but Ben wouldn't let me work. It would just be the scene for another argument or another fight. In order to escape from the brutality at home and from the difficulty of raising three little boys, I decided to start my own business in my home. It seemed like such a simple solution. I really was good at sewing and good at work with my hands, so I became a seamstress. Women customers used to come into the house for fittings, and I always made sure to schedule them when Ben wasn't around. If he should be around at that time, I would be afraid that I would lose my customers through some of his nasty comments. I also didn't want him to know how many customers I had, so that I could save some money, and save it I did. I have a little bank account now that he knows nothing about, all made out of the business money that I did in those years. That's my safety account. If things really, really get bad today, I will take that money, and I can leave. It's my security blanket, even though I'm not sure I ever will use it.

Maria is another woman who was able to save some money. She managed to put away a dollar here and a dollar there out of her grocery money or household money that her husband would give her to spend for the family. She never told anyone that she was putting this money away, but saved it for emergencies. On one occasion, she had to use the money for emergency surgery for one of her children, but slowly she was able to replace it. During the interview, Maria said that she had, after twenty-three years, been able to save about $650. She was very proud of being able to save this much money. It struck me as sad that it would probably not be enough to buy her a plane ticket and to pay a deposit and the first month's rent on an apartment.

The women whose stories have been told here are the more fortunate ones. These are not the women who cannot afford bus fare to another town. These are not the women whose batterers take away their cars so they cannot even seek safety across town. These are not the women who show up at safe houses, shelters, churches, and other refuges with nothing but the clothes they are wearing and their children. I did not get to meet many of these women unless I went to the refuges and safe houses and interviewed them there. Their stories all were similar. Brutality and economic deprivation went hand in hand. I did not choose to use those stories as case studies because I am interested in demonstrating that socioeconomic level does not protect a woman from being battered. Having money does not ease the pain or comfort of a woman who is being battered. Some women may use their money to buy a night's lodging in a motel or a trip to Europe, but it does not lessen either the physical or the psychological pain of living in a violent love relationship.

7

Family Discord

Most little girls dream of living in a happy family "forever after." Battered women particularly want this dream to come true. However, as in other areas of the battering relationship, the family's function is disturbed. The disturbed family structure includes the parents and relatives of both the battered woman and her batterer, and their children. Often former spouses and stepchildren are also involved. The family structure of older battered women may include their children's spouses and their relatives and their grandchildren. Despite the mobility of families in American cultures, the families of battered women tend to be within close geographical reach. Sometimes they live in other states, but the family manages to visit and communicate fairly regularly. Battered women do not always suffer alone. If the family is nearby, the battering cannot be kept a total secret. Much of the pain is shared, although a conspiracy of silence often develops. In most cases, the women interviewed felt that while their families could not initiate intervention, they would help them escape from the battering situation if asked—although there were some instances when families deserted the women or encouraged them to endure the violence to preserve the family. The catch was that these women had been trained from earliest childhood not to leave: "Marriage is forever," "You made your bed, now lie in it," and "Divorced women are responsible for their marital failures." The decision to terminate a violent marriage had been taken away from these women by society's expectations early in their childhood.

How do children learn the messages of their culture? Psychologists are just beginning to learn about the effects of growing up in a home where sex roles are stereotyped. Sexist attitudes teach little boys and girls that little boys are stronger than little girls, and that boys deserve the very best. Little girls learn to be nurturers. The not-so-hidden message contained in female nurturing behavior is that girls must expend their energy in supporting boys to achieve success. This is translated to mean that it is really all right for men to coerce women into doing what they want them to do, because men know best.

We also teach our children certain beliefs about violence. Despite any wishes to the contrary, we are a violent society. We are beginning to understand that when we use coercion to discipline our children, we make it easier for them to become more tolerant of coercive force as they grow older. This rewarded coercive behavior then leads to more frequent acceptance and use of violence. This pattern is confirmed by studies of child abuse and other forms of violence. One consistent finding is that, as noted earlier, most people who batter their children were themselves battered as children. Child abuse thus becomes a vicious cycle. People who have been battered learn to use battering behavior as a means of getting what they want. Secondly, studies of the effects of violence and of viewing other people's violence reveal that the more violence you observe, the more tolerant you become of violent behavior. That is not to say that you must use violent behavior yourself. What it does suggest is that you permit it to be used in front of you. Much of the testimony in government hearings concerning the effect of television violence on children has shown these findings to be consistent.

Sociologists studying violent behavior among family members report that there seems to be a violence level permitted and tolerated in each family. Family members decide on the level. Some families thus may tolerate a great deal of violence before it becomes defined as troublesome to other family members. Richard Gelles's work at the University of Rhode Island indicates that abnormally high levels of violence seem to pass down from generation to generation in different families. We thus have some subcultures where violence against family members is a norm. It is only when the level of violence in the family rises above the normally tolerated level that people within that family are willing to consider themselves victims. Many incidents of battering thus take place in a family situation which neither party is willing to label as battering behavior. It is interesting to consider why such coercive behavior is tolerated at all. Why would people, specifically women, permit themselves to be regularly coerced into doing some things they did not want to do? Why do battered women remain in their violent homes? These questions have been the most perplexing ones for me to answer.

Battering is usually approved as acceptable behavior when it is relabeled "strong discipline." From the point of view of the batterer, such discipline is regarded as permissible if it helps to achieve a goal. From the point of view of the victim, such discipline is acceptable if she feels she deserves it or if she benefits from it. Such discipline is thought to be an effective teacher. There is no doubt that strong discipline or punishment will suppress undesirable behavior. It is quick, efficient, and permits someone to discharge his/her anger at another person. It is such an effective tool of control that those who routinely use this discipline speedily realize that often just the threat of the behavior will elicit the desired results. If you remove the threat of force, however, then that person is free to behave in whatever way he/she wishes. So we see that controlling someone's behavior through the use of violence only works temporarily, while the battering or the threat of battering is actually present. Then, too, over a period of time more violence is necessary to accomplish the same results. Violence as a discipline does not cause a permanent change in the way someone will behave unless the victim believes that the possibility of violence is always present. However, batterers are very accomplished at getting their victims to believe that it is. A climate of fear is established which is maintained by the ever-present potential for extremely violent explosions. There does not need to be a steady reign of terror for the family atmosphere to be emotionally charged. Rather, the stage needs to be set through prior incidents for all to understand that another violent explosion is a certainty—the only variable is when it might occur. Many of the battered women believe their men have extraordinary insight into their thoughts and actions. The men also are seen as omnipotent in terms of their ability to survey their women's activities. Thus, battered women feel as though all of their thoughts and behavior must be perfect or they may precipitate the inevitable acute battering incident. In this way, the constant potential for violence controls the lives of battered women.

Threats of violence also to the battered women's families were standard routine for the batterers in my study. They often described exactly how they would torture and maim family members who got in the way. Usually, such threats were directed at female members of the woman's family. The men in her family—fathers and brothers, particularly—were usually secondary. The woman really believed that her batterer would commit such violence. After all, she knew him to be capable of committing violence against her and her children, the very people he was supposed to love. Therefore, she usually allowed him to isolate her from her family; or, in some cases, she saw her family without him. In any event, she believed she could not depend upon her family to protect her from him.

Child-rearing patterns in this society sanction the use of physical control and violence against children. This is the norm rather than the exception. Schools resort to corporal punishment, including child beating and battering. Children learn that people who love you have the right to hurt you in the name of discipline—for your own good. The comparison between children and battered women is not far-fetched. Men see women as children. Women who are infantilized may themselves believe that they need to be disciplined. When it is permissible to beat up your child in the name of discipline, then it becomes acceptable to beat up your woman. If the blame for the incident can be transferred to the woman, then a beating can be excused in the name of discipline. Men say, "I wanted to teach her a lesson."

In analyzing the kinds of dissonance that occurred within the families of these battering couples, it is important to identify the battered woman and her batterer as the core of the nuclear family. Most battered women do have children, from either their present relationships or previous ones. In an unusually high number of cases, these women became pregnant with their first child prior to being married. At the same time, they held traditional beliefs about children coming after love and marriage. Staying together for the sake of the home and family was often cited as a reason for allowing victimization to continue. All of the women interviewed stated that they did not want to deprive their children of their fathers by breaking up their marriages. There is a selflessness that goes along with grinning and bearing an intolerable situation for the sake of the children. Impressive data, however, demonstrate that children who live in a battering relationship experience the most insidious form of child abuse. Whether or not they are physically abused by either parent is less important than the psychological scars they bear from watching their fathers beat their mothers. They learn to become part of a dishonest conspiracy of silence. They learn to lie to prevent inappropriate behavior, and they learn to suspend fulfillment of their needs rather than risk another confrontation. Like many children who suffer from overt physical child abuse, these children learn to be accommodating and cooperative. They blend into the background. They do not express anger. They do not acknowledge the tension. They do expend a lot of energy avoiding problems. They live in a world of make-believe. When the screaming and yelling begin they stare transfixed but inconspicious, watching in terror. Sometimes they turn up the stereo or television to block out the noise. Other times they fall asleep, pretending it is not happening. When they are older, these child victims report enormous feelings of guilt that they chose to conceal and deny these incidents rather than to attempt to intervene. They often assume responsibility for the beginnings of a fight.

Women with younger children often denied that the abuse these children witnessed or experienced affected their growth and development, although sometimes they could recognize signs of emotional disturbance in their children. The children often suffered from severe learning problems in school. Imagine trying to concentrate on schoolwork while wondering whether your mother would be alive when you got home that day. Compliance and cooperativeness typify the children's behavior in school. Outside of school, however, these children are often impulsive, unruly, and aggressive toward other children. They have learned many different coping styles in order to spare themselves from being beaten. I observed the behavior of school-age children in safe houses in England and in this country. Such safe houses tend to be very crowded, noisy, and chaotic; yet the children were able to tune out the chaos and stare for long periods of time at a television set. Direct physical contact was often needed to get their attention. Their mothers vacillated between being overprotective and ignoring them.

The presence of children in the home affects the frequency of the battering cycles. The number of acute battering incidents and the number of times the cycle occurs seem to increase at three distinct periods. The first is during pregnancy, when there is a rapid escalation of physical abuse toward the woman. The second period occurs when there are infants and small children present in the home. Small children demand an enormous amount of a woman's attention. It is also more difficult to stop a small child's pleas for assistance and to control their demands. Women who have suffered battering when their children were small often cite the batterer's jealousy of the time spent with the children as the precipitating event for the abuse. The third period when violence escalates is when the children are adolescents. This is a period of high stress for normal families as well as those experiencing domestic violence. Adolescents can no longer stay neutral in their parents' battles. The battered women in this sample report that their children chose one of two tactics; either they became supportive of their mother and attempted to stop the batterer from harming her, or they identified with the batterer and began to abuse their mother themselves. It is not clear why the adolescents chose the responses they did. What is clear is that no matter which response they choose, they have ambivalent feelings toward their mother. They both love her and hate her. They want to protect her, but they also feel that she deserves the abuse. In many cases, they feel angry that she has abandoned them to meet the consuming needs of the batterer.

June's story is a good illustration of how this alienation can occur. When she was interviewed, she was a twenty-one-year-old college student, the oldest daughter in a family of four children. She had a sister seventeen, a brother fifteen, and another sister eight years old. Her father had battered her mother for as long as she could remember. She herself was abused as a child.

I never realized that my family was different from the other kids I grew up with until I was in third or fourth grade, I think. At that time I remember coming into school with black-and-blue marks all over my arms and legs where my father had beat me the night before. I remember the teacher making a big fuss over it and taking me down to the principal's office. A woman came out to talk to me. I think she was a social worker. I just remember her being very nice and sweet and asking me how I got the bruises. Somehow they gave me the message that I shouldn't talk, that it would be wrong to tell them the truth, that my father had done it and had also battered my mother that night, so I didn't say a word then or afterward, until last year when I finally told someone other than my family.

Growing up, I can remember sometimes when my father and mother would be having big battles, my mother would take me to my grandmother's house or to my aunt's house. I would sometimes spend a couple of nights there with my brother and sister. Later on, after the baby was born, my mother really needed me to be a substitute mother to Lisa. I guess I didn't mind, usually. I was glad to be able to help my mother. She was trying to work and get ahead and buy things for us as a family. I think she was trying to cover some of my father's debts; but it was always hush-hush, and we never talked about it. Anyhow, I would be the one who would get everybody ready before I went to school. I had to make lunches, and I had to feed the baby in the morning so that my mother could sleep. When I came home at three o'clock, my mother had already left for work, and my father was taking care of the baby. He worked nights. My mother would come home just about when my father was ready to go to work, so they really didn't see each other all that much. Anyhow, it was my job when I came home from school to take care of the baby, so my father could get some sleep so that he would be able to work all night at his job. I remember getting beaten a lot of times by my father for not doing things right. It wasn't until I was a teen-ager that I realized some of the fights my father would have with me were exactly the same as the fights he would have with my mother. I remember vividly going to her one day and crying about what was happening at home when she was at work. I know I was angry with her, but I also needed her protection. She made it very clear that she couldn't give it. She cried with me, too, and told me how much she loved me, but she said there was nothing she could do about it, that we all had to do the best we could. She pleaded with me to try to stay away from my father and not get into trouble with him. It was as though some of her knew that it wasn't really my fault, just as the beatings weren't really my fault, but the other part of her knew that she was letting me take the rap for her, that I was getting beaten instead of her. We never talked about things like that, but I still knew it was true.

I remember trying once to talk to my grandmother, who was really like another mother to me. I started crying to her and telling her my new revelation, and she just looked at me and said, "Hush, girl, hush. You don't know what you're saying. Don't say things like that, girl. That's just not true. You know your mother loves you; you know she's trying hard for you and for the other kids. You've got to do your part, too. We know your father's difficult to live with at times but you have to be strong. You have to bear it."

When I went away to school, I felt so guilty, like I was really deserting my mother. As I would have predicted, my father's beatings of her started to increase while I was out of the home. There was nothing I could do. If I went back to that house, I would get the beatings and she wouldn't or at least not as many. But I felt like I was going crazy, that I had to get out and run while I could, and going away to school seemed like the best thing to do. I still feel guilty sometimes, but I know it was the right decision, even though now I'm not allowed back in the house at all. That was because at Thanksgiving, when I went home, my mother and father were at it all day long, the fighting, the yelling, the bickering, my mother trying to shush us all, keep us quiet, and keep us out of it, and my father raging and screaming and yelling and putting us all down. I couldn't take any more of it, and I finally told him to knock it off, and he started in on me and then my mother got involved and got in the middle between him and me, one of the few times she really stood there to protect me. The screaming got louder and worse, and my brother and sisters were about to jump in on the whole thing when I ran screaming and crying, and my father started beating my mother. His punches were flying, and he was shoving us both all over the kitchen. The other three kids just stood there watching in the doorway, both not knowing who to jump in on first. God, it was awful! I ran out of the house when I could, still screaming and yelling, and I called the police. I decided that was it, no more. I wasn't going to put up with it anymore, and my mother didn't have to either. Well, the police came. I walked in the house with the police. They sat us all down, and I told my side of the story, which was the truth this time. They looked at my father and my mother, my mother with bruises all over her, tears still in her eyes, and my father all disheveled, still not calmed down yet, and my brother and sisters terrified, but still in that whole conspiracy of silence. They asked my mother, "Did he do this to you?" My mother looked at me, looked at the other kids, and looked at my father, and then looked at the policemen and said, "No, it was just a family fight."

Well, I screamed and yelled and tried to persuade my brother and sisters to say something, but nobody would. They were just like I was for all those years, but I decided no more for me. I do the best I can, but I can't protect them anymore. So I left home that day, and I haven't been back in that house since. It's seven months since then, and I miss them all terribly. I get to see my brother and sisters sometimes at my grandmother's house, and I talk to my mother a lot. I haven't talked to my father since then, and I don't think I ever will. Although I know never is a long time, I'm just still too angry at him to be able to even talk about it. I'm angry with my mother, too, for all those years, but I love her and I know she loves me, and I know someday I'll have to work that out, too. The saddest part is my sisters and my brother, especially my little sister. I wish I could get them out and save them, but I know I have to save myself and finish school; then maybe I can go back and help them.

When I met Molly, she was a forty-five-year-old welfare recipient. She had three teen-aged children, two boys and a girl. When she heard that I was doing interviews of battered women, she called and asked if I would talk with her. She made it very clear on the telephone that she was not being battered by her husband; in fact, she had no husband. The people who were doing the battering were her children.

My husband took off about ten years ago when my oldest child was eight and my youngest was four. I've been alone ever since. Oh, I've had some relationships with men and occasionally somebody would move in for a while, but not too often. Mostly, I had to do it on my own. I had to raise those children and I had to support us. I did O.K. sometimes. I got a job as a hairdresser, which I really like doing, and sometimes I really could make good money. Lately it just hasn't been that way. I've been too tired and haven't been well, and I've been on welfare for about a year and a half since my operation. I think that's when the kids' beating me up started, too. I don't think they did any of that before I went in for my operation.

Although they used to yell and scream at me a whole lot. When they were very little, their father did beat me, but I don't think they saw it, and I don't think they knew it. They were really too little. Besides which, their father was really good to them. He never hit them. In fact I'm embarrassed to say it was me who hit them. He would beat on me sometimes, and the tension would be so bad, and those babies, I had three babies, they'd cry and they'd whine and they'd get on my nerves. It used to seem like I never could do anything right for any of them. I couldn't please my man, and I couldn't please my babies, especially my middle one, my daughter. She was so difficult to raise. She would cry, and she would whine, and she would always want something, and always at all the wrong times, too. I did beat those babies at times. Maybe that's why they beat me now. I don't know.

The kids and I—well, we get along all right most of the time. It's only once in a while that they start to get pushy with me. The funny thing is, it's usually after I get my welfare check. Then each of them starts demanding money; and before you know it, the whole check is gone before I even get anything for myself out of it. I've asked them a hundred times to get a job if they really wanted more money. But they're lazy kids, and they're not about to work if they can get money from me. My middle daughter is the one who does the worst damage. She's had a lot of trouble with both alcohol and drugs. I worry about her so much sometimes, but then I get so angry with her. If I give her any advice or tell her what to do, she turns on me and screams and yells, then starts slapping and punching and kicking. My social worker tells me to tell her to leave and let her go out on her own, but I just can't do it. All those years I sacrificed to give those children a better life. I loved those kids. I know they don't mean to hurt me, and maybe they're doing it because I used to hit them to get them to mind me when they were little. I just don't know.

It is interesting to watch battered mothers play with their children. In most cases, it is difficult for them to get into a playful mood. Once they do, however, they jump in totally and laugh and romp like a child with their children. I have observed similar interactions between batterers, their women, and their children. Batterers tend to be enormously playful and childlike, causing lots of laughter with their practical jokes. At times, their playfulness borders on outrageousness. Their silliness flouts social rules. For example, they may sneak into an apple orchard and steal an apple, delighting their children with stealthy antics; or they may make fun of other people. Practical jokes are frequent, with someone else always being the "fall guy." It is sometimes difficult to stop the practical joke before someone gets hurt.

Phyllis talked about how Jim created a feeling of family togetherness for her and the children. Much of it seemed to center around traveling together. They owned a camper; and when the children were young, they would all go camping together.

> When Jim would decide that it was time to go away for the weekend, the kids would start looking forward to it. Oh, I don't blame them. I was the one who would do all of the work. I had to go shopping and pack up the food, get their clothes ready, and pack, and close up the house before we would leave. It was worth it, I used to tell myself, because the kids used to have such a wonderful time. I must say that there were some moments on those camping weekends that were the nicest ones we ever had. When Jim would relax and feel good about himself, about me and the kids, life was just beautiful. You never knew, though, sometimes those wonderful moods could change just as fast as a storm could come up over the lake. All of us learned to recognize when his mood was changing from a happy, playful one into a mean, demanding, cruel one. At that time, though, it was hard to get away from him, all six of us crammed into that camper. It was hard to keep the kids quiet. They didn't understand. Just a little while earlier, their father was singing and playing ball and running and cracking jokes with them. Then, just as quickly, he would turn and start yelling at them to sit straight, to be neater, to stop making noise, and to stop irritating him. We just never knew which was going to happen when.

Most of the child abuse reported by the women interviewed occurred when the children were infants and preschoolers. The child abuser in about one third of these cases was the father. The man abused the woman and he abused the children. In about another third of the cases, the woman also was a child abuser, as was Molly, cited previously, whose three teen-aged children abused her. In the other third of the cases, there was no report of child abuse other than the indirect kind that occurs when a child lives in a home where the mother is battered. Douglas Bersherov, director of the National Center for Child Abuse and Neglect in Washington, D.C., submitted testimony to Congress that indicated that in child-abusing families where there was known wife abuse, too, in 70 percent of the cases the men were the child abusers. In child-abusing families where there was no known wife abuse, then only 40 percent of the abusers were the men. There is no doubt that a strong relationship exists between child abuse and wife abuse. Sometimes the child abuse took the form of incest or seductive behavior toward the girl children. In fact, there seems to be a fairly high relationship between fathers and brothers committing incest upon the children in the family and those men battering their women. Boys who grow up in a family where the father abuses the mother frequently become wife batterers themselves. There is no doubt in my mind of the connection and interrelatedness between rape, battering, and incest upon girl children. All are crimes against women committed by men.

Jeannie talked about how she protected her infant daughter from the brutal blows when she was being battered.

Stacey was a sweet little baby. She rarely cried except, it seemed, when Vic was having problems of his own. One night Vic came home in a horrid mood. I knew there would be trouble, so I fed Stacey and put her to bed a little earlier than usual. She was real good and played in her crib for a while until she fell asleep. I managed to keep things calm and thought I was about to avert an explosion, when later on that night, Stacey got up and was crying. I got out of bed and went into her room to hold her and calm her down, and decided that maybe she was hungry and that I needed to give her another bottle. At that point, Vic came in the room and started screaming and yelling at me. I had just had oral surgery and my gums were feeling pretty badly, but Vic started beating me on the head with castanets that we had brought back from one of our trips. He banged one of them so hard across my mouth and across my head that the beads flew all over. As soon as he started coming at me, I went to sit on the bed with the baby and rolled up so he couldn't reach my face, so he was banging more on my back and my head. Once the castanet broke, he then took off his shoe and started beating me with it, all over my legs, my head, and my back. The baby started crying because the bottle was knocked out of her mouth. He pulled me off the bed, with the baby in my arms, by my feet. I had to protect that baby. I landed on the floor, and I took all the bruises. He didn't say a word while he was beating me. He seemed to be so calm, no rage. I was so scared he'd hit the baby, or he'd do something to the stitches in my mouth. I didn't think he was going to beat me to death this time, but I thought he'd do it to that baby. I protected her that time. I don't know why he stopped, but all of a sudden and almost as fast as it started, it was over.

Julie had a harder time protecting her daughter. She was no longer married to the baby's father and was living with another man, who turned out to be cruel to her as well as to the baby. Julie only lived with him for two months when her daughter was about two years old, but enough happened in that short time so that it will not be forgotten.

Nick really seemed to like my daughter. I mean, she's cute and pretty and bright and was just at the age when she was starting to talk when I met him. We would all go out together, and he seemed so proud of her. He would show her off like she was a little doll and told people she was his daughter. In fact, it was funny sometimes, he would like to make believe that we really were married, and we really were a family. It seemed as important to Nick as it did to me. But there were other times when he was mean and cruel, when he had something inside of him that could only come out by hurting us. He didn't really know how to be a family. I knew after he moved into my apartment that it was wrong. All of a sudden, the baby started getting on his nerves. She liked to keep a night light on because she was afraid of going to sleep then, and Nick wouldn't let me put it on for her. I couldn't stand her screaming and crying at night. She was so little and so afraid, but he wouldn't let me go to comfort her. If she woke up in the middle of the night with a nightmare or just wanting me, he would keep me in bed and

wouldn't let me go to comfort her. If we would be in bed
making love and she would start to cry (I don't know why, but
she always seemed to do that, like she really knew the time), he
would become enraged with me and with her. When he would
be in an ugly mood and he'd be yelling and putting me down,
putting my mother down, he would also find things wrong with
the baby. He'd tell me how dumb she was, how she wasn't
saying enough words yet, or she wasn't toilet training fast
enough. I mean she was only two; what did he want from her? I
guess I knew that things were really weird when Nick decided
that he was going to take over her toilet training. Since he was
home so much, I had very little time to spend alone with her,
and he really did take charge. If she would have an accident, he
would spank her so hard I just wanted to cry with her, but it
was what he did to her when she was good and went to the
bathroom that frightened me even more. After she would finish
going to the bathroom, he would tell her that he was going to
wipe her off. He would go into the bathroom with her and
would start to fondle her genitals. He would start putting his
hand up and down the crack by her rectum and start making
nice to her little bottom in ways that I knew were wrong. She
and he would make a game of it. She would laugh, and he
would laugh. The day I caught him putting his finger in her
little vagina was the day I packed her and me and left. I really
think that he would have had sex with her if she hadn't been a
little baby. What a monster!

Julie saved her little girl by paying attention to what she
saw. The number of little girl children whose fathers or
brothers commit incest upon them is unknown. Researchers
and other people working in sexual-assault centers around the
country know that this is not an unusual incident. Little girls
are sexually fondled and seduced from the time they are two
all the way through adolescence, often by the same men who
beat their mothers. Many of the women interviewed in this
research tearfully broke down and admitted that they suspected that their men were seducing or sexually assaulting their
daughters. Many more were unaware of this sort of behavior
until someone else pointed it out. The women never brought it
up in the interview unless they were specifically asked wheth-

er or not their batterers behaved in a sexually seductive manner to their daughters. These women found it very hard to deal with their own guilt over allowing their daughters to be at the mercy of these violent men. They felt they should have known and stopped it. Yet they were hardly to blame in this horrible triangle. Both they and their daughters were victims of their men's abhorrent and inexcusable behavior.

Marilyn's reaction was typical.

I never realized that he was being seductive to my daughter until just now. But that must have been it, wasn't it? All those times when we would go traveling together, I would sleep with one girl and he would sleep with the other in those double beds that you have in family motels. My little girl used to come to me crying, saying she didn't want to sleep with Daddy, please don't make me sleep with Daddy, let me sleep with my sister. He insisted that it wasn't right, that the girls shouldn't see the two of us sleeping in bed together. They might think that we were having sex and that would be terrible. It would distort their minds. My God, what a fool I was to believe him. It's funny, you know, he would never let the girls go out on dates. When Ilene was a senior in high school, he didn't let her go. She cried and pleaded with him to let her go to her high school formal, and he said no. Strange, because when Jennifer wanted to go this year, he finally gave in and said she could go. Then he took her to the department store to pick out her dress, and I have to tell you I never saw such a sexy dress. It was black and low-cut and had a slit up the sides. It made Jennifer look like she was a hard twenty-year-old, instead of the pretty seventeen-year-old that she is. There's no satisfying him. He's either jealous of her having a boyfriend or he dresses her in provocative clothes. I've tried to stay out of their relationship. When he's busy and preoccupied with her, then he leaves me alone, and I don't get battered. I guess I'm wrong for not protecting her, but the truth is I don't think I could have protected her anyhow. He wouldn't listen to me. It would have only made things worse.

Jennifer, Marilyn's seventeen-year-old daughter, did not agree. She was seen at a community mental health center after running away from home. It was difficult to tell with whom she was more angry, her father, who brutally beat her when he suspected she was having sexual relations with a boyfriend, or her mother, who she felt never protected her from her father's sexual advances. Although Marilyn denied such knowledge, Jennifer felt her mother knew what her father was doing and was an accomplice because she did not stop him. She was sent to live with an aunt in another state, probably the only workable solution in her particular family situation.

Battered mothers are not the only ones who enter into the conspiracy of protecting the batterer. Other family members do, too. Some of the people who called to participate in this research identified themselves as sisters of women who were being battered. In a few cases, mothers of battered women called. Although it was impossible to corroborate their stories with the battered women themselves, it seemed evident that they knew what was happening and still chose not to intervene. When some of them had intervened earlier in the relationship, they found that neither the battered woman nor the batterer would take their advice. Now they felt the most helpful thing they could do was to protect her from embarrassment and him from being found out. In most cases, they were willing to help protect the children when asked. But battered women rarely ask for family help because they fear the consequences of involving their family members in the violence.

Although most of the battered women interviewed came from close families, they often reported difficulty in expressing their anger to their families. Their parents could evoke great amounts of love, guilt, and anger in them, but the women had difficulty handling those feelings. Sometimes, the women used the batterer as a buffer between themselves and their families. His saying no was often used as an excuse to avoid directly refusing family help. However, while the women only wanted a buffer, the men often erected impenetrable walls. Most of the time, the women did not tell their families what was happening in their homes. As if it were a game, both families and women pretended not to know what was happening, while both knew all too well.

In a large number of cases, the most helpful family member was the batterer's mother. She was the person to whom the battered woman would run in the middle of the night if she was bruised and terrified. She could be trusted to know when medical attention was necessary or when it was safe to go back home. She salved the wife's wounds, gave her a pep talk, and sent her on her way. Often the mother-in-law would commiserate with the battered woman, telling her she understood just how she felt because she, too, had experienced battering in her marriage. "Stress the good points," the mothers-in-law would say. "Don't dwell on these bad moments, they pass. I had it worse than you do, dear. I know what you're going through, but thank your lucky stars that it's not as bad as it could be." On the one hand, the mother-in-law endeared herself to the battered woman by offering her refuge and solace. On the other hand, the battered woman often blamed her mother-in-law for many of her beatings. She blamed her for not treating her husband better during his childhood. At the same time, she was understanding of this woman because she knew the batterer's father was also cruel and demanding. The battered women interviewed said their men had ambivalent feelings about their mothers. The men both loved and hated their mothers, and feared their power. Many women reported that battering incidents became more frequent when their husbands spent time with their mothers. This was true also if their fathers were present. In either case, the women felt they took the brunt of their husbands' anger toward their mothers. They often said of their batterers, "They hate women, especially their mothers."

The nature of the batterer's relationship to his mother and father is unclear. There were obviously disturbed relationships between the batterers and their parents in this study. Just exactly how that relationship influenced their behavior as adults needs further study.

We felt the question of whether a particular ethnic or religious group imposes its values on family relationships was an important one. We had to consider how the religion that women practice relates to their remaining in a violent home. Is violence a subcultural norm in different ethnic groups? But it turns out that if religious or cultural values do play a role in the battering relationship, that role probably has to do with the maintenance of the family as a unit rather than the encouragement of overt violence.

The Latin culture is often stereotyped as producing hot-tempered men and women. Does this stereotype increase the amount of violence in a battering relationship? Based on our research with a representative number of Hispanic women, this did not seem to be so. Their culture did not encourage men to hit women any more than others did. The difficulty in these cases was that the "machismo" factor put the women under a double strain not to report their husband's brutal behavior. To do so would cause him to lose face and would label her a betrayer. In any culture where losing face is important, battering relationships become even more concealed. I am convinced, however, that violence is not encouraged in the ethnic and family values of any one culture. In Western boom towns, where energy is being rapidly developed, or in rural Appalachian areas, where violence becomes a way of life, it is the perpetuation of the violence that is encouraged—the cessation of violence that is not encouraged—rather than its inception in the first place. Men do not have to beat their women in order to gain the respect of their community, although they do have to dominate them. The domination factor, however, is evident in all ethnic cultures.

Religious values weigh heavily in the stories of the women interviewed, since most grew up in homes that practiced some religion. Their religious values favored keeping the family together at all costs—even the woman's life. The religious groups that were most overt in denying any help to the woman were the conservative fundamentalists and some orders of Catholicism. While they might assist the woman during a crisis period, they would send her home to "preserve the family" when the need for immediate safety passed. Separation and divorce were unthinkable. In story after story, women told of being instructed by their religious adviser to go home, pray for the batterer's soul, and hope that he would become a better person.

At the time of this writing, a new focus seems to have emerged within the religious community. Churches are beginning to establish safe houses to assist battered women. How they will resolve the conflict between the religious value of keeping the family together and the need to separate the family when the relationship is violent will be interesting to see. The beginning is there, and that is encouraging. I believe that religions should protect individual souls rather than the collective family; and as long as it is detrimental for the woman and her children to remain in a violent relationship, I feel confident church groups will take measures to assist her in rearing her family as a single parent, much the way they have responded to women who have become widows.

In summary, the family unit, traditionally considered the cornerstone of our society, becomes terribly distorted in a violent relationship. Children are seriously damaged, both physically and emotionally. Fortunately, many of these families can become reasonably healthy families when the mother, as a single parent, acquires adequate economic and emotional support.

8

Social Battering

He's a good person, Walter is, not a bad person. He believes in
giving to the public. He wouldn't hurt a soul. Why me? He
pushes himself day and night to get his programs through. It's
nonstop work all the time. I can't remember the last time we
had a real vacation, just the two of us, without reporters or staff
aides sharing time. "Working vacations," Walter calls them.
"Don't have time to relax," he says. "Too much to do in too
little time."

I suppose I shouldn't complain. I get to have my staff aides,
too. I don't have to cook or clean house, just organize the whole
damn thing. But I don't feel like doing that, just letting
someone else do it. You know it's amazing how alone you can
feel even with a house full of people.

Sometimes I even like the glare of public life. Certainly it
forces Walter to pay attention to me when others are around.
But shut off the TV cameras and he's mean and nasty and
ignores me as usual. I don't know how much longer I can go on.
Alcohol doesn't help nor do pills. I've tried them and just got
put away in a fancy hospital. I can scream and shout for
attention, but all I get is more sneers, more verbal abuse, and
more pity. Now that we're public figures, Walter rarely hits me
anymore, but his cruelty remains. He'd die if he knew I was

here talking with you. Me, a battered woman? Ha! He would never believe it.

He encourages me to get out and do something for myself, but then he puts me down for every mistake I make. You aren't allowed to make mistakes, to experience failure, if you are part of Walter's life. I suspect he'd divorce me if he didn't need the image of a wife so badly. He doesn't need me for sex. He certainly seems to have enough other women. I'll bet any woman would give her eyeteeth to spend some time with him. They don't know. Yet I couldn't leave him. It would ruin his career. Ha! He'd never let me anyhow. I'm sure he'd use his power to get rid of me. You know, like they did to Martha Mitchell when Nixon was President. He could do it, you know. Walter could.

The inconsistency between the image of a man who beats his woman and the man who devotes his life to community service is apparent in Renée's story. She agreed to an interview provided the details were changed to conceal her husband's identity. There were many other Renées and Walters in this study. These were the women who were trapped by their husbands' high-powered jobs, careers, or community positions. They were military wives, corporate wives, politicians' wives, and wives of other prominent men. In the eyes of the public, the activities of these women reflect on their men, and the men are well aware of the possible negative consequences. Frequently, the women were not permitted to engage in activities unless first approved by their men. While we do not normally think of such restrictions as battering behavior, they result in the same kind of social isolation, dependency, and loss of individuality that physical brutality produces.

The use of social isolation and humiliation as a coercive technique in battering behavior generally involves psychological coercion. The threat of physical violence, however, is always present. These women get the message that if they do not obey orders, they will be seriously harmed. They also know that no one will help them. First of all, no one wants to believe that the men, who are pillars of the community, are capable of the kinds of abuse the women report. In addition to not being believed, these women also feel that no one would dare to take action against their husbands. They see the husband as more powerful than anyone else who might attempt to save them. The inability to seek help is further complicated when the batterer is a prominent member of a profession, such as the law, which is supposed to provide protection for the woman. A policeman's wife, a psychologist's wife, a physician's wife, a judge's wife, a mayor's wife, a military wife, a Member of Parliament's wife, a news commentator's wife—all have a difficult job in receiving such protection. In most cases, these women realize that their husbands' influence within the community will make it harder for them to get assistance. They are also painfully aware that if they attempt to seek out help, they must be prepared for immediate publicity, embarrassment, and the potential ruination of their husbands' careers. A double system of tacit cover-ups and concealment thus results. Everyone around the batterer becomes an accomplice to his violence. Because those who are associated with the batterer derive their self-esteem from being associated with him and his position, no one will take the chance of toppling him, for they all stand to lose.

Renée's story is similar to that of a corporate executive's wife who wanted to participate in my project anonymously. I agreed to a telephone interview, provided she would agree to mail back a completed set of questionnaires. Although I never learned her name, her story is too similar to others not to be true.

> When we were married twenty-five years ago, we both came from extremely wealthy families. Both of our families were just delighted that we married. It was, as you would say, keeping up the family status. Three weeks after we were married, the abuse started, and continued pretty seriously while my children were little. I finally went back home to my parents. My father had a long talk with my husband, and he swore he would never do it again. My father also made sure that we had plenty of

household help, so that if there were any more beatings, they would tell him about it. It's funny, because if they ever told my father, he never did anything anyhow.

The first five years of our marriage I really loved him, and I thought I could help him. I was going to be his psychiatrist. After a while, though, the fear of being killed took over. He would come home from cocktail parties and go to his gun collection and wave them and yell, "I'm no good and I'm going to kill myself! And I'm gonna kill you and the children, too." I really believed him. I was afraid he would kill himself, me, and the children. When we would go to bed at night, he would reach out and kick me out of bed for no reason at all. Many nights I would spend in motels, or in another part of the house, making sure one of the maids would sit up outside my room all night. I laugh now when I think about it, because I don't think she could have stopped him if he wanted to get into that room. But somehow it made me feel better then, like I really was protected.

I've always known that my husband was more powerful than the court. If I went to court or called the police, he would kill me. He's bigger than the law. When he would come home, he would batter down the doors if there was any room that had a closed door in it, so I used to make sure that all the maids left the doors open. Many nights he would come home and start banging on them, and I would wrap up the children and go to drive-in movies. I always knew it was going to be bad when he would go to see his mother. She had had lots of mental problems and had had a lobotomy when he was younger. Going to see her always seemed to set him off.

He's very good at what he does. If it weren't for him, this community wouldn't have a lot of the extra cultural things that his money has provided. Our relationship is so strong that it can't be broken. I know things about him that he'd kill me before he'd let them out. When things get so bad that I can't stand them anymore, I pack up and go to Europe and travel for a couple of months and then come back. That helps, even though it's still very lonely. When my youngest child was twelve and the other kids were in school, I packed her up and we lived in Europe for a whole year. That was one of the best years that I can remember. I don't know what I'm going to do. He'll kill me if I try to leave. The best thing I can do is try and recognize when he's in that kind of mood and just get away from him for a while. I couldn't live any other way. I need his success to be my success. Without him, I'd just be nothing.

Lorene was married to a high-ranking military officer. His initial success was due to his superb performance as a combat officer during the Vietnam War.

Living as an officer's wife has its ups and downs. It's nice to know that you're being protected, that you can get your food at the commissary, that you can go to the officers' club, and that you can participate in all kinds of activities that are set up on the base for officers' wives. There's always a support system there, lots of others who are in the same situation you're in, especially if your husband is away on overseas duty. But it has its bad points, too. You really aren't seen as a person yourself. You're seen as your husband's wife. In fact, all of your activities are called military wives' or officers' wives' activities, and sometimes you have no choice but to participate in them. I've learned to hate the officers' wives' groups. They're as regimented as you could expect in the military. I remember once wanting to play bridge with a woman I had met. She was the wife of another officer, and we had children the same age; in fact, we had a whole lot in common. We began to play bridge together, and we would see each other socially, until one day my husband told me that I could no longer see her. I couldn't understand it until he explained that he had been getting a lot of complaints from his commanding officer that I was spending too much time with her. Her husband was much further down the military social ladder than my husband was, so I wasn't allowed to be friends with her. The only women that I was allowed to be friends with were women I could not share things with.

Lack of freedom to choose one's own friends is not limited to the military. Batterers in all social groups usually insist on approving, if not choosing, their wives' friends. Battered women are consistently isolated by their men from women friends, especially those who are viewed as having some influence with the battered women.

Battered women are expected to maintain social contacts for their husbands. They are generally expected to entertain their batterers' clients or business associates. These women often report that they would rather do this kind of business entertaining than attempt to entertain their own friends. The unpredictable nature of the man's explosiveness makes it difficult for her to plan a party in advance. She knows, however, that if the party is with his business associates or clients, he will keep his temper under control. It is hardly a wonder such women believe that there is something wrong with them when their men can demonstrate self-control if it is to their advantage and unrestrained violence when no one is looking.

Social battering may take the form of extreme social isolation. In some cases, batterers refuse to go to social functions that their women wanted to attend. Professional women also need to entertain clients and business associates, yet their men refuse to play the escort role. Battered women cannot count on their men in social situations and often choose to forgo social events rather than deal with their batterers' unpredictability. Those women who attempt to have some kind of social life never know whether their batterer will be charming company, leave the party, become inattentive or bored, or verbally humiliate them.

The battered woman finds herself making excuses and defending her man's behavior. He may blame her for causing his behavior. She may accept the blame because she feels everyone recognizes his behavior as punishment for her wrongdoing. She feels humiliated and guilty and winds up rationalizing the battering. In relationships where alcohol exacerbates the problem, social events often take on an additional aversive quality for the woman. She knows her husband may drink too much and violence may follow. Her plight is described accurately by those women who have joined Al-Anon, a self-help group designed to provide support for families of alcoholics. Whether she attends a social event or stays home, she fears being abused.

Batterers often use social events as a weapon. For example,

if the woman is making plans to go somewhere, he may refuse to give her a firm decision as to whether or not he will attend. He will often act coercively by telling her that if she does something he wants, then he will go and behave nicely. This kind of behavior perpetuates the woman's vacillation in making her own decision as to whether to go alone or stay home. She constantly hopes that at the last minute he will come through, yet she cannot predict his moods and fears further trouble. This coercion encourages manipulative behavior on her part as she tries to smooth over any minor battering incidents in order to keep his mood peaceful. Very often at the last minute he will refuse to go, thus forcing her either to cancel or to make excuses when she arrives alone at her destination; or he will attend the social function but be obnoxious, rude, and brutal. This behavior is successful because of its sporadic nature. Sometimes he will be charming and delightful and sometimes he will not. The woman never knows when she is going to get the payoff.

Jeanette's report of the following incident is typical.

I knew things were getting bad. The tension had been building for the last two or three weeks. There were many more minor incidents. It was taking more and more effort for me to smooth them over. I really began getting worried. My sister was getting married on Sunday, and I knew I'd die of embarrassment if George went to the wedding and was rude and obnoxious to my family. I just couldn't bear it.

Thursday evening George came home in an absolutely vile mood. He banged the dishes around and started drinking pretty heavily after dinner. At first I tried to stay out of his way, but after a while I couldn't stand it anymore. His picking and picking just got on my nerves, and I was worried about Sunday. How was I going to handle it? Did I have to cancel and not go myself? Should I go alone? All of a sudden George started screaming at me, his usual stuff. I couldn't stand it anymore and started screaming back at him. I knew he would explode. It just didn't seem to matter. It seemed better to get the explosion over with than to keep it going for another few days. I couldn't stand the tension. Besides, I knew that if George got the beating over with tonight, by Sunday he would be contrite and sorry. He would try to make it up to me by acting just as nice as could be in front of my family. That was really what was important that night, how to get George to go to my sister's wedding and make me proud.

Jeanette did not provoke an acute battering incident because she liked getting beaten. Rather, she had been through the battering cycle before and knew that during the third stage her batterer would be a charming, loving partner with whom she could attend her sister's wedding. That was her reward. Unfortunately, she had to suffer a beating to get it.

Women who have great difficulty in dealing with this kind of social battering tend to isolate themselves further. Many of them report that the tension surrounding the manipulative behavior spoils the pleasure they might have gotten in attending a party. They do not go out as frequently as they would like, and slowly cut themselves off from others. They fear accusations of jealousy that result from social events. They begin to turn down all invitations, and eventually the invitations stop coming. They find themselves alone more and more with their batterers, and become more dependent upon them for their social outlet. The more time they spend together, the more angry feelings escalate into further batterings. Those women who do develop a social life spend a good deal of time going places with other women friends. They play cards, attend religious activities, or go to the movies. These activities cause further jealousy and possessiveness on the batterer's part, and the vicious cycle of battering behavior is perpetuated.

Verbal battering may well be the most powerful coercive technique experienced in a battering relationship. Despite having suffered severe physical injuries, most of the women interviewed in this sample reported that verbal humiliation was the worst kind of battering they had experienced. They were constantly harassed by verbal humiliation, a more observable form of social battering than social isolation. Most of us can recall being with a couple who are always arguing. The nasty retorts flung back and forth become oppressive, and we find ourselves making excuses to avoid being with them again. Verbal humiliation often extends beyond a social event itself. Social interaction is a fertile ground upon which to find reasons to batter women. The batterer may criticize the woman for the way she dresses. She is too provocative, too plain, or too dowdy compared to other women. He may accuse her of flirting with other men, and he generally subjects her to a rehashing of every social contact she has made during the evening. No wonder battered women fear social events and tend to eliminate them from their lives.

One of the reasons that social isolation has such a tremendous impact in controlling women's behavior is that women are particularly vulnerable to social embarrassment. Women have been trained to be ladies and to behave properly in public. Once they are effectively isolated, they have little opportunity to learn about other people's behavior. Battered women seldom know other battered women. They believe that the violence they are experiencing is unique. For most of these women, the last thing in the world they want is to be seen as a castrating bitch or to be viewed as less than feminine, so they either isolate themselves or allow the public humiliation and embarrassment to continue rather than fighting back. If the battered woman does fight back, she is censured for her behavior not only by her batterer but also by society at large. The woman who uses the safety of a country club, restaurant, or friends' parties to wage her warfare against her battering husband is often viewed critically. People do not understand that she chooses such territory because it is the safest for her. Many of the women in this sample said that they waited until they got into a social situation with a number of other people present before they began to let some of their anger out at their partner. While they felt they had little control in stopping themselves, it was the only time they felt safe in expressing their anger. They knew it was inappropriate, and felt guilty. They also suffered the private escalation of abuse that followed the event. But they needed to express their anger where others could help control the batterer's response for the time being. For a woman, fighting in the social arena may provide controls that fighting at home lacks.

Once her social isolation has become complete, a woman begins to suffer from extreme feelings of helplessness and powerlessness. These psychological changes have been occurring all along during the battering relationship; however, the psychological devastation becomes total when she is isolated from other people. After a period of such total helplessness, even if a woman is literally guided step by step out of the relationship, she is still paralyzed and unable to act on her own. This condition of learned helplessness is similar to severe psychological depression. An overwhelming feeling of hopelessness envelops her. She feels she cannot control her destiny, and she virtually gives up. Whatever confidence she once had in her own capabilities deserts her and she suffers from a massive ebbing away of self-esteem. The very energy that she now needs to propel her out of this violent situation is lost. She dislikes herself even more for being unable to act. She defines it as laziness rather than depression. This further perpetuates a negative self-image, making it even more unlikely that she will be able to reverse her victimization alone. She has now learned that nothing she does really matters anyway, so she settles into a routine attempting to minimize her pain and suffering. When this happens, the battered woman's victimization becomes complete.

Some women fight depression to the very end. In many cases, suicide seems the only alternative. It is not known how many women have successfully committed suicide to escape battering. Quite a few of the women who participated in this research discussed attempts to kill themselves. Most of the other women said they thought of it from time to time. In many cases, remaining in such a violent home was indeed a form of self-destruction. This was true especially when the woman believed that the only way their relationship would end would be when one of them died.

Maureen's story is typical. Her husband was on the medical school faculty. She knew that he would suffer severe embarrassment among his colleagues and possible loss of his job if his battering behavior was revealed, so she suppressed the truth until she could not endure her situation any longer. At one point, Maureen was hospitalized in a local mental hospital for severe depression. During her entire course of treatment, she kept the battering relationship a secret. She never discussed it with her therapist, although it was certainly a prime reason why she was so emotionally disturbed. After having been out of the hospital for several months, the battering resumed, and Maureen again became seriously depressed. She feared going back to the hospital, because she thought this time they might make her tell about the battering. On the other hand, she knew that if she did not discuss the battering with her therapist, she would never get well. Feeling trapped, she decided to seek out the support of one of her husband's colleagues and a trusted friend.

I finally went to see Eric when I knew there was nothing left to do. I felt myself more depressed, and I knew my therapist was going to recommend hospitalization again. I couldn't stand that, so I called Eric and asked him to have lunch with me. I invited him over to the house, because I didn't want anyone to hear in a restaurant or in the office. Eric agreed to come, although I could hear the hesitation in his voice. I didn't tell my husband for fear he would suspect something and become jealous of Eric's coming over. I also asked Eric to keep it quiet at work, which he agreed to do. When he got there, I was so relieved to see him, I burst into tears. I thought he was going to run out of the door at that time, and so I pulled myself back together, took him into the dining room, and served him a sandwich. I then began to tell him the whole story. As I began to talk, I knew Eric didn't believe me. Finally, after ten minutes, he stopped me. "Maureen," he said, "have you told this to your therapist?" "No," I told him. "I couldn't tell anybody. Don't you understand that? I can't tell that information to anybody." "Well, Maureen, I really think that you have to tell your therapist all about this. I'm the wrong person to tell." I realized that maybe he was right. Maybe I was making a mistake, but once I had started talking, I just couldn't stop.

"But, Eric," I said to him, "don't you understand what he's doing to me?" Eric looked at me and said, "Maureen, I really think you do have very serious problems. I don't know whether this is true or not, what you're saying. It just sounds too bizarre to really be that way. Somehow I just can't see him doing that to you. I know him very well. He just wouldn't do it. I know you've been under a lot of strain, Maureen, lately. Don't you think that this is part of the strain?" "No," I wanted to scream at him. "It's not part of the strain, it's the cause of the strain." But at that point I felt what was the use? I looked at him, and I just said, "What would you do if you knew it really was true?" He looked at me and said, "Look, if it really is true, then I think you ought to just kill yourself and get it over with, because he'll do it or you'll ruin his career, so why not just kill yourself and get it over with?" At that Eric got up and said, "Look, Maureen, I have to go back," and left the house.

I remember just sitting at the table looking at the empty chair and realizing that my last hope was gone. I had waited all these years to finally tell someone; and when I did, he didn't believe me. I started to think about his advice then and thought killing myself might not be such a bad idea. I wouldn't be hurting anyone then. Everyone would get along just fine without me. They certainly managed when I was hospitalized. I went into the bathroom, and I found a couple of bottles of pills. I didn't even know what they were. I opened up the bottles, and I put them all in my hand. I swallowed as many of them as I could and lay down in my room. I was lying there just thinking about what it would be like to die, when all of a sudden, my husband walked in the house. Since I knew he had a class then, I became very frightened. He came storming into the bedroom and started screaming at me for having told Eric. Apparently Eric went back and told him what I had said during our luncheon date. He looked at me, and then looked at the empty pill bottles, and yelled at me, "Oh, my God, what are you doing, what are you doing?" I remember just being very calm and saying to him, "Eric told me to kill myself and that just seems to be the best thing." He looked at me and tears streamed down his face and he said, "O.K., if that's what you want to do, maybe that will solve everything. I'll lie down right next to you until you die," and he did. The next thing I remember was being waked up in the hospital. I couldn't understand what had happened. Fortunately, my daughter had come home from school and had found me lying there and

Daddy sobbing, "Mommy's killed herself." She had been through enough battles that she knew what to do and called the police, who sent a rescue squad and they managed to save me.

I'm glad now. My husband faced arrest on charges of attempted murder. He has been suspended from his faculty position and may lose his medical license. I'm sorry about that, but now that we haven't lived together for a couple of months, I'm really glad for me.

Maureen was probably one of the lucky ones. She was busy making a new life for herself when I interviewed her. Her bouts with depression were far less extreme, although they were not completely gone, and she still was in psychotherapy.

Some of the interviewed women had chronic debilitating illnesses that trapped them in battering relationships. Most of them reported that when they were ill, their batterer became kind, gentle, and took excellent care of them. As long as they allowed him to determine the kind of treatment they needed, they would be cared for. Psychologically this makes sense. If the batterer needs his woman to be dependent upon him, and illness is certainly an extreme form of dependency, then he can be the kind, gentle caretaker she needs. Physical illness does indeed restrict a person's freedom. The batterer can relax his vigilance when his woman is ill, because he knows she cannot go very far. It seems entirely plausible that battered women who remain in such relationships also suffer from many different forms of illnesses. It is not clear how many of those illnesses are psychosomatically caused. We are learning that generalized stress reactions can produce psychophysiological disease. In addition to allergies, skin disorders, ulcers, hypertension, chronic fatigue, chronic back ailments, and migraine headaches, generalized stress reduces the body's natural immunological defenses. Cancer, respiratory illnesses, cardiovascular problems, and other diseases have been linked to changes in the body's immunological system. A number of the women in this sample suffered from disabling illnesses. In each case, there were secondary gains from these illnesses: their husbands ceased their violent behavior and adopted kind, nurturing, caretaking behavior instead. Being sick or disabled provided these women temporary freedom from battering. Many of them feared to leave their batterer because they would have no one to care for them when they became ill again.

Diana was such a person. She was in her early thirties and had been married for fifteen years. Although she never suffered from physical abuse, her battering history was typical in every other aspect. Her husband was possessive and jealous beyond any legitimate cause; he sexually abused their thirteen-year-old daughter; his temper was short; and he frightened and terrorized everyone in the family. Diana had no job skills and had never worked except as a homemaker. She was expected to be at her husband's beck and call. The only relief Diana ever got from her household duties and responsibilities was when she was sick. During the interview, Diana demonstrated both very childlike and adult thinking patterns. Her voice actually changed from a little girl's to a more mature woman's, depending upon which mood she was in. This was most apparent when she discussed her various illnesses.

Johnny really is a wonderful nurse, you know. Sometimes I wish he could do that for a living instead of having to prove himself as a salesman. I think he'd be a lot happier. He just loves to take care of me when I'm sick. A couple of years ago, I developed gall bladder problems, and I had to be in the hospital. Johnny came two, three times a day to see me. I mean he was there more often than any of the other women's husbands in the room. He was always bringing me things, like flowers and candy and cookies, and he'd treat the nurses nicely, too. He was always checking up to make sure I was comfortable. He was like that every time that I had an illness. Even if it was just a little cold, he'd make me get into my nightie and get into bed, and he'd make me get the covers up around my neck to keep me warm, and he'd bring me hot tea, soup, and juice. Every few minutes there would be something else waiting for me. I usually get sick a lot during the winter. I don't know, I'm susceptible to every bug that goes around; and every time I get sick, Johnny spends time with me. It doesn't matter, even if he's in a bad mood. If I get sick and get into bed, then he's right there to take care of me; he's kind and sweet and loving.

This last time, with my back, he really was super. I just don't know how it happened. I woke up in the middle of the night, and I couldn't move my back. I just couldn't move. I woke Johnny up in the middle of the night, and he rubbed my back down, and he gave me some medicine, and he even put the heating pad on my back to see if that would help. In the morning when my back still wasn't any better, Johnny called the office and took the day off, and he took me down to the emergency room. When they couldn't find anything wrong after taking some X-rays, he decided to take me to that new neurologist in town. I really didn't know if I wanted to go to all those doctors, but I knew I had no choice. I had to let Johnny run the show, or he wouldn't take care of me at all, so I let him make all those decisions. Well, that day I saw the neurologist and another orthopedist. I would have liked to have called my own doctor. I trust him, but Johnny wanted to try these new ones first. Well, the neurologist decided to put me in the hospital, and he was considering doing surgery the next day. I was not sure that was the right thing to do and pleaded with both him and Johnny not to do that to me. They put me in the hospital where my own doctor couldn't come. I guess all my pleading and my crying made them postpone the operation for three days. They decided to try some physical therapy first. It didn't help. Instead, things just got worse and worse and worse. The day before they were supposed to operate, I cried and cried and cried and begged Johnny to let my other doctor see me. Johnny agreed and bundled me up and took me to his office, telling the nurses he would bring me back to the hospital, that he was just taking me out for lunch. My doctor examined me and said to Johnny that I didn't need an operation, that as far as he was concerned, it was the same old back problem that had always bothered me, and what I really needed was some bed rest and some physical therapy. Well, I didn't know what to do then. Neither did Johnny. How could I make such a decision? I told Johnny, "You make it, Johnny; whatever you decide, I'll go along with." I really didn't have much choice, you know. He had to make the decision, or he wouldn't have taken care of me. Our family doctor said he would put me in the other hospital. Johnny agreed. I don't know whether he just didn't want me to be operated on or whether he thought it would be cheaper to be in the other hospital. Anyhow, he called up the neurologist and told him that we were going to try something different. And it worked. After about two weeks, whatever it was just seemed to go away. Maybe it was a pinched nerve, like the neurologist said, or maybe not. Maybe I just needed a rest. It sure was nice not to have to do everything around the house.

Other women who have reported illnesses say some of the same things Diana said. As long as they gave their batterer control over making the decisions about what would affect their bodies, their men took good care of them. As soon as they began to challenge his authority to control their bodies, he became brutal again. In Diana's case, it is difficult to say what caused the original back problem. That there was real pain and real trauma to her body is evident. Whether severe tension had something to do with the trauma to her back is another question. In any event, illness often helps the woman and protects her from responsibilities, provided she lets the man totally take over.

As these women become older, they are even more susceptible to various kinds of illness. I wondered what the response of battered women and their men would be to normal aging. Certainly the problems of loneliness affect all women. Although a small number of older women came forward voluntarily to tell their stories, I decided that I needed to seek out the geriatric population more directly if I was to get enough cases to make adequate comparisons. I visited several agencies serving older people and asked for volunteers from among their clients. I was able to arrange interviews in the homes of a sizable number of older women who had been battered or who were still being battered. Some of them had been living with their batterers for thirty or forty years. Although I cannot generalize from this limited number of cases, these women reported that their batterers tended to mellow with age. Many times, however, the battering only moved away from physical to more verbal abuse. Then, too, the mellowing process did not always take place. In fact, many kind and gentle husbands became more violent as they aged. Much of this behavior was attributed to problems of senility and hardening of the arteries of the brain. I have told of the woman beaten with her husband's cane after never having experienced violence in her marriage before. Others related similar episodes that seemed to be directly related to the physiological changes brought about by the aging process.

Many of the women interviewed stated that they had stayed with their batterers all these years in order not to be left alone as they aged. Most of them feared growing old; they wanted companionship, and they were willing to put up with violence in order to have it during the last years of their lives.

Elsie was seventy-six years old when I interviewed her. Her husband had died several months earlier, and Elsie was still mourning him. Married after they both graduated from a prestigious Eastern college, they had lived together for fifty-three years. I was impressed because in the 1920s it was rare for a married woman to be educated. As Elsie talked, I realized she did not fit the stereotype I had of women growing up in that era. She described growing up in a home that was very nurturing. Her father insisted that she go to college to become a university professor. Elsie met her husband while in college, and they shared fascinating careers. They were unusual in that their education and their fame were equal. "Are you willing to believe an old woman?" Elsie asked me as we began the interview. When I assured her that her story was valuable, she proceeded, haltingly at first, but stronger as she went along.

> We loved each other, you know, although I don't think we loved each other when we were first married. It was exciting, the prospect of beginning a career together. Women didn't do that in those days. In 1923, when we graduated, you couldn't get a job very easily, but we managed to find one, both of us together in the same university. Even that was strange then. I never knew when the fights would start. Sometimes it was jealousy because we both worked in the same place. Other times that helped, because we couldn't fight too much there. I think it helped, too, because we always shared everything together. I don't know whether he could have let me go work

someplace different. In any event, that would have been un-
heard of in those days. A nice woman was supposed to stay
home, you know. She didn't go off teaching on a college
campus if she was married. In many ways, our relationship was
very strange.

Well, he started hitting me soon after we were married.
About a year later, I became pregnant. When I told him, his
reaction was so violent that I thought to myself, This is
absolutely ridiculous. I can't bring a baby into this world. So I
had an abortion. I told him it was a natural miscarriage. But I
found a doctor who was willing. You know, they did have them
in those days, too. All this rigamarole about abortion today
makes me laugh sometimes, as though you young people think
that it didn't exist then. But it did, and I used it. I became
pregnant two more times and two more times had abortions. I
didn't tell him the next two times. I just went and did it. The
last time, I pleaded with my doctor to make sure that I would
never have any more pregnancies. I guess after the third
abortion, he agreed to do it, and so he fixed me so I couldn't
have any children. Sometimes when I see some of my other
friends here with their children and grandchildren, I'm sorry
about that. But I knew having a child in that marriage was the
worst thing to do, and I would never bring a child up in that
world. So I'm not sorry for that.

Our worlds revolved around each other, you know. We did
everything together. We went to work together. We had entertainment together. We lived together. I loved him, you know,
even when he was brutal and mean; I loved him through the
whole thing. I'm sorry he's dead, although there were days
when I wished he would die. I'm sorry now. He was my best
friend. He was the person who shared everything with me. I bet
you must find that strange, don't you? Sometimes I do, too. He
beat me right up to the end, you know. Oh, it wasn't as hard
later on, but it still didn't matter. I couldn't do anything right
when he was in those moods, and other times life was just
wonderful together. It was a good life, and I really do miss him.
There weren't too many men who would put up with a woman
like me in those days. They didn't want any independent
women like today's men like. It was better to live with him than
not to have been married at all.

Elsie's feeling that it was better to have been married to a
batterer than not to be married at all is pervasive amongst
battered women, no matter what their age. The fear of being

alone causes women to put up with indignities no human being would believe they could endure. Woman after woman would tell how much better it was to be married to a batterer than to live alone—until they actually left. Once they made the choice to live alone, they found themselves very happy that they had done so. The sense of well-being and relief after living in such terror carried them through the days when nothing went right and they wished they had someone to depend on again. In most cases, the women left their batterers several times before they were willing to end the relationship permanently. There was no doubt that the day-to-day monotony of the routine job and the trials and tribulations of being a single parent forced many women back into their battering relationships.

I first met Karla when I was doing interviews in the hospital. She had seen me on the floor several times interviewing different women and had asked if she could participate. She was in her early thirties and had been hospitalized for the third time with a recurring malignancy. About five years earlier, she had had a radical mastectomy. Since then, she had had recurrent malignant tumors in other parts of her body. When I met her, it was uncertain whether she would live or die. She was in the hospital having cobalt treatment for a newly discovered malignancy. Karla's story was typical of other battering relationships. She had married her husband when they were very young. The battering started soon afterward. She had a child, in the hope of making their relationship better. She felt that things were going from bad to worse when it was first discovered that she had a breast tumor. After her mastectomy, her husband became a loving and tender caretaker while nursing her back to health. Karla thought that maybe her illness was a good omen, that their life together would change and they would become a more normal family. This happiness was short-lived.

As good and kind as he was, I knew I couldn't count on him after a while. The incidents were small at first, like I'd have an appointment to go for radiation therapy, and he would take the car and not be home on time, so I'd miss my appointment. Or I'd ask him to pick up our little girl at play school, and somehow he'd become involved or forget. The play-school director then would call me an hour later to find out where he was. If I would nag at him, it wouldn't help; he'd only get more cruel. One day I remember the pain was so bad that I pleaded with him to please plug in the heating pad behind our mattress. My arm still wasn't healed yet, and I couldn't move the heavy mattress to reach the plug. He plugged it in at another spot in the room so I couldn't lie down with it. I remember crying and pleading with him to move it, but he refused and stormed out of the house. It was then, I think, that I knew I had to leave him no matter what. While he was gone, I went to the phone and called my friend who was an attorney and told him this was it, I needed to get a divorce. I don't understand why, with all those years of cruelty, I waited until I was riddled with a disease like cancer in order to end that relationship. In fact, some of my friends have asked me why then, when it seemed as though I needed him most. I guess that is why. I know that with a disease such as cancer and all the times that I've had repeated tumors, that I might not have much longer to live, and I decided that whatever time I had left had to be in my control and had to be the best I could give myself. I was responsible for whatever time was left, not him. Obviously, his cruelty made it impossible for him to give me what I needed. It's my right to a little happiness, too. Even if I don't have much time left, I'm going to feel good about what I do for myself and for my kids.

As I write this today, Karla is still alive and still battling the dread disease. She says she is doing well, although she has her bad days. From her description, the bad days do not sound any better or any worse than those of other women who have attempted to take responsibility for their own lives. Their fears of living alone have been exaggerated. Most of them say that the loneliness they suffered living in a battering relationship was far worse than the occasional loneliness that occurs when you actually do live alone.

PART III

The Way Out

Introduction

Today providing help for battered women is fast becoming a national priority. There has been a complete about-face in the three years I have been studying this problem. As recently as 1974, people were still questioning whether significant numbers of battered women really existed. Now Congressional committees, civil rights commissions, and other government agencies are studying the problem. Laws to protect battered women are being introduced in legislatures in most states, and a national plan has been introduced in Congress. My own state of Colorado assigned top priority in the 1978 legislative session to revising legislation for battered women, and the enforcement of existing laws is finally beginning to take place. Concerned groups are lobbying to gain adequate funding and services. At the International Woman Year's National Women's Conference in Houston in November, 1977, resolutions recommending increased services for battered women were passed overwhelmingly. These resolutions stated:

> The President and Congress should declare the elimination of violence in the home to be a national goal. To help achieve this,

Congress should establish a national clearinghouse for information and technical and financial assistance to locally controlled public and nonprofit organizations providing emergency shelter and other support services for battered women and their children. The clearinghouse should also conduct a continuing mass media campaign to educate the public about the problem of violence and the available remedies and resources.

Local and state governments, law enforcement agencies, and social welfare agencies should provide training programs on the problems of wife battering, crisis intervention techniques, and the need for prompt and effective enforcement of laws that protect the rights of battered women.

State legislatures should enact laws to expand legal protection and provide funds for shelters for battered women and their children; remove interspousal tort immunity in order to permit assaulted spouses to sue their assailants for civil damages; and provide full legal services for victims of abuse.

Programs for battered women should be sensitive to the bilingual and multicultural needs of ethnic and minority women.

A multilevel, systematic approach, used in the mental health profession for health service planning, is needed to develop new services and strengthen existing ones for battered women. This system has three levels: (1) primary prevention; (2) secondary intervention; (3) tertiary intervention. I would like to sketch out how this three-level system could work to help battered women.

1. PRIMARY PREVENTION

This includes public education programs, as well as direct work with agencies, institutions, and other support groups, to eliminate social problems which either directly or indirectly cause the condition. A primary prevention campaign is already being waged by the media in the United States. As information becomes more available, people are beginning to change their attitudes about battered women. Television shows, magazine articles, and books are being devoted to battered women. Much remains to be done, however. In particular, we must:

a. *Eliminate sex-role stereotyping during child development.* For example, books, movies, commercials, and television programs must reflect equality between the sexes. The Equal Rights Amendment in this country must be passed. The National Plan of Action passed by the National Women's Conference must be implemented.

b. *Reduce the violence in our society.* The television and motion picture industries must be persuaded to reduce violence in their programing. The chic brutality in advertisements must cease. As an example of one possible way this might come about, the women's movement has suggested an economic boycott against record companies displaying such brutality on jacket covers.

c. *Reduce the harshness in child discipline.* We must learn to use positive discipline rather than the negative and physically abusive punishment that our society sanctions. Children need to be taught that people who love them do not have the right to hit them, even for their own good.

d. *Understand the victimization process of battered women.* The public should be made aware of the cycle theory of battering and the various forms of battering behavior. We must reduce the learned helplessness phenomenon found so commonly in women and replace it with assertiveness and equal opportunity among men and women.

Level 1, primary prevention, also involves consultation with agencies, institutions. and other support groups dealing with social problems. Work in this area has also begun on behalf of battered women; however, more intensive efforts are needed in several areas:

a. *Agency personnel should be taught to be more supportive of women.* Besides being trained to work with battered women, they must become educated in the entire scope of the problem and learn new effective techniques for working with these women and their families.

b. *Institutions and agencies should be encouraged to enforce proper rules and regulations for treating battered women.* This need is especially evident in the court system. Probation officers, clerks of the court, attorneys, and even judges often deny battered women fair and equal rights.

c. *New laws should be introduced and rules and regulations should be rewritten to implement existing laws.* The division of the legal aspects of wife battering into civil and criminal remedies needs serious study. Social service departments need to revise their guidelines in order to assist battered women and their families effectively.

d. *The development of new community support groups for women should be encouraged.* Such groups will continue to provide consultation and education services long after the initial thrust for development of new services is over, thus maintaining the prevention work begun during this period.

If primary prevention is successful, we will eventually eliminate all domestic violence and never know who battered women might have been. In working with the primary prevention model, society is treated as a whole, not as a collection of individuals. Most individuals are not identified. Primary prevention is the long-term goal. If it is successful, the attitudes and values of a whole culture will be changed. People will use negotiation rather than coercion in their relationships.

2. SECONDARY INTERVENTION

Individuals are treated and labeled as battered women. Early identification facilitates this intervention. The earlier they are treated, the more potentially successful the intervention. The least restrictive kinds of interventions are most appropriate at this level; e.g., home visits, telephone hot lines, outpatient clinic visits, crisis intervention counseling, legal advice, financial assistance, and information distribution. The goal of secondary intervention is to help the battered women resolve their situations with the least amount of interference from others. Helpers must take their cue from the women as to what kind of support they need. The strengthened agencies, institutions, and support groups developed through primary prevention often provide these services in the secondary intervention process.

3. TERTIARY INTERVENTION

Here the battered woman needs a totally supportive temporary environment before she can attempt to make any independent decisions. Safe houses, immediate hospitalization, and long-term psychotherapy provide such an environment. Most often this tertiary intervention is required immediately in order to provide optimum safety. These women will be unable to arrive at realistic decisions or act upon them unless they have this safety. The safe houses, refuges, and/or shelters which have sprung up across England and more recently in this country have been an essential element in the treatment of battered women. The length of time a woman spends in such a controlled environment depends upon the individual. This time is used to regain the natural resources lost during her battering experience. Many women do become frightened at the prospect of being totally responsible for their lives and return to their violent relationships. However, such women, if permitted, will quickly leave their battering situation again and return to the safe environment. This back-and-forth movement often occurs three to five times before a woman is able to detach herself permanently.

All three levels of intervention, primary, secondary, and tertiary, must go on simultaneously. If a woman remains in a safe house long enough to remove herself permanently from a battering situation, she must then be able to shift to a less controlled environment where she can rebuild her life. But only a change in popular attitudes will enable society to be ready to receive her. There are many women who do not need to go to a safe house to rebuild their lives, and for them secondary intervention is enough. They, too, however, would greatly benefit from the infusion of primary preventive efforts into society.

Treatment alternatives dealing with the battered woman's need for safety and care span most of society's public and private institutions. They include safe hiding places for them and their children, a fair law enforcement and criminal justice system, emergency medical services, responsive social service departments, job protection, career counseling and job training, and a community support system. Awareness of the necessity of providing for the battered woman's safety beyond just the safe house has been growing in this country and Europe and reflects the current understanding that these women have been victimized by an indifferent society as well as by their men.

9

Safe Houses

Last Thanksgiving time, while I was shopping in the super-market, I saw a battering incident. The supermarket was crowded. Along one aisle a woman was pushing her cart hurriedly, choosing items from the shelves. Beside her was a man who looked tense and agitated. As I passed them, the woman removed an item from the shelf. The man glared at her and said, "Now you've done it. Now you've done it. You've made me mad. If you don't put that back, you will make me even madder. Do you know how mad you are making me? Now you've gone and done it!" She turned to him and said quietly, "We need this for dinner." He looked at her with fury and said, "You've made me mad. Now you've really made me mad by saying that. You can just forget about your hairdresser's appointment. I can't stand it when you make me mad this way!" The woman looked rather nervous, obviously concerned about her companion's loud behavior. She said something like "Let's go." He yelled back, "Don't tell me 'Let's go' now! You've really made me mad." He started to hit her arm. At this point, the woman, looking embarrassed, pushed her cart rapidly through the crowd. The man followed, continuing to swing at her. She took a place in line with the cart, while he became more abusive. I reached into my wallet and took out a card that had the name, telephone number, and additional information about our local safe house. As the man continued his badgering, I unobtrusively slipped her the card. She glanced at it and put it in her pocket. Without a word, she left the cart and ran outside. Several people were able to detain the man for a short period of time by blocking him on the check-out line. How grateful I was to have that information for her. Six months before, if I did anything, I would have had to call the police, who would probably have sat them down for a little chat, telling him not to do it again, and empathizing with him about how difficult it was to shop in a crowded supermarket around holiday time. According to stories that battered women have told me, I am certain that this couple would have gotten no farther than outside the store and the man would have begun his attack all over again. Scenes like this are not uncommon. Now there is somewhere a woman can go to immediately.

Safe houses, refuges, or shelters have become the cornerstone of treatment for battered women who do not wish to return home. Erin Pizzey founded the first known refuge in England in 1971. The house was donated by the local housing council and became known as Chiswick Women's Aid. Originally it served as a meeting place for women who wanted to talk. Almost immediately, however, women who were being beaten and did not want to return home came for safety and refuge, not just to talk. The need for such places was evidently extraordinary, as every such refuge that has since opened in England, Wales, Ireland, Scotland, Europe, and the United States has quickly overflowed capacity. Pizzey's Chiswick Women's Aid grew from one house to a current network of over twenty-five houses. Other refuges developed simultaneously throughout the British Isles. Although they all used Chiswick as their model, many modifications were made.

Almost all the English refuges are now coordinated through the National Women's Aid Federation, a central agency supported by local and national government funds. As of June, 1978, over 150 were operating in the British Isles. Similar refuges or groups also exist in the Netherlands, West Germany, France, and the United States, but none has developed extensive networks like the English. While we do not have an accurate count of the safe houses operating in the United States, my estimate is that there are about sixty. The National Coalition Against Domestic Violence, which includes most of the shelters in this country, is currently in formation. Further information can be obtained from Bonnie Tinker at Bradley Angle House, P.O. Box 40132, Portland, Oregon 97240. All refuges, shelters, and safe houses provide some assistance to battered women, even if only a place to sleep. Other services may include medical help, vocational training, counseling, and rehousing. In England, although the national medical service is available for those women and children who need physical care, psychotherapy is not routinely available as it is in the United States. The usual stay in an English refuge is six to twelve months; however, the housing shortages in England may force battered women and their children to remain longer.

Most of the differences between refuge models deal with the degree of community established among members. All are successful because they provide a community support system that nurtures these women and children which did not exist for them in their original communities or families. One current issue for most safe houses and refuges is the degree of independence or responsibility demanded from battered women upon their initial arrival. They all have various rules to be followed and all of them appear to function successfully.

Chiswick Women's Aid was founded on a total therapeutic community model. This means that everyone is expected to be responsible for herself and for others' welfare, too. Decisions are made by consensus and everyone has an equal stake in running the house. But assumption of full share of responsibility is based on ability to do so at any given time. It is a slow, gradual, and structured therapeutic process. Women initially are housed in a crisis-oriented receiving center. An open-door policy guarantees that no battered woman or child is ever turned away; this policy results in chaotic, overcrowded conditions, but it undoubtedly saves lives. The telephone number and address of Chiswick Women's Aid are widely known. Irate batterers have arrived there only to be frightened away by the large numbers of people in the refuge. When I visited Chiswick during the summer of 1976, there were 138 women and children living in the crisis center. People were literally everywhere. Despite the large numbers, a great sense of organization and purpose was evident among the women interviewed.

When a woman arrives at Chiswick, she is greeted by a reception group of staff members and members of the house. She is given some personal items, if she has brought none, and allocated a bed and a place to store her things in a dormitory-style room. If she has children, she is given the option of having others in the house share the responsibility of caring for them. She can have her children sleep with her or in the children's dormitory. Because refuges have little money, self-help is a necessity, and all meals, chores, and finances are the responsibility of the collective group. Independence is encouraged by a slow assumption of responsibility for oneself and others in a sheltered and protective environment. Women learn that they can trust others to help them and that they can be successful in helping others—the necessary elements for fostering the development of interdependence. This is what is meant by a therapeutic community. Critics of this approach argue that the mere presence of these elements does not guarantee the achievement of long-term therapeutic goals. At best, they say, a crisis house provides short-term safety; at worst, it encourages further dependence, as these battered women are not forced to accept the responsibility for their own lives.

However, women are encouraged to leave the crisis house for one of the second-stage houses as soon as possible. Second-stage houses are also managed communally, but every woman is expected to share equally in the process. These houses are located throughout London, its suburbs, and in several other cities. The largest, a former hotel, houses eighty women and children; smaller ones have an average capacity of around twenty. Battered women and their children are eligible to receive financial support under the social security system, and they remain in the house until they are ready to leave. They must either provide their own housing or wait their turn on the housing council list. Some women choose to continue to live indefinitely in this communal style. For these women, a third-stage housing arrangement has been established which has less mobility and more sense of permanence. The oldest in the third-stage housing group is located in an old vicarage in Bristol. The longest stay in this house has been four years. The women and children there have developed a remarkably close sense of community fostered by their years of living together. During my visit, I was struck by what a beneficial alternative to the nuclear family this arrangement was for these women and children.

Other refuges established in England, as well as in this country, do not always copy the Chiswick model. Rather, they support a greater degree of independence, both initially and throughout the battered woman's stay in the refuge. These refuges are smaller than Chiswick, usually housing from twelve to twenty women and children. Camden refuge, a member of the National Women's Aid Federation, does not advocate community responsibility for children, finances, or meals. Each woman has her own kitchen closet to store food, which she purchases out of her social security allowance. Independence in food shopping, meal preparation, and budget control is the desired norm. Women are *encouraged* to learn from one another, but this is not done systematically. A paid housemother is hired to assist the process. During my visit to Camden, I did not sense the warm communal support that I felt at some of the other refuges. Several women complained of having their meager food supplies stolen. Rarely was child care shared. If a mother had to go on an errand, her child was not tended by the others unless she specifically requested such help. The children at Camden relied more on each other than they did on the adults for support and care. I can only speculate that the stress on independence and the need to keep the nuclear family intact, rather than the communal approach, were responsible for these differences.

Swindon refuge encourages independence by insisting that its women apply for their own social security benefits. Many of these women are middle-class industrial wives or farm women who have rarely had to deal with government bureaucracy. A local support committee sets up strict house rules which include allocation of house maintenance chores and the regulation of visitors, especially men. Other refuges leave house management strictly up to the women residents. In one group, the members exercised their decision-making rights by voting to withhold their rent payments to the refuge. This action put the support committee in a dilemma. They now had a group of battered women who were independent enough to challenge authority (theirs), but they were also faced with having to close the house for lack of rent money.

In almost every case, initially refuges were established by support committees which knew very little about the problems of battered women. Other than the Chiswick Women's Aid network, which provided its own staff training before a new second-stage or third-stage house was opened, the refuges throughout Britain have begun with good intentions, little money, and little government assistance. (This pattern has also been followed in establishing safe houses in the United States.) In England, the National Women's Aid Federation network provides technical assistance and resources for the entire country. The main office in London sends regional representatives to visit the various refuges several times a year. Regional coordinator meetings also are scheduled, and large annual conferences are held. Founded on feminist principles, which mandate that no one person take a leadership role but that leadership be shared among numerous women, the National Women's Aid Federation assumes a low profile in establishing and maintaining these refuges. Regional coordinators are not permitted to serve for more than one year. While this procedure makes sense in terms of maintaining a horizontal leadership structure, it also means that those women providing the best leadership and resource information must leave their positions just at the peak of their effectiveness. We must learn how to share power yet not be cruel to our hard workers.

For fuller descriptions of the British refuge system, I refer you to summaries written by Marjory Fields and Rioghan Kirchner, available by getting in touch with them at the Brooklyn Legal Aid Services; Erin Pizzey's book *Scream Quietly or the Neighbors Will Hear;* Del Martin's book *Battered Wives;* Rebecca and Russell Dobash's articles on refuges in Scotland, available by writing them at the University of Edinburgh; the HEW monograph on the Services to Battered Project founded by the Office of Human Development, and my chapter published in Sage Publications' Women's Policy Studies Series, Volume III, *Victimization of Women,* edited by Jane Chapman and Margaret Gates.

In the United States, the development of refuges or safe houses is in the infant stage compared to the movement in England. Women's groups in this country have provided temporary housing on an informal basis. National Organization of Women (NOW) chapter headquarters, women's resource centers, and feminist bookstores have been the most reliable sources. Church groups, local YWCAs, and community mental health centers are now also beginning to function in this area. Untold numbers of battered women have also sought safety in motel rooms and in the homes of friends and family members. Some of the helping groups provide counseling for battered women and their families. New programs are developing, some under the Victim/Witness Assistance Program, funded by the Law Enforcement Assistance Agency (LEAA). Safe houses are now available in many metropolitan areas. The Colorado Association for Aid to Battered Women is currently conducting a federally funded study to determine the usefulness of safe houses and other community services to battered women. In order to locate a safe house in your community, get in touch with the Center for Women Policy Studies, 2000 P Street, N.W., Washington, D.C., for its current list of services to battered women.

The importance of the shelter movement is that it provides a sense of community and a support system. As soon as battered women walk through the door, they are no longer helpless victims. They begin to realize that they do have power over their own lives, that other people care enough to risk helping them, and that the institutions of society can and will come to their aid. Here battered women learn to try different life styles by watching staff members and other residents. Most battered women have been isolated from other people, and the sharing of commonalities and differences with others helps to offset their previous deprivation. They experience the benefits of being able to make the system work.

The amount of time that women spend in a safe house varies. Most shelters in this country find between four and six weeks to be the optimum stay. It takes three or four weeks for a woman to adjust to the fact that she is not going home. Once she has accepted this reality and begins to mourn her past, she is ready to use her energy to start planning her future. During the first phase, with the aid of staff and other women, the battered woman takes an inventory of her skills and her particular needs in order to plan the next phase of her life. During the fourth to sixth weeks, she usually begins concrete steps toward reaching those short-term goals. Hopefully, she is also on her way to long-term life planning. Battered women come to a shelter or a safe house terrified of their future. By the time they are ready to leave, they generally have confidence that they can make it alone.

Many battered women are mothers. As was pointed out in Chapter 7, few of them have much energy left over for their children after coping with their batterers. The stay in a safe house gives them the opportunity to become reacquainted with their children without the threat of violence. They actually learn to be better parents through direct staff intervention or by contact with others who have different ways of interacting with their children.

About 50 percent who stay longer than one week in a safe house will not return to live with their batterers. This percentage rises dramatically if the safe house remains open to those women who return home and then want to come back to the refuge. As noted earlier, this back-and-forth process may occur as often as five times before the battered woman is able to leave home permanently. It may be that these women need to experience the inevitability of the battering cycle several times after they have learned to identify it before they can accept their inability to control it. Women who remain in shelters until they feel comfortable with themselves rarely get involved in another battering relationship.

There are some definite limitations to the refuge or safe house concept. First it provides an artificial sense of community. However, many women cannot cope with the real world unless they have such a support system. A natural support system network in the community does not exist yet, although many groups have begun the process. In communities where safe houses have existed for a number of years, such as St. Paul and Minneapolis, Minnesota, widespread community support has already begun to develop. Sharon Vaughn and other women from Women's Advocates, the original safe house in that area, have managed to untangle bureaucratic snarls in the social security system, in social service agencies, and in police departments; this has encouraged others to continue to try to do the same in their own communities.

Many other groups that have not been able to afford safe houses have concentrated on strengthening potential support systems within the community. Their work has concentrated on encouraging existing helping agencies to become more responsive to the needs of battered women.

Another drawback to safe houses is their limited potential for educational or vocational training. Some shelters have made arrangements with local schools or job-training programs, but most have their hands full coping with the basic physical and emotional needs of their clients. Although women from many different social, cultural, educational, and economic levels utilize safe houses, unless they have job skills prior to entry, they will probably not be economically self-supporting when they leave. Without the potential for economic independence, these women will still be at the mercy of the state or another man. It is perhaps unrealistic to expect a battered woman to begin career planning immediately after entering a safe house. Generally, during the first few weeks, all of her energy is spent putting the past to rest. Vocational counseling and training are most meaningful after that process has taken place, during the last few weeks that a woman is in a safe house. Women in Crisis, a safe house recently opened in Denver, is making arrangements for job training to continue for their women after they leave. Again, members of the safe house staff have acted as advocates in encouraging other community agencies to begin providing the specific services these women need. Rainbow Retreat, a safe house in Phoenix, Arizona, for women from families where alcoholism has been a contributing factor, has scheduled vocational counseling as part of its treatment program. In many cases, even women with jobs must leave them when they leave the battering relationship in order to be truly safe. If they remain, their batterers can still trace them. Career counseling thus is as important for women with job skills as for those who have not worked outside the home.

Children provide still another problem in safe houses. Many

of them are emotionally disturbed, and others have serious learning problems. While refuges have attempted to provide care for infants, preschoolers, and even school-age children, they generally don't have the resources to deal with them adequately. Local school districts often refuse to accept these children because of the short periods of time they expect to be there. If schools do admit them, they generally do not provide the special services the children need, and thus their learning is interrupted further.

Space is a problem in safe houses for younger children who need room to run and play. Other children, especially the adolescents, engage in various acting-out behaviors that make communal living in cramped quarters a horror. They often destroy the meager furnishings. Adolescent boys can be as violent as their fathers, and often find willing younger versions of their mothers in the adolescent girls. The theory that an abusing family begets a new generation of abusers is painfully observable in these safe houses. A good deal of time, energy, and money is spent trying to reverse this trend to prevent the children from perpetuating violence.

Crowding is another problem. Refuges are filled with so many people that the noise level is often deafening. There is no privacy and not much room for individuality, although this becomes less of a problem if short-term occupancy is encouraged. Most safe houses are in physical disrepair because of overuse. Washing machines, if they exist, are often broken, as are most other appliances; they simply cannot stand the wear they are given. In one safe house I visited, the women were unable to repair their overworked washing machines, so they took over a local laundromat several evenings a week. They persuaded the laundromat owner to remain open beyond his usual hours so they would not interrupt service to his regular customers. They had enough laundry to utilize every machine. Doing the laundry this way was more efficient than the constant hassle of repairing their own washing machines and dryers.

A critical problem in safe houses is widespread sickness. Colds, stomach ailments, and other contagious diseases run rampant through houses because ill members usually cannot be isolated. Women and children whose previous isolation has actually protected them from many childhood illnesses become easy prey for rounds of chicken pox, measles, mumps, and other diseases against which they have not been inoculated. Finances make it impossible to staff the houses with doctors and nurses, so professionals must donate their time. As dismal as this picture may appear, it is crucial to understand that, both here and in England, women *choose* to live in a safe house rather than in their quiet, clean, spacious, disease-free homes with their batterers.

The last major problem in the safe house or refuge movement is the treatment program for the men. The batterer is ignored unless he comes after his woman. If he does, he is generally turned over to the law enforcement authorities. If the batterer were to stop his problem behavior after his victim left, he would not be a concern to those interested in helping battered women. This, however, does not seem to happen. It is more likely that he will either become psychotic, seriously depressed, or, even worse, find another woman to batter. To date, there are almost no facilities anywhere in society, not just in safe houses, for dealing with batterers. This is most likely because until very recently their behavior has not been regarded as abnormal. Mental health workers do not yet know how to treat these men. Nor are any other agencies able to provide adequate services. It is unfortunate, although understandable, that these men generally do not get any treatment.

In several refuges, batterers have been involved in treatment. Rainbow Retreat in Phoenix states that 60 percent of their batterers participate in group, family, or individual therapy. Chiswick has set up a separate house in London in which batterers may live or meet in groups. Although neither refuge reports the same kind of excitement and success with the men as with the women, at least initial steps have been taken. At the American Lakes Veterans Administration Hospital in Tacoma, Washington, a new program for batterers is beginning. The focus of treatment in this unit will be to eliminate the violent behavior of these men. Hospital administrators have noted that often after a woman leaves a batterer, he is admitted to the psychiatric ward of this hospital. Any patient admitted to the hospital psychiatric ward who also has a history of wife abuse can volunteer to be put in one special ward. It is hoped that new treatment procedures will develop from this experimental unit.

Safe houses have many other problems. They are expensive and difficult to operate. Staff turnover is high, as the staff is typically underpaid and overworked. In many cases, staff training prior to working in a safe house is limited. Most refuges give staff members several days off a month to recuperate from the stress and workload they must endure. Funding is a constant problem. Support groups lose enthusiasm and frequently shift allegiances. Keeping safe houses running after they finally are opened takes enormous energy.

Despite all the problems associated with safe houses, they truly are the cornerstone of battered women's programs. Battered women cannot cope in the outside world without some assistance and intervention. Death and murder are part of this scene, as are other atrocities. Even when the batterer and the woman live apart, harassment and tragedy befall them. One woman told of having her house set afire by an irate batterer who had already moved out. Another discussed the apparent murder-suicide of her ex-husband and his current fiancée. A third was severely beaten at the bus station by her former husband. Still others talk of kidnapping and child beating after they have separated from their batterers. Safe houses help women prepare themselves to cope with these problems and, through their advocacy, assist other agencies in dealing with them, too.

All shelter members become saddened when a former member or child is killed, an event which happens far too often. They assume guilt for the death, thinking, If only we had done better, she might have stayed. In one group that I visited, I entered a room where about a dozen women, several staff people, and a local police officer were all sitting weeping. A former member had killed her baby the night before. Losing this baby was particularly difficult for the group to accept because they had supported the woman's request to have an abortion when she first learned she was pregnant. She had seriously abused her three other children, after being brutally battered herself. The request for government funds to pay for the abortion was denied, despite the intervention of the support staff at the safe house. Soon after the child was born, the woman placed a pillow over her infant and smothered it. Needless to say, this tragedy might have been prevented. It is simply one of the many tragedies that the staff of a safe house must cope with daily.

Although safe houses and similar helping organizations are just a step in the right direction, at least they are so much more than ever has been available before. They provide some direct services to the victims, their children, and occasionally the batterer, too. More importantly, they are advocacy groups which mobilize lots of other services to these troubled families in a community. There is much more that still needs to be done. Yet all of the difficulties in starting and operating the safe house disappear when the battered woman shakes off her victim mantle. The successes achieved make the many problems surmountable.

10

Legal and Medical Alternatives

In designing treatment alternatives for battered women, the first and, of course, most obvious necessity is to halt the battering. Anyone working with a battered woman must immediately assess the degree of physical danger her current living arrangement poses. Once her immediate safety is assured, further treatment alternatives can be recommended. The various services, agencies, and groups dealing with battered women within a community should take steps to insure that their efforts be coordinated. Emergency help must always be available. Even when a woman's safety has been assured temporarily, it can change rapidly. In some rural communities, emergency housing is provided by a trailer type of recreational vehicle which not only can house a woman and her family overnight but also transport her to a safer environment when necessary. The van can be parked outside the police station, if necessary. Not all battered women need emergency services. For some, a visit to a lawyer's office may be the decisive incident that helps them escape. Others use a doctor, a psychotherapist, a teacher, an employer, or a good friend to propel them into action. They, too, need supportive services to protect them from their batterer's anger, yet they do not need the protective environment of a safe house. These women will use other treatment alternatives to reorder their lives.

LEGAL ALTERNATIVES

The legal alternatives necessary for battered women include: adequate police protection, easy access to restraining orders, facilitation of prosecution procedures by assault victims, provision for temporary support and maintenance, speedy divorces, regulated child visitation, and legitimate legal procedures for battered women as defendants.

Adequate Police Protection

Battered women uniformly report that police do not provide adequate protection from their batterers. Of the women interviewed in this research, only 10 percent ever called the police. As noted elsewhere, these women stated that the best they expected from the police was to quiet the batterer down, decide whether or not the women needed medical attention, and try to make them both promise to stop fighting. As soon as the police left, the batterers resumed their abuse. It does not take long for a battered woman to learn that calling the police will result in another beating. Thus, she stops calling altogether, or if the police do arrive (frequently called by a well-meaning neighbor), she may side with the batterer in order to minimize his anger when the police leave. It is estimated that out of the 10 percent of the battering cases reported in this study, at least half never got recorded in official police reports, for when such records were requested, they were unavailable. While about 90 percent of those women who did report assaults to the police actually signed complaints, less than 1 percent of the cases were ever prosecuted. It is up to the district attorney's office to decide whether or not to prosecute, and the cases are rarely followed through because the rate of conviction is so low. This is doubtless because, as in rape cases, the only witness is usually the victim. Police protection for the battered women in my sample was as ineffective as that reported by other battered women.

The reason for police ineffectiveness in dealing with battering relationships is not entirely clear. Police understand their responsibility to be to maintain public law and order. Most police officers feel, however, that those acts taking place behind a family's closed door are not subject to police intervention; rather, they are *private* acts between men and women. Police officers are frequently men who have been socialized to believe that a man has the right to discipline his woman. An unusually high incidence of wife beating is reported among police officers. It is thus difficult to expect that these same men will be able to protect other men's women adequately. Morton Bard, the police psychologist at City University of New York, has been training police to respond as both protectors and social workers in New York City. There is a controversy concerning whether or not police make effective conciliators when they intervene during an acute battering incident. Certainly when a raging phase-two battle is occurring, reasonableness is ineffective and authoritarian separation of the couple is called for. Nonetheless, in those police departments which have accepted this additional role, reports are positive. Both police and citizen fatalities have decreased. There are also fewer repeat calls. The Hayward, California, Police Department has hired special counselors to follow up police domestic violence calls. This method also has proved successful. In many cases, police departments that have set aside special bureaus to work closely with women's resource centers or crisis shelters also report positive collaboration. The system used in Missoula,

Montana, between the police and a support group called Women's Place is a model of such effectiveness. In areas where police and LEAA programs interact to provide training and referral sources, battered women usually receive more protection.

The largest number of police fatalities in the line of duty occur when police respond to domestic violence calls—approximately 25 percent of all police fatalities. That figure rises to 40 percent if all police injuries are included. Thus, not only do police agree that they are ineffective in providing alternatives for battering couples, but they also view responding to such requests as personally dangerous.

Police departments themselves have been wrestling with this problem. In a revealing presentation to the American Bar Association convention in 1975, Detroit Police Commander James Bannon admitted that interpersonal violence had been escalated by the difficulty police have had in providing adequate protection. He stated that the number of calls to police departments in battering cases is extremely high. (An especially interesting statement in view of my sample, in which only 10 percent of the women had called police.) Calls from battered women are usually screened by the police dispatcher. Only calls from women who seem to be in imminent danger are answered. Repeat calls to the same residence are common. These women quickly learn to tell the police dispatcher that the man has a gun, in order to get prompt response. When the police arrive, they often become angry when they find that the woman has only minor injuries, and they may not respond so quickly next time.

A recent study by the Kansas City police indicated that homicides in battering relationships could be predicted on the basis of police-call patterns. Fifty percent of the fatalities had called for police intervention at least five times prior to their deaths. Eighty percent had called at least once. Thus, deaths in battering relationships might be preventable with adequate police protection. Although police may log in their domestic violence calls, the data are largely irretrievable. Such data should be made available to document the scope of the battered woman problem.

Successful programs such as those in Hayward, California, and Missoula, Montana, indicate that inadequate police intervention should no longer be tolerated. There are innovative ways that police departments can become more responsible to meeting the needs of battered women and their families.

The battered women themselves suggested ways to improve police intervention. First, the police should be able to prevent the man from committing further immediate violence against them. The most effective way to guarantee such protection is for the police to treat the domestic violence call as an assault and arrest the batterer. The police should also sign the complaint. The state, represented by the police, then is responsible for pressing charges, as it is in any other assault case, not the battered woman. It is unrealistic to expect the victim to sign the complaint and press charges when she is given no protection from further assaults. Most police officers state that they lose interest in protecting battered women when the women repeatedly drop charges. They interpret this reluctance to press charges as a desire to remain battered rather than fear of violent punishment by their batterers for pressing charges. In treating battering as an assault, police should include both married and unmarried couples. Police should also have the right to request a temporary restraining order forbidding the man to harm the woman further or removing him from the premises, as they may in many states in child abuse cases. Although some police officers state that police issuance of a restraining order or a peace bond may limit the psychological effectiveness of the fear it evokes when the judge so orders, the women interviewed stated that no matter who issues such an order, most batterers respect it. Finally, police should be given responsibility for enforcing restraining orders. The issuing court, if there is one, should send copies of these orders to the local law enforcement agency, rather than requiring the victim to show the orders to the police. Entering it into the computerized informational system which police use is most effective. Many battered women report that their restraining orders are immediately ripped to shreds by the batterer long before the police arrive. The courts should therefore issue these restraining orders directly to the local police department, so the local police have the authority to protect the women.

In New York City, a class action suit against the New York City Police Department, the probation officers, and the clerks of the court has been filed on behalf of twelve battered women. These women, and several others who have been added as plaintiffs, are being represented by attorneys from the Center for Constitutional Rights, Brooklyn Legal Aid Services, New York Legal Aid Services, and the New York MYF Corporation. The suit requests a declaratory judgment to force the defendants to perform their duties to protect the battered women. In addition to prompt and adequate intervention, the other major issue raised in the suit is the provision of temporary restraining orders upon request and need. The complaint states that probation officers and clerks of the court have denied these battered women access to judges, who are the only ones who can issue such restraining orders in New York City. Inadequate protection for battered women is not unique to New York City. Battered women everywhere do not receive protection under the law. In most states, married battered women do not even have the benefit of any law other than those in domestic law. A thorough review of pertinent legislation can be found in Del Martin's *Battered Wives.* A 1976 Denver study citing the violation of civil rights of battered women also has been released by the United States Commission on Civil Rights. Testimony presented to the United States Commission on Civil Rights in January, 1978, details these violations further.

Easy Access to Restraining Orders

One of the most controversial areas has been the issuance of temporary or permanent restraining orders and peace bonds. In issuing a restraining order, the judge, in effect, orders the batterer to stop his assault and to stay away from the battered woman and her home. If the couple is not married and does not own joint property, the order is issued quite simply upon evidence of violence. If the couple is married, however, judges are reluctant in most states, and forbidden by law in others, to enjoin a married man from using his property. Unless divorce petitions are filed, most married women have extraordinary trouble getting temporary restraining orders. Disobeying a restraining order usually results in a contempt of court citation and an immediate arrest order. Yet the punishment is rarely more than a small monetary fine and/or up to one year in jail. Despite the relatively minor penalties, restraining orders are the legal profession's second most potent technique in dealing with offenders, arrest and prosecution being the first. This is due to the fear batterers have of arrest and being in trouble with the law. They tend to mask this fear by pretending the law can't touch them, but over 80 percent are said to obey restraining orders.

Each state has its own method for obtaining such an order. A temporary restraining order usually is issued first, which then becomes permanent unless the assailant shows cause why it should not. A peace bond is similar to a restraining order in intent, the difference being that the peace bond usually requires a financial commitment from the assailant, which is then confiscated if the order is violated.

Many attorneys do not find restraining orders particularly useful, as they feel the batterer will not obey them. These attorneys claim that a restraining order or a peace bond is simply a piece of paper which cannot force a batterer to cease his violent behavior. Obtaining restraining orders also involves an inordinate amount of attorney and court time. In those states where divorce papers must be filed simultaneously with a request for a restraining order, the attorney's time involved becomes out of proportion to its immediate need. In fact, many attorneys report that by the time they finish filing all the papers required by the court, the effectiveness of the restraining order has been diminished, and the batterer is in his phase-three contrite, loving behavior. Nevertheless, the battered women who responded to this research all stated they felt that the restraining order was extremely successful once they obtained it. Although many felt that they had to engage in manipulative tactics with their attorneys in order to obtain such relief, once they had the restraining order in their hands, they felt safe. This study showed that 80 percent of the batterers were violent only in their domestic relations—80 percent of them had never been brought before the criminal justice system prior to the battering incident. It is reasonable, then, to expect that the psychological force of a restraining order would weigh heavily upon these men in determining their future behavior. In fact, that is what was reported. Most men whose women had a restraining order issued against them ceased their assaultive behavior. In those cases where the couple was no longer living together, the men stopped harassing the women and lessened their surveillance. The inequities and hardships experienced by battered women in obtaining such relief certainly need immediate attention. Legislatures must make laws that remove the inequities experienced by married women in obtaining restraining orders.

Facilitation of Prosecution Procedures by Assault Victims

Immediate prosecution is another potent technique that the criminal justice system has at its disposal to halt violence against women. Unfortunately, it is rarely used. In this study, less than 1 percent of the women interviewed actually completed prosecution against their batterers. Such low statistics are commonplace all across the country. The fact that batterers suffer no legal consequences for their assaults serves only to perpetuate their violent behavior. Why is this so? In interviewing district attorneys, judges, lawyers, and the women themselves, we learned there were several reasons. The most important one, of course, has been mentioned previously. The social mores which permit a husband to beat his wife in the name of discipline pervades the very basis of our judicial system. This is clearly evident when one examines the procedures required to prosecute a batterer.

In most states, counties, and cities, the woman is required to sign a complaint against her batterer before the prosecutor will even consider prosecution. Even when she does sign such a complaint, and has witnesses, it is still left to the district attorney to decide whether or not to prosecute. While accurate data do not exist on the number of complaints signed versus the number of cases that actually go to court, informal data conclude that the percentage is minimal. When questioned about this low prosecution rate, most parties concerned stated that the battered woman often changes her mind and refuses to serve as a witness or withdraws the complaint prior to prosecution. Others stated that cases do not come to trial because of inadequate corroborating data. There are few, if any, witnesses to the private assault, and prior evidence is usually not sought, even when it is available. This is true even when police have been witnesses to the assault. In fact, most police departments admit when questioned that they do have legal authority to sign the complaint themselves if they either have witnessed the assault or have adequate reason to believe that the man did perpetrate an assault upon the woman involved. Even in repeat-offender cases, police departments choose not to exercise this right. It seems highly unfair to expect a victim to become the state's main witness as well as to act on behalf of the prosecutor.

Most women interviewed stated that they would continue to press charges if they had support in doing so. States which have Victim/Witness Assistance Programs show this to be true. Victim advocates associated with the Harborview Hospital program for rape, battering, and incest assaults in Seattle, Washington, have obtained one of the highest prosecution and conviction rates of violent male offenders. Women victims are provided with an advocate to accompany them through the entire legal bureaucratic procedure. The stories of long waits outside offices and run-arounds from agency to agency diminished when an advocate was present. Advocates smooth the legal process for women and encourage them to follow through in securing their legal rights.

Another state which has made an attempt to facilitate the prosecution of cases involving battered women is Florida. Under a grant from LEAA, a Citizens' Dispute Settlement Center has been established in Dade County. Its purpose is to reduce potentially violent situations and lessen the need for prosecution by obtaining, through arbitration, a mutual agreement to stop the violence. Of course, this implies that the woman is an accomplice in her own victimization. Trained volunteers serve as the arbitrators. Referrals come from police and state attorney's offices. When a case comes before the Citizens' Dispute Settlement Center, both parties are mandated to appear before an arbitrator. At that time, arbitration continues until a mutual agreement is reached. The two parties sign the agreement. If the agreement is violated, a letter threatening prosecution is sent to both parties. Unfortunately, this is where the system breaks down. The arbitration hearings are confidential and are not permitted to be introduced as evidence in subsequent prosecution cases. So there are no real penalties for violating arbitration agreements.

One arbitration that I observed at the Center indicated that unless the arbitrator was experienced in working with battering relationships, he/she could miss important aspects of the case. In this case, a woman brought her estranged husband to the Citizens' Dispute Settlement Center because he had poured acid on all of her clothing. First, the arbitrator neglected to ascertain that the couple was no longer living together. More importantly, he did not ask whether or not there had been previous instances of violence. The woman, however, had indicated in her original complaint that the man had been harassing and brutalizing her. She chose to use the Citizens' Dispute Settlement Center as a way of threatening him to stop his behavior. She was not permitted to obtain a restraining order, nor was she afforded the opportunity of prosecution until she had gone through unsuccessful arbitration at least once. When questioned, the arbitrator became defensive about his lack of ability to perceive the true situation. He stated he did not believe it was the function of the arbitrator to go into the prior history of the couple, but simply to resolve the incident as reported.

In all fairness, another observed arbitration was highly successful. The arbitrator was well trained and knew what questions to ask and how to obtain a history of violence. In this case, the arbitrator required the man to put in writing that he would cease and desist from physical or verbal harassment of the woman as part of his arbitration agreement. The man was clearly told that he would be prosecuted under criminal law if he violated this agreement. In most cases I reviewed, the agreement was honored by the batterer. The extent of the usefulness of this kind of arbitration has not been systematically evaluated. The probability of its success seems dependent upon the quality of the arbitrator. Such programs have not won wide acceptance owing to the difficulty of providing well-trained arbitrators. Successful arbitration demands that two equal parties enter into fair negotiations. Given the difference in power between the batterer and his victim, arbitration is not automatically recommended but may have potential in the future.

There is no doubt that effective prosecution can diminish the rate of violence against women. Adequate record keeping is especially important, as impressions and interpretations are useless in a courtroom. Everyone associated with a battered woman should keep accurate records that will hold up in a court. In my work as a psychologist, I have been training other mental health professionals to document all instances of battering that they observe in their clients. This may mean keeping a Polaroid camera in their offices so that they can take color pictures of a woman's bruises. It may also mean collecting tattered shreds of clothing to use as evidence. Clear descriptions of the exact incident reported and of the woman's injuries are needed to prosecute effectively. Effective prosecu-

tion requires that people who are aware of a woman's battering must be willing to testify on her behalf in the courtroom.
In many cases, batterers go free because no one corroborates
the woman's story. Use of an expert witness in these cases is
highly recommended. Battered women's stories are difficult to
believe. The fact that they have continued to live under such
brutality is used to their detriment in any legal proceedings,
and knowledgeable family members often refuse their support.

Provision for Temporary Support and Maintenance

There has been a good deal of controversy over whether to
use civil or criminal remedies for prosecution in these cases. If
a battered woman prosecutes her husband in criminal court
and he must serve a jail sentence or pay a large monetary fine,
she may suffer, too. If she is economically dependent upon
him, and he may lose his job, then she has no support. Even in
those cases where the woman has financial resources, a large
fine may be more than the family's finances can stand. Social
embarrassment caused by court proceedings, especially if the
man is found guilty, is another deterrent to following through
on criminal charges. Thus a movement has begun to decrimi-
nalize some of the wife-assault cases so that they can be held
in civil court, where penalities are not as severe. In Pennsylvania, legislation which permits cases to be tried in civil court
has been well received. The new law permits a civil court
judge to issue a separation order, a restraining order, separate
maintenance payments, and temporary child custody and
visitation orders, all at the same time, upon evidence that the
man has battered his woman. Although many civil libertar-
ians feared that the rights of the batterer would be violated by
granting such easy remedy, in the hundred or so cases already
adjudicated no man's legal rights reportedly have been violated. In each case, the court had the authority to adjudicate
these questions temporarily up to one year without requiring

that permanent divorce petitions be filed. The simplified procedure has reduced attorney's fees, bringing this sort of legal relief well within the range of most battered women. Furthermore, men are not as apt to lose their jobs or damage their social positions because of the disgrace associated with criminal proceedings.

Because of the overwhelming success of the Pennsylvania statute, other states are beginning to consider similar legislation. In Colorado, such a bill is expected to be introduced in the state legislature in the 1978–1979 session, with the support of groups such as the District Attorneys Association, the Colorado Association for Aid to Battered Women, NOW and other feminist groups. Such legislation will not prevent criminal proceedings when they are appropriate; rather, it will give attorneys, district attorneys, and battered women a choice of legal alternatives.

All available data indicate that less than 25 percent of women who have been granted a separate maintenance financial agreement, which includes alimony and/or child support payments, ever receive this money. The federal government has attempted to collect child support payments without much success. Battered women probably have a lower percentage of collection of such payments, as the batterers are often unable to earn sufficient amounts of money once they are living independently because they fall apart emotionally and/or physically. Oftentimes, the battered woman needs to receive a larger share of joint property in order to assist her in meeting later financial obligations of raising her family. To date, the court has not taken this into consideration when awarding property, child support, and alimony to battered women.

Battered women who flee their husbands should be exempted from potential desertion charges. Documentation from any of the previously mentioned support groups is needed by attorneys. Battered women also need to be informed of their rights in any potential divorce action. Many women are ignorant of property distribution and child custody laws.

Some safe houses and legal aid services across the country are providing excellent legal defense for battered women. Private attorneys need to follow suit. Places such as the Center for Women Policy Studies in Washington, D.C., have been a major source of aid and information for groups across the country. Originally funded by LEAA, the Center provides assistance to victims of "sensitive" crimes. Initially this term referred only to rape, but it has now been expanded to include technical help to any organization providing services for battered women and victims of incest. The Center publishes an information newsletter, *Response,* which is distributed without charge.

Speedy Divorces

Legal rights for battered women who enter into separation and divorce actions also need to be considered. The women involved in this research have expressed the feeling that their legal rights have been violated because they were battered women. In some states where fault is still used as grounds for divorce, these women are often accused of desertion by their husbands. Property distributions are adversely affected when this occurs. Battered women who wish to seek divorces prior to leaving their husbands are often unable to receive assistance from the legal aid services in their community. Legal aid services are usually inundated with divorce cases, and thus set income limits based on total family income to determine eligibility for use of their services. This system provides a particular hardship for the woman who has no income of her own but who is married to a man with a fair-sized income. As a result, obtaining adequate legal representation is usually determined by the amount of money a woman has. She not only needs money to pay for the divorce, but she also needs to know that her attorney has her interests at heart. Many attorneys discount a battered woman's stories of violence and minimize the risk these women undergo when they ask their husbands for a divorce. Many of the women interviewed who finally were divorced stated that they had retained two or three attorneys before they found one in whom they had confidence. This situation only puts more stress on a woman already functioning at a high level of tension. In many cases, the women also reported that their attorneys did not inform them of their legal rights. Whenever I refer a battered woman to a divorce attorney, I inform her or him that the client I am referring is a battered woman and initially will need more support, information, and legal advice than many other women seeking a divorce. The attorney also needs to be especially careful about the safety needs of her and her children.

Regulated Child Visitation

Child custody and visitation rights are of paramount importance in divorce proceedings of a battering couple. Batterers commonly engage in child custody battles. For some, such battles are a way of prolonging the inevitable disintegration of their family. Others use child custody as a weapon to keep the woman from going through with a divorce. Still others genuinely want custody of their children and fear that once the divorce takes place, not only their wives but their children, too, will be lost to them. Once child custody has been determined, many women report that the batterers do not exercise their visitation rights. In other cases, however, there have been reports of kidnapping, especially when the children were very young. When the threat of kidnapping is reported by a battered woman, it must be dealt with immediately by the attorney. Sometimes a temporary suspension of child visitation rights or close supervision is appropriate.

Children involved in battering incidents also need to have their rights legally represented. This is true especially for girl children who are victims of sexual abuse by the batterer. Most attorneys will not ask about potential sexual abuse unless their client mentions it. All attorneys who deal with battered women or their husbands should question the legitimacy of automatic visitation rights. If necessary, a petition may be made to the court either to suspend visitation rights or to have the court assign an attorney to represent the children.

Legitimate Legal Procedures for Battered Women as Defendants

A new legal concern is the battered woman as a defendant. A number of women have been brought to trial because they have assaulted or killed their tormentors. Most times, the woman killed her batterer. As mentioned earlier, I have been involved in several of these cases. In three cases, I served as an expert witness at the request of the defense, and in several others I consulted with the defense attorneys. In one assault case, I assisted the district attorney in prosecuting the man. Several factors were common to all these cases. First, each woman stated that she was convinced the batterer was going to kill her. Violent assault had taken place previously in all of these cases. In the final incident, however, something different was noted by these women which convinced them that the batterer really was going to kill them this time. In each case, the woman stated that she did not intend to kill her batterer, only to stop him from killing her. In fact, this was the basis of my testimony on grounds of self-defense. None of the women realized that their batterers were dead. In fact, months after the incident these women still talked about their batterers as though the men could still control their behavior. All reported being terrified of their batterers. To them, the men were omnipotent; the women felt they had no place to hide. No matter where they went, the batterer would follow. In each case, the batterer's violence was extraordinarily brutal. In the end, these women had to resort to the most extreme kind of force—use of a lethal weapon—in order to prevent the batterers from killing them.

To provide a legitimate defense for such women, several

legal questions must be resolved. In most states, self-defense is defined as the use of the least sufficient amount of force to prevent bodily harm. Under the laws of self-defense, therefore, unless the woman truly believes that her batterer will kill her imminently, she does not have the right to kill him. The law in most states requires that the woman exercise the least possible force necessary to escape the batterer. A central question in these cases is why she did not leave prior to the final assault, why she did remain in the battering situation. If it can be proved that the psychological bond between the defendant and her batterer was equivalent to being physically restrained, acquittal on the basis of self-defense can be justified. In most battering relationships, both the woman and the man are psychologically dependent upon one another. It must be made clear to the court that the woman is a victim because of her extreme dependence upon the batterer. She does not believe that she can be a totally independent person. Death is a more acceptable alternative to separation. Similarly, the batterer would rather die or kill his woman than voluntarily leave her or let her leave him. The Center for Constitutional Rights in New York City has established a special division to assist in preparation of defenses for women victims of violence, directed by Chris Arguedas.

MEDICAL ALTERNATIVES

The staffs of hospital emergency rooms generally see battered women following the phase-two acute battering incident and as they move into phase three, loving behavior. Most emergency room doctors do not have time to question the battered woman about the origin of her injuries. Even when they do ask, they often do so in a suspicious, callous, hostile, or indifferent manner, which only causes the woman to become defensive. The women interviewed reported that if the emergency room doctors had not seemed too hurried, they might have told them the truth. However, they did not believe the doctors would consider their injuries as life-threatening as those of the person in the next examining room.

Nurses in the emergency room have the most continuity with repeat patients and are most likely to spot battered women, especially if they have had awareness training. The staff at Denver General Hospital, which has the largest emergency room facility in Denver, has received training in identifying and supporting battered women. Many of the nurses reported incidents in which a badly injured woman was sitting in the waiting room when a man rushed in and pulled her out with him into the night. A system to escort such women immediately into a private waiting room was then instituted. There a trained social worker assists her as soon as possible, and the nurse on duty assesses the severity of her physical injuries. This is now routine procedure for all women coming into the emergency room, alone or without a man. Any injured woman waiting with a man is watched carefully to determine whether abuse might be involved. If a nurse suspects battering, the woman's chart is tagged to alert other emergency room staff. The woman is examined and interviewed alone. This procedure is unusual, as most emergency rooms permit accompanying people to be present during examination. She is asked if her injuries are the result of a beating. Confronted directly, it is difficult for her to conceal battering, unless she is totally terrified. Whether or not she admits to being abused, she is given the telephone number of the nearest helping agency, usually one dealing with women victims. I have known battered women who kept such a telephone number hidden for six or more months before they used it. If the injured woman admits to being battered, all details of the incident and complete descriptions of her injuries, as reported, are entered on her chart. The chart may serve as valuable legal evidence later on.

Whenever possible, a battered woman should be admitted to the hospital. She is usually physically and emotionally exhausted. Hospitalization not only hastens her healing process, it also provides a temporary refuge. During hospitalization, both the battered woman and the batterer are forced to deal with the consequences of the violence. If they try to deny or minimize her injuries, as is so common, hospitalization prevents them from doing so. Even in cases where hospitalization is impossible, hospital staff should attempt to impress upon the couple the seriousness of the woman's injuries. In the hospital, the battered woman has time to think and perhaps decide on a course of action. Although most women return home after hospital treatment, for many it is the first step toward independence. Wherever possible, hospital personnel should encourage the woman to go to another home to continue her recuperation. Often the battered woman will listen to professionals if their advice seems sound.

The injuries of battered women treated in hospital emergency rooms fall into several categories. The first is serious bleeding injuries. Wounds requiring stitches to close them, especially around the face and head, are common. Facial wounds often cause a great deal of bleeding, and here shock is always a possibility. The second category is internal injuries which cause bleeding and malfunctioning of organs. The women interviewed reported damaged spleens, kidneys, and punctured lungs. A third category includes bones: cracked vertebrae, skulls, and pelvises, as well as broken jaws, arms, and legs have been treated. Women with injured ribs, collarbones, or pelvises often are not seen for several days. It is only when the pain from the broken bones does not subside that the battered woman seeks medical attention. Many times, X-rays show broken bones that have healed incorrectly because of lack of medical attention. (I have been told that it is possible to note on X-rays the difference between fractures that occur in a normal accident and those which occur from twisting, as in broken arms.) A fourth category is burns. Cigarette burns and burns from hot appliances, stoves, irons, acid, scalding liquids, and similar things show up in the emergency room.

Most women who arrive in the emergency room have multiple injuries. The sense of overkill that is part of a phase-two acute battering incident is all too obvious: the batterer does not stop with the first observable physical injury; he continues until his rage subsides.

In another category are the women who come to the emergency room with less observable physical injuries. They often arrive with acute anxiety attacks resulting in heart palpitations, hyperventilation, severe crying spells, and the like. Others come with a host of psychophysiological ailments that tax the diagnostic skill of attending physicians. While many emergency rooms routinely call in a mental health worker to talk to women whose injuries seem to have psychological as well as physical causes, they often neglect to inquire as to whether she is a victim of battering. Sensitive interviewing can elicit the true home-life situation. It is important to determine whether such women are suicidal before administering barbiturates or tranquilizers. Fortunately, most emergency rooms dispense only small doses of such medications. However, many of the women interviewed stated that they were able to amass enough of these medications from several emergency room visits to kill themselves if things got too bad. A study by Yale Medical School's emergency hospital room physician, Ann Flitcraft, demonstrated the dangers of such indiscriminate drug dispensing. Immediate referrals to mental health facilities where specific services for battered women exist would be the most helpful alternative for these women. Teams of paid staff and volunteers are now on call on a twenty-four-hour basis in communities as diverse as Missoula, Montana; Seattle, Washington; Miami, Florida; New York City; Denver, Colorado; and others. In the final chapter, I shall tell you how to make such contact.

Private Physicians and Clinics

Private physicians and clinics do not see as many battered women following a phase-two explosion as hospitals do. Many women say they are too ashamed or frightened to confide in a family doctor and prefer the anonymity of large hospital emergency rooms. Private physicians generally see battered women during the first, tension-building phase of the battering cycle. As the tension begins to cause more anxiety, women request medication to help them feel calmer, to sleep, to relieve backaches and other stress symptoms. Elaine Hilberman reports a group of rural battered women who, at great risk to themselves, sought out services from a comprehensive health clinic without their batterers' knowledge. They received supportive counseling and medication to relieve stress symptoms and facilitate sleep.

Many battered women come to the attention of medical personnel during pregnancy. They usually seek routine obstetrical care, which provides some continuity with a clinic or medical staff. This is a good opportunity for helpers to confront the woman about her suspicious bruises and to recommend positive alternatives.

Company Medical and Counseling Departments

Company medical and counseling departments are another natural community resource that can help provide safety and help for battered women. Many batterers are well known to their wives' co-workers. The batterer may hang around the wife's office without much reason, usually not causing trouble for her until near the final stages of phase-one behavior. The woman will sometimes seek counseling or medical help through her company, so that the batterer does not know. Anxiety and lack of sleep often hamper her efficiency. If she can get sent home on sick pay, she tends to use the time to try to reduce the tensions that have been building. She usually stays out for several days following an acute battering incident. If she has been injured, she waits until make-up can cover the bruises. She often sees the company physician to check for broken bones, especially broken ribs, for which she can put off treatment about four days until the pain worsens.

Some large companies have programs for battered women employees. For example, one company physician who has studied the battered woman syndrome will place such a woman on disability if her medical conditions warrant it, and will suggest referral sources for psychotherapy. The woman can remain on disability with full pay and all medical expenses covered until her psychologist feels she is ready to return to her job. This type of program assures battered women job protection while giving them time to cope with their crises, including the option of going into hiding for short periods of time. Many battered women are considered hypochondriacs because they visit their doctors so often; yet they have few other sources of professional assistance. They regard it as less of a risk to see the doctor for physical complaints than to seek psychological help.

11

Psychotherapy

In a country such as America where there is a kind of reverence for the practice of psychotherapy, it should not be surprising that battered women and their families have sought the services of psychotherapists. As is true of other helpers, however, professional psychotherapists (including psychiatrists, psychologists, social workers, and psychiatric nurses) have also been inadequate in helping the battered woman. The women interviewed reported that most therapists refuse, directly or indirectly (usually by omission), to deal specifically with acute battering incidents. Instead, the therapists concentrate on the psychological consequences such incidents produce. It is to be expected that women who have been abused repeatedly will have enough psychological symptoms to keep a therapist busy. Many psychotherapists interviewed have admitted not realizing that their clients were being brutally beaten over long periods of time. Such failure to identify battered women becomes even more frequent when the results of the violence have not been severe. Psychotherapists have been trained to believe that victims often provoke their assault. Nowhere has this belief been more in evidence than in their dealing with the psychological aftermath of violent crimes against women. Psychotherapists, often inadvertently, have added to the woman's loss of self-esteem by joining in the conspiracy of silence that surrounds battering incidents and by concentrating on women's "provocative" nature when such incidents are revealed in therapy sessions. It is no wonder, then, that most of the battered women interviewed felt psychotherapeutic intervention was not useful for them.

Battered women have recounted stories of being treated as though they were engaged in "crazy" behavior. They told of seeking psychotherapy for their batterers only to be told that it was *their* problem. Many women in the sample were involuntarily institutionalized. Others spoke of voluntarily seeking admission to a mental hospital in order to escape temporarily from the battering situation. In several cases, the women were given so many shock treatments that their memories were impaired permanently. Other women were diagnosed as paranoid schizophrenics, the evidence for which was their suspiciousness and their lack of trust of people they feared might say the wrong things to their batterers. In a paranoid way, they concealed their actions, wrote and stashed away secret messages on tiny pieces of paper, and constantly worried about manipulating other people's behavior so as not to upset the batterer. As previously noted, rarely did these women report that they discussed the fact that they were being brutally beaten at home. In those cases where the women reported that battering behavior was discussed in their treatment, the purpose of the therapists was always to discover what they were doing to provoke this kind of abuse. The assumption was that the woman needed to be beaten in order to expiate her alleged sins. Others in the sample reported being treated for serious depression, which no doubt served to protect them from the constant level of stress in their unpredictable lives. For too many women, their justified and perhaps motivating anger was mellowed by indiscriminate use of tranquilizers. The acute stress reactions these women were experiencing were diagnosed as more serious emotional disturbances. This probably occurred because the environmental situation was not considered seriously enough by those psychotherapists providing treatment.

Many battered women's coping techniques, acquired to protect them from further violence, have been viewed as evidence of severe personality disorders. These women suffer from situationally imposed emotional problems caused by their victimization. They do not choose to be battered because of some personality defect; they develop behavioral disturbances because they live in violence. My grant proposing further systematic research into battered women's personalities was funded by the National Institute of Mental Health in 1978. The goal of this project has been an assessment of both the strengths and the weaknesses in battered women as compared to women who have not experienced living in violence. It is hoped that such data, when compiled, will end the myths and misinformation that have perpetuated some psychotherapists' attitudes. Other psychotherapists, however, are just starting to do good work with battered women and their families, using the new information we have begun to gather. Because battered women are telling their stories and are being believed by mental health professionals, progress in this area is occurring.

As a psychologist and a psychotherapist, I am poignantly aware of how inadequate my training and that of my colleagues has been in understanding and treating violent family relationships. It is only within the last ten years that we have begun to wrestle with the problem of treatment for child batterers. Although we are learning how to provide psychotherapeutic services for rape victims, we still have limited techniques available to help us change the rapist's behavior. So, too, for battered women and their families. We are learning how to support and provide psychotherapy for battered women. Less is known of how to treat their children or their batterers.

There are two kinds of treatment available to battered women and, in some cases, to their families. The first is supportive counseling provided by paraprofessionals or non-professional persons trained in specific counseling techniques for working with violent families. The second is professional psychotherapy provided by psychotherapists. In both types, additional training in current techniques is necessary to provide adequate therapy for the battered woman.

I strongly recommend that at this time only women psychotherapists treat battered women. Battered women are similar to rape victims in that they respond more easily to a female therapist who is trained to understand the effects of such victimization. These women need to learn to trust other women as competent, strong professionals. The role model that such a woman therapist provides for the battered woman facilitates therapy. Then, too, women can share intimate problems with other women in a way that also facilitates therapeutic progress. While it is not impossible to do this with a male therapist, treatment by a male therapist takes longer. It is also useful not to have the added complication of relating to a male therapist in a seductive or a manipulative manner, as most battered women are accustomed to doing. Thus, I would suggest to a battered woman interested in finding a psychotherapist that she needs to consider choosing a woman therapist who has had some recent training in working with battered women. It is perfectly acceptable to ask a potential psychotherapist what her/his values and training are in this area.

Psychotherapy has generally emphasized the value of keeping families intact whenever possible. In working with battered women, however, psychotherapists must encourage breaking the family apart. The major difficulty in providing psychotherapy is that most battered women want the therapist to stop the batterer from abusing them, but they do not want to break up the relationship. The women are as dependent upon their men as the men are dependent upon them. The relationship becomes symbiotic; neither can manage without the other. This creates a kind of bonding between the two that becomes terribly difficult to break. Psychotherapy modalities which strengthen the battered woman's successful coping strategies while helping her overcome her sense of powerlessness are effective in this regard. Supportive psychotherapy during the separation and divorce period has proved to be most successful. Rarely do battered women who have received such therapy get involved in another battering relationship. The kinds of psychotherapy may vary in technique and scope, but the goals remain constant. Current behavior is the focus, although exploring the past is sometimes helpful in interpreting present problems. It is important to clarify the ambivalent feelings of the battered women. They center around issues of love and hate, anger and passivity, rage and terror, depression and anxiety, staying and leaving, omnipotence and impotence, security and panic, as well as others. A combination of behavioral, insight-oriented, feminist therapy has proved to be the most effective therapeutic approach. The therapies with the most success for battered women to date have been reported to be crisis intervention, individual psychotherapy, group therapy, and, in a limited number of cases, couples therapy.

CRISIS INTERVENTION

Crisis intervention techniques are often very appropriate after an acute battering incident, as they focus on a specific critical incident. Battered women or batterers are usually concerned enough then about their lack of control to want to understand and change their behavior. The goal is to teach the client how to resolve possible future crises by applying conflict resolution techniques to the present crisis while motivation is still very high. This is the one time that battered women are consistently able to persuade their batterers to come into psychotherapy treatment. The batterer, too, is afraid of the uncontrollable rage he has just experienced. In using crisis therapy with battered women, it is important to label the women "battered." The use of denial is a typical coping mechanism which prevents them from considering action. The details of the battering incident that the woman reports should be documented. If bruises are noted, they, too, should be documented. As mentioned before, it is also helpful to take Polaroid color pictures of the woman's bruises in case she needs them for a possible court appearance. The battered women interviewed reported that it became easier to relate the details of their experiences to a crisis worker when the worker asked specific questions and did not appear squeamish when presented with the gory details.

In interviewing the batterer, crisis workers must be sensitive to his difficulty in reporting the details of an acute battering incident. From the batterers that I have worked with, I have learned that they find it difficult to discuss anything other than what the battered women did to deserve such beatings. They seem to need to justify their violent behavior by concentrating on the details of the incidents that led up to their loss of control. Most justify their violence by saying that the women deserved it. Some insist that they were justified in their brutality because it was their role to teach the women a lesson. Crisis workers need to point out the batterer's rationalization by stressing that no matter what the precipitant, his violent behavior had dire consequences. Immediate psychotherapy techniques should be utilized to teach the batterer ways of controlling his anger. Sometimes hypnosis, relaxation training, and biofeedback are useful.

Women and men should be seen individually unless, in the judgment of the therapist, there is little likelihood of further battering. Then, some time together in a joint therapy session is permissible; but this is rare. The therapist should not expect much trust initially. The stories of the battered women interviewed in this sample indicate that they have little reason to trust a therapist. When interviewing battered women on a crisis intervention basis, therapists should set aside at least two to three hours. Once battered women begin to tell their stories, they need the time to share them all. They have often held back for so long that when they find someone who is genuinely interested, they cannot stop until their stories are told. This contradicts previous beliefs that too much sharing is to be discouraged in an initial session for fear the client may be unhappy about losing control. It is more difficult to get the men to talk initially. For them, it may take several sessions before they willingly share their stories. It is important to help the battered woman and her man follow through in making changes whenever possible. However, it is more important to be understanding and accept the woman's ambivalence about making immediate positive changes in her life. Although some battered women can do this, most need more time. Thus, crisis intervention therapy, which is designed to be intensive and short-term in nature, is usually only a beginning in the psychotherapeutic process for battered women.

INDIVIDUAL PSYCHOTHERAPY

Individual psychotherapy, which is long-term in nature, has the potential to be a most useful therapeutic intervention for battered women. Stopping the battering is the immediate concern, but the long-term expected outcome is economic and psychological interdependence. To be interdependent means to be as capable of either independent or dependent behavior within a relationship as is appropriate. Each person in an interdependent relationship can provide strength (independence) which the other person can lean upon (dependence); while, at the same time, the person who is independent can depend upon the other for certain needs, too. Most people value independence without accepting the fact that dependence is also mentally healthy, providing there is respect and trust in the relationship. A mutuality exists within such interdependent relationships that relies upon flexibility rather than fixed roles. Although interdependence is usually used in context with emotional feelings, it can also apply to economic status. In an interdependent relationship, the woman needs a skill which enables her to be financially independent at any time. She must be capable of meeting her needs economically as well as emotionally. This then leaves her free to choose to enter a relationship, rather than feeling it is her only alternative. Most relationships involving battered women are not interdependent in such a way. The woman becomes the victim because of her extreme dependence upon the batterer. She does not believe she can be a totally independent person.

Interestingly enough, neither does the batterer believe he can stand alone. A bond seems to exist between the couple that says, "We may not make it together, but alone we'll surely perish." Both typically are traditionalists who fear the religious, social, emotional, and economic ramifications of divorce. As we have seen in the previous chapters, death is a more acceptable alternative. It is essential to understand this conviction when working with such a couple. The woman sees death as the only way out of her situation, both the batterer's death and her own. The batterer similarly would rather die or kill her than voluntarily leave—or let her leave. Since, as we know, the best treatment alternative for the battered woman is to get out of the battering relationship, the resulting dilemma is enormous. For the batterer, however, the most beneficial life is one in a warm supportive family relationship. If the woman leaves him, the probability that he will become mentally ill or commit suicide is extraordinarily high. It is more difficult for the batterer to learn to be independent than it is for the battered woman. Such a dilemma becomes difficult for a psychotherapist to reconcile when working with both the man and the woman. Thus, individual psychotherapy, with the woman in treatment with one therapist and her batterer in treatment with another, becomes imperative. What is good for her therapeutically may not be good for him.

Many of the women in this sample indicated that they began to seek a therapist during the first phase of the battering cycle. This is different from seeking crisis intervention help after an acute battering incident, which is the end of phase two in the cycle theory. The women indicated that they recognized the rising tension and felt the inevitability of the forthcoming battering. They sought therapy believing that if they could rid themselves of their provocative behavior, their batterers would then become model phase-three men all the time. They asked the therapist to teach them new techniques to cope with the battering behavior. Their goal was to stop the abuse by controlling the batterers' behavior themselves. But as I've already explained, this tactic just could not work. Battered women who seek therapy often do so at great personal risk. They do not dare tell their men they are in therapy initially, although most of the women in this study said they eventually did. They sometimes give the therapist an assumed name and invent excuses to account for their whereabouts while they are in their therapy sessions.

It is important for psychotherapists to understand the battered woman's need for such duplicity. By accepting her secretiveness and protecting it, the therapist gives the battered woman the clear message that she will not place her at greater risk. She also lets the battered woman know that she believes she is in danger and that she respects the woman's own strength in utilizing appropriate survival techniques. For therapists who work in a mental health center or other clinic, it becomes important to intervene in the standard bureaucratic procedures in order to preserve the woman's right to privacy at all times. This may mean changing computerized billing procedures so that the woman is permitted to pay in cash or in some other convenient manner, rather than having statements sent to her home address. Sometimes the therapist must be creatively manipulative in order to protect her client's individual rights.

Bonnie was a good example of the need for therapist support. When she first came to me for psychotherapy, she gave me a different name. As part of my practice as a feminist psychotherapist, I do not charge for the initial psychotherapy session. (A number of feminist therapists have decided that this is one way to encourage consumerism on the part of women clients. It gives both the client and the therapist the opportunity to evaluate whether or not entering into a psychotherapeutic relationship would be beneficial.) A woman in her early forties, Bonnie was referred to me by her family physician as a last resort before scheduling her for exploratory surgery. Although she had never been physically assaulted, the psychological battering she suffered was thought to be the cause of her physiological ailments.

"I'm really not sure why I am here," said Bonnie while wringing her hands nervously during that first session. "I think it's important for you to know that I can't tell you who I really am because I'm afraid that my husband will find out. I know you work with battered women and I'm sure I'm a battered woman even though he has never hit me. I just know he can," she said in a quivering voice. "I just know if I push him, he will."

I told Bonnie it would be all right not to tell me who she was until the end of our first session. At that time, I explained to her I felt a need to know her name and how to get in touch with her in case I had an emergency. "No," she emphatically stated. "You cannot get in touch with me." I protested that I would not want her to come for a therapy session if some emergency prevented me from being there. "It's all right," Bonnie said. "I will take that chance. If you are not there, I'll wait awhile and then I'll leave you a note and go home." "But can't I call you with some kind of prearranged signal?" I asked. "No," said Bonnie. "If the phone rings, I would have to make up a story as to who was on the other end. He couldn't ever know. And he might listen in on the extension, or maybe my daughter might hear, and if she heard, she might use that and spill the beans in a fight or something like that. No," she stated again, "you cannot ever call me."

I decided to respect Bonnie's wishes and not discuss it any further until we finished the first hour. Bonnie began to tell a story that was similar in nature to that of other battered women. She told of marrying her husband at a young age, after having been raised in a traditional manner, expecting all men to treat her as Daddy's little girl, and fully accepting her role as a mother, homemaker, and her husband's helpmate. It was his responsibility to earn enough money to support the family financially, while her responsibility was to keep the home intact. Her first clue that this might not be the happy dream she had expected was when she continued to work while he completed his education. Bonnie was accused of infidelities with everyone at work. As soon as she was able, she quit working and stayed at home. It then became her responsibility to bring her husband his morning coffee at the office, have lunch prepared when he came home at noon, keep the financial records for his office, and other similar chores. As long as she did these activities well, his explosions were less frequent. Nevertheless, she was never able to avoid them entirely. "Life could be smooth," she revealed, "if I followed his orders at all times." The moment she began to display some initiative, he became verbally abusive, withdrew his caring, and acted mean. As the first interview progressed, it became clear that Bonnie was terrified that someone inadvertently would set off her husband's cruel behavior toward her. "I hide things from him," Bonnie said, "because I never know how he will react to them. It might not bother him at all sometimes, or he might get very angry and hold it against me. The thing I can't stand the worst is when he tells me over and over and over again how I did something wrong. If I were to tell him that I was coming to see you for therapy, he probably would then be able to tell me how crazy I was and how it was always my fault when he lost his temper. I can't do that. I just don't want him to know."

I agreed to see Bonnie in therapy after that first intake. Part of her compromise was that she told me who she was and how I could locate her if it really was an emergency. We devised an elaborate system that I agreed to use if I needed to reach her. She asked to pay me in cash at the end of each session, which I agreed to. Later on in treatment, after I had observed her taking dollar bills out of different compartments all over her purse, she told me how she had to hide things in order to protect them from discovery. If her husband saw that she had accumulated so many dollars over the period of a week, he would begin to question her as to how they would be spent. It was easier to avoid his questioning, and thus her strange hiding behavior became understandable.

After several months of Bonnie coming into therapy sessions and beginning them with her stories of how she had to manipulate and oftentimes lie in order to have our time together without anyone else knowing about it, I confronted her and asked her why she would not tell her husband she was coming to therapy now. It was clear that her family physician had recommended psychotherapy in order to reduce the stress that he believed was precipitating some of her physical ailments. Thus, she had a valid excuse if she did not wish to discuss the battering incidents with him. Bonnie countered by saying, "I would rather lie and make up stories as to where I'm going, instead of telling him that I was in psychotherapy. If I told him, he would want to know what I said to you after each session. I don't want to have to lie and make up stories about what we talk about. That's my time, and it's my private business. He has no right to ask me about it. And maybe he will force me to tell him what we really talk about. I would rather go through the trouble of making up stories to cover where I've been for this time, instead of having to make up stories about what we talk about. This is much easier for me."

I could certainly understand Bonnie's need for secrecy. My respect for her ability to maintain the status quo at home while attempting to strengthen her own emotional well-being was important. As of this writing, Bonnie is still living with her husband. She is no longer in therapy. I do not know whether the battering has increased or decreased. But I do know that Bonnie's ability to seek out independent activities for herself without being immobilized by the terror of provoking a battering incident has been strengthened by therapy. She has made important decisions about an inheritance that will come her way. Through therapy, she was helped to allow her daughter to live her own life without being responsible for her mother's well-being, and Bonnie feels much better about herself. Although these gains may seem small, they can be enormously important in a battered woman's life.

The battered woman who comes to the therapist during phase one of the battering cycle is usually trying to cope with her feelings of guilt, anxiety, and anger. The therapist can help her express her guilt by having her recount the details of battering incidents in which she could not stop her own battering. The feminist therapy approach, which tries to separate the woman's personal issues from common issues shared by other victimized women, is most effective. It is essential to confirm society's lack of adequate help for her, but also to be encouraging about the potential for change. Control of anxiety may be accomplished through relaxation training, hypnosis, or recommending that the battered woman join a health club so as to focus on positive body feelings. The one area over which the battered woman does have total control is that of her body. She has usually developed a lack of body awareness in order not to feel the real pain of her battering. Thus, it is important for her to begin to build self-esteem and a sense of power through body exercise. It is also important to help the battered woman recognize and control her anger. She should be encouraged to experience anger each time it occurs, rather than suppressing it and releasing it all at once, perhaps triggering an acute battering incident. The difference between feeling anger and expressing it must be clearly underscored. It does the battered woman no good to feel her anger and then express it to her batterer. Generally it gets her another beating. Rather, she needs to be taught to feel her anger, control it, and utilize it to help propel her out of the battering situation.

The realities of present alternatives and future goal planning are explored in individual therapy. The battered woman needs to recognize concrete steps she can take to improve her situation. Like Seligman's dogs, discussed in Chapter 2, she must be dragged over her escape route numerous times before she can be expected to do it on her own. If the therapist encourages her to utilize the legal system for remedies, she must be prepared to advocate for the battered woman during these procedures. Intervention and collaboration with other helpers are important corollaries of individual psychotherapy. This may mean getting in touch with a lawyer, the district attorney, a social service worker, rehabilitation or vocational counselor, or whoever else may be involved in helping the battered woman remedy her situation. If the woman chooses to use the court system, the psychotherapist can accompany her client or volunteer to testify on her behalf. These are important tasks an individual psychotherapist can undertake, in addition to facilitating the psychotherapeutic process.

If the battered woman's goal is to remain with the batterer, even temporarily, then therapeutic goals of strengthening her independence within the relationship become important. Career goals need to be explored. Reinforcing the positive in the battered woman's life, using successive approximations from minimum to maximum independence, is important. Progress is often slow, and patience is necessary. Individual therapy concentrates on the present but may use the past to promote understanding of the current situation. The therapy is more action-oriented than analytic; unstructured psychoanalysis is too risky. The battered women interviewed all stated that psychoanalysis did not help resolve their battering situation. In fact, in many instances, its emphasis on self-analysis served to perpetuate their abuse. As therapy progresses, other adjunctive therapies can be recommended, such as assertiveness training, parent education, vocational counseling, and couples therapy.

GROUP THERAPY

Group therapy as another therapeutic format for battered women has some advantages over individual therapy. Battered women are usually isolated and rarely meet other battered women. Friends in whom they can confide are few. A group composed of all battered women can thus be an extremely valuable therapeutic experience. Such a group combines the best of the consciousness-raising groups with the expertise of (preferably) two therapists familiar with group process. It is difficult for private psychotherapists to provide groups for battered women, because the therapists usually do not see enough battered women to form a group. However, a number of agencies are now conducting women's groups for victims. Usually six to twelve women and two therapists make the best combination. It is often necessary to provide individual appointments during crises that occur for group members. This is one reason for having two therapists working together in the group. Women describe having derived a sense of strength from all of the other group members that is more difficult to provide on an individual basis. Therapy is action-oriented, with the focus on changing behavior. Group norms are established that make behavior change imperative in order that the battered women continue to feel supported by the other women.

It has been found that two kinds of groups are needed when working with battered women: a first-stage and a second-stage group, each having different therapeutic techniques and goals. First-stage groups tend to be more crisis-oriented in nature and generally include women who are beginning to leave the relationship with their batterer. Thus, some women in the first-stage group may have already left home; others may still be in the process of leaving. First-stage groups usually meet weekly over a period of several months. Members depend upon one another for emotional as well as informational support. It is common for one member to assist a new member in criminal justice and social service agency procedures, or sometimes even with just the mundane details of how to select and move into a new apartment. Group members are encouraged to exchange telephone numbers and be available to help each other. In one group that I have been associated with, the women call each other and discuss whether their momentary problem is of sufficient magnitude that it warrants an emergency call to the mental health center. Such consensual validation encourages battered women to make better use of the services that are available to them. The group therapists take an aggressive role in encouraging women to action when appropriate.

In one group in Seattle, an advocates division has been established to help women victims use the criminal justice system. This is necessary to help battered women overcome the immobilization that their terror brings. As women witness other women successfully making changes, they themselves are more likely to try to change. This is true whether the groups meet on an outpatient basis in a community mental health center or are conducted in a women's resource center or a battered women's shelter.

Second-stage groups tend to resemble many other kinds of women's therapy groups. Here is where the therapy concentrates on rebuilding lives. Psychological issues, such as effects of their early childhood, are explored as well as the practical concerns, such as how to trust men again. For battered women, the critical focal points are their relationships with men and women. They are fearful and untrusting of men, yet desperately seek out their company. If loneliness sets in, then their batterer begins to look good to them again. The trials and tribulations of living alone are shared in the group. Single parenting, too, becomes a critical therapeutic area. Relationships with women are also distorted and need clarification. Battered women fear conflict of any kind. Thus, they will often give up a friendship rather than fight with someone. They tend to nurture a friend, become angry at feeling taken advantage of, and then begin to feel furious. Rather than expressing their anger slowly or asserting their rights, they save it up and then explode in rage or just break off a relationship. They have difficulty with intensity in relationships, too. All of these issues are directly handled in a good therapeutic second-stage group.

Very recently there have been attempts by male therapists to provide group therapy services for batterers in several mental health centers. The therapeutic techniques are still experimental, but the psychotherapists report exciting results. One of the most significant changes is that the men who attend group therapy sessions are less likely to become depressed, suicidal, or psychotic during treatment. This is true even though the men have joined the therapy fully expecting their participation will keep their women from leaving them. In cases where the women were in one group and the men were in another, each received a sufficient amount of psychotherapy to permit them to break the symbiotic bonds and begin new relationships without using coercive techniques.

As mentioned earlier, the American Lakes Veterans Administration Hospital in Tacoma is in the process of creating an inpatient men's unit for batterers. Dr. Ann Ganley, the unit psychologist, states that many batterers are admitted to the hospital with acute psychotic episodes, which often occur after the battered women leave. Dr. Ganley and her staff are attempting to develop psychotherapeutic techniques which will be successful in eliminating the batterer's need to behave in a violent manner. Recognizing his impending tension and anger and utilizing hypnosis or biofeedback techniques to teach control have been proposed as an adjunct to psychotherapy.

There is often a risk factor for psychotherapists who lead these groups. Some batterers have indeed unleashed their rage on the therapist. Once the Seattle group was held at knife point for several hours by a patient. Another patient drove a car through the front door of a safe house. Other terrorizing threats have been reported. Perhaps one of the most harrowing incidents occurred during a group therapy session at a mental health center where I am a consultant.

It was about a half-hour into the group therapy session when the women were interrupted by the sound of piercing screams. They attempted to ignore them for a few seconds until it became clear that no one else was responding. The women showed visible signs of anxiety, greater than would have been expected with an average group. One woman sat and became rigid. Another put her hands over her ears and began rocking back and forth. Several started speaking rapidly and incoherently. The therapists realized that they needed to take some action before the therapy session could continue. They went to the window and looked in the direction of the screams. To their horror, on the sidewalk below them, between the mental health center and the police station, there was a man beating a woman. They all stared in frozen silence until one of the therapists suggested that they call the police. Upon the interruption of the silence, each woman in the group began shouting another alternative. "Let's go downstairs and break it up," said one woman. "No," said another, "he'll kill us, too." "I think we should scream out the window," suggested a third. A fourth woman became concerned about what was happening to their children, who were meeting simultaneously next door. "Could this affect them?" she wondered out loud. During the initial moments of this incident, no one was quite sure of what was the best solution. While the telephone call to the police was being made, the other women all sat without purpose. Before the incident was reported to the police, several of the women and another therapist began to run downstairs, thinking perhaps they might be able to stop the beating. The therapist wisely realized the futility of such an action and its possible dangerous consequences to her clients. With the call placed to the police, it seemed appropriate to expect immediate intervention would take place. To everyone's dismay, it seemed like an eternity before the police responded to the call. During this time, the women moaned, rambled, cried, and openly feared for the woman being beaten. In a sense, she was each of them and they felt their impotence, rage, and frustration all over again.

Psychotherapists who work with battered women must be prepared to deal with this kind of trauma. Reports of batterers banging on the battered women's doors, kidnapping their children, terrorizing them with guns, and committing suicide are daily problems to be faced in group therapy sessions. This is true especially for stage-one group therapy.

In second-stage groups, the immediate crises are less frequent. It is in these groups that the women learn to rebuild their lives without interference from their batterers. Once the emergency nature of life diminishes for battered women, they must learn to deal with the problems of single women. They must learn to adjust to being alone without slipping into more serious depression. They need to structure their lives in a way to bring them maximum satisfaction. They need enormous support in coping with children who have been badly scarred emotionally, and they need to learn to trust men again. Issues of dating become important in working with second-stage groups. Developing male and female friendships also is stressed. Many battered women need to relearn interpersonal relationship skills that they have lost. Changing faulty behavior patterns and unnecessary attitude expectations is a major job in group therapy during the second stage. Working together with other women in such a group is usually rewarding. The primary goal of such psychotherapeutic intervention is to strengthen the battered woman's self-esteem and help develop her skills so that she can protect herself and will never be battered again.

COUPLES THERAPY

Couples therapy is the therapeutic technique that most psychotherapists, helpers, battered women, and batterers count on to make everything all better. Battered women in particular feel that if they can get their men to participate in therapy, then they will stop their abusive behavior. This assumption is not necessarily true. Very few traditional techniques of couples therapy apply to battering couples. Many of these methods include teaching couples how to fight fairer and better. I am in total disagreement with such techniques; battering couples do not need to learn new fighting behavior. Rather, they need to learn to control their anger. Nonfighting techniques need to be stressed instead. Another difficulty with traditional couples therapy is that it includes the goal of helping the relationship become better. Individual needs are subordinated to the survival of the relationship. With battering couples, the survival of the relationship is secondary. The goal is to strengthen each individual to be able to build a new, healthier relationship. Success is achieved if the individuals are strengthened, even if the relationship itself is not able to survive.

Recognizing the need for new treatment techniques for couples therapy, my late husband, Dr. Morton Flax, a psychologist, and I developed a procedure which has been successful in limiting the severity of battering incidents, although it has not, as yet, eliminated battering incidents completely. This procedure is based on the cycle theory of battering and utilizes a behaviorally oriented communication-training approach. Most couples in a battering relationship have extremely poor communication skills. Their verbal and nonverbal communication is fraught with distortion and misinterpretation. Individually, they continuously engage in making assumptions about the other person's behavior that may be inaccurate. The relationship has unusually strong symbiotic dependence bonds that need to be broken before new communication patterns can be established. It is therefore more important to work on the two individuals within the relationship, rather than dealing with the relationship itself. Ultimately, the goal is interdependence for each.

Our treatment procedures begin with clearly stating that the couple is seeking psychotherapy because the man is a batterer and the woman is a battered woman. These labels help overcome the denial of the serious nature of the violence they experience. Male and female co-therapists must work with the batterer and the battered woman, respectively. Initially, the man and the woman work separately, and the couples live apart. After a short period, upon the advice of their respective therapists, they are allowed to move back together, and they begin joint therapy sessions. These joint sessions are occasionally supplemented with individual therapy when appropriate. The issues discussed in therapy deal with strengthening each individual, so that the relationship becomes free of all coercion. We begin by teaching the couple a signal to use with each other when either one begins to feel tension rising in phase one of the cycle. Often it takes a lot of work to teach the couples to recognize their own cues. Once they learn to feel their tension at minimum levels, we can begin to prevent the tension build-up that causes an acute battering incident. We've used a hand signal in the shape of a little "c" and a simultaneous verbal message that have been most successful. Thus, one or the other signals his or her partner by saying a prearranged word or phrase (in most cases our couples have chosen "Walker-Flax" as their verbal reminder) and simultaneously flashing the little "c." In addition to providing a neutral stimulus to mean "Stop whatever you're doing immediately because it is causing me to become upset," the prearranged signal keeps the batterer's hands from reaching to touch the battered woman and the verbal message prevents threatening words from being uttered. Upon receiving this signal, our clients are taught to cease immediately the offending behavior and not to discuss it for a prearranged period of time. Time-out periods of a half-hour are usually the most beneficial. However, if it takes longer than half an hour for the anger to subside, we allow one more time-out period before discussion begins. Sometimes the first discussion is to negotiate for a longer time-out period. If the couple is unable to discuss the incident without anger rising, the man and the woman are instructed to write it down and bring it to their next therapy session, where the four of us will analyze the situation and problem-solve together.

In the beginning of couples therapy treatment, the therapists must assume control of the batterer's and the battered woman's behavior. Each of them must contract with his or her therapist not to engage in any violent behavior without first attempting to reach his or her therapist. We have arranged that initially our couples will call us daily to check in and report on their behavior for the day. As treatment progresses, daily contact is reduced. However, initially it serves the purpose of helping each to control his or her anger. It prevents the woman from using denial and ignoring her response during phase-one tension building, and it teaches the man that he has alternatives to coerciveness and can prevent violent reactions.

During couples therapy, the couples learn how to ask for what they want from each other without being limited by often erroneous assumptions. They are taught to recognize their own behavior patterns in their unique battering cycle, so that they can become aware of the danger points. They are taught to agree to do one or more things for each other which are called contingency reinforcement management procedures. Natural positive reinforcers are strengthened. Therapy time is spent strengthening the positive and dissecting the negative to prevent explosions in the future. Behavior rehearsals, psychodrama, modeling, and role playing are techniques that are used. We use mirrors, audiotapes, and videotapes in order to demonstrate inconsistencies between verbal and non-verbal behaviors.

Such psychotherapy is time-consuming, expensive, and exhausting for both the couple and the therapists. Initially, the couple becomes extremely dependent upon the therapists in order to prevent further violent incidents. As the dependence lessens, so does the potential for new explosions. It has been impossible for us as therapists to have more than two such couples in treatment at any one time. We have been unable to introduce this kind of couples therapy into mental health center and clinic programs because of the cost factor involved. Thus, it has limited potential.

Although problems do exist with this type of therapy, couples benefit. They attend regularly, and their life improves. The women do not work as rapidly toward independence as they do in individual or group therapy, but they lose the pervasive terror that immobilizes them, and they learn to express anger more constructively. The men learn to be more assertive, too, asking directly for what they want without having to threaten the women if they do not satisfy them. They are also better able to cope with their periodic depression. As difficult as it is, couples therapy is a viable treatment alternative for battered women and their partners. However, it should only be used in cases where both insist on keeping the relationship together.

ATTITUDES AND VALUES OF THERAPISTS

Battered women and their batterers have been identified and available for psychotherapy intervention only recently. The modalities discussed here are just a beginning. The ultimate goal is to promote interdependence so that psychological and physical battering behavior ceases. The most effective means to reach this goal is the separation of the couple. Other treatment alternatives provide some relief. Psychotherapeutic interventions are now beginning to deal with the effects of victimization. In addition to competent psychotherapeutic training in specifically working with battered women and their families, the standards of competencies required to provide adequate psychotherapy include specific attitudes and values. Such therapists must:

1. Support women who have been victimized.
2. Not accept stereotyped myths about battering relationships.
3. Appreciate natural support systems in the community.
4. Be willing to help create new support systems.
5. Be willing to cooperate and untangle bureaucracy for unskilled clients.
6. Collaborate with other professionals.
7. Deal with their own fear of violence.
8. Understand how institutions oppress and reinforce women's victimization.
9. Be willing to be role models for their clients.
10. Be willing to deal with complicated cases.
11. Appreciate the work of noncredentialed paraprofessionals.
12. Be able to formulate their own outlets for anger.
13. Tolerate clients' anger.
14. Tolerate horror stories and terrorizing events.
15. Allow their client to work through her issues without pushing too fast.
16. Allow clients to return to a violent relationship without becoming angry with them.
17. Respect and believe in people's capacity to change and grow.

There is a body of knowledge demonstrating that women often do not receive adequate psychotherapeutic intervention owing to sexist attitudes held by psychotherapists. Dr. Phyllis Chesler's book *Women and Madness* began to detail such practices. The American Psychological Association has produced several studies documenting the existence of such sexist attitudes and has recommended changes in the training of psychotherapists in order to overcome the negative effects these biases can produce. I have been a participant in a project sponsored by counseling psychologists to define standards necessary for effective counseling or therapy with women. I also chair a task force within the women's division in psychology (APA Division 35, Psychology of Women) that is currently translating our knowledge into curriculum, so that all psychotherapists will learn how to work with women in their training programs. Psychologists are now required to spend varying amounts of hours in continuing education courses each year in order to renew their licenses to practice psychotherapy. Other mental health professionals must do the same. This requirement means that already licensed professionals have the opportunity to learn new techniques from a feminist perspective that will permit them to provide the kinds of psychotherapy I have outlined in this chapter. Newly trained psychotherapists have the opportunity to study the problem of battered women during their training. While such training has not been widespread, I am confident that the beginning efforts will be expanded so that battered women and their families will receive the kind of psychotherapy that will eliminate violence from their lives and prevent it from recurring in the future.

12

Designing a New Tomorrow

In this section of the book, I had hoped to be able to design a future society in which battering behavior was extinct. Having spent so much time describing the brutality and the toll on human lives that this kind of violence has taken, I wanted to end on an optimistic note. Now that I have reached this point, I am aware that the task of designing a new tomorrow is overwhelming. I can only offer here a few suggestions that perhaps can serve as a beginning toward that goal.

My first concern is with relationships between parents, children, and the family unit. When I speak to audiences concerning my findings to date on violent families, one question I am always asked is "What will happen to the family unit if we develop the kinds of institutional remedies you suggest?" I have no specific answers, but I will say that the traditional family must change. Our expectations that the family will provide a refuge and peaceful oasis from the burdens of the outside world are patently untrue. Whether the family ever did provide such tranquility I cannot speculate. It is clear, however, that it cannot do so in today's world. Rather than being a unit of refuge, one out of every two families, I estimate, contains violence. This violence is almost always committed by a man against a woman. In a small number of cases, it is the woman who commits violence. I would imagine, however, as I have stated elsewhere, that in most of these cases the woman's violence is probably retaliatory in nature. This means, then, that our dream of the happy family is inconsistent with the reality that family living actually provides.

I suspect that the cause of this situation is not the family as an institution, but rather the demise of the extended family and the rise of the nuclear family unit. The stresses and pressures that a man and a woman and their 2.25 children must cope with in American society today are too much for most to handle. The extended family could provide a support system that would prevent the use of violence as an alternative when the going gets rough. Specialists in studying the family have found that the presence of another family member in the home reduces the amount of violence immediately. Thus, the nature of the family, rather than its elimination, needs to be further explored. Perhaps smaller community support systems can substitute for the loss of the extended family. These systems can only be successful if the historical sociological stereotypes that are designed to allow wife abuse are overcome. The anti-woman bias in society, and especially the degradation and exploitation of women, must change. A feminist perspective stressing cooperation among people must prevail.

Relationships between parents and their children also need further exploration. I cannot help but be impressed by the fact that when we correct our children by hitting them, we teach them that it is possible to love someone and physically hurt the person at the same time, all in the name of discipline. We need to find ways of disciplining our children that do not include transmitting this message to them. Social-learning theorists know that the most effective way to teach children behavior is to give them positive incentives to repeat that behavior. We need to find ways to teach children what acceptable behavior is, rather than to expend the kind of effort we do on punishing maladaptive behavior. Although we know that punishment techniques only suppress behavior temporarily and when the punishments are stopped such behavior rises to a higher level, we persist in using negative discipline in our homes and in our schools. We must learn to accentuate the positive and ignore the negative behavior in children without resorting to violence.

Hopeful signs that I see are the new parent-education classes currently being offered through mental health centers, YWCAs, church-sponsored groups, and other community agencies. Such classes are also being introduced in the public schools, so that tomorrow's parents can learn good parenting techniques in a systematic way. It always amazes me that I have spent over ten years learning to be a psychotherapist, and yet I have never had any formalized training in being a parent. I suspect that I have far more influence over our six children's lives than I do over any of my clients' lives. Now that we know what kinds of behavior make for good parenting and what creates poor parenting, we must transmit this information to future parents in a systematic way. I am hopeful that these new parent-education classes will reduce the amount of inappropriate violence committed against children.

Sex-role stereotyping in raising our children must also be eliminated. Boys and girls must be encouraged to become the best people they can, without regard for limiting masculine and feminine stereotypical roles. From my research, I have no doubt that child abuse, wife abuse, rape, incest, and such forms of violence against others have their roots in both familial and societal dissonance.

Another question that I am always asked is "How can you recognize a potential batterer?" The answer to this question also has to be, I really don't know. About the best I can do is to point out some characteristics that might identify a potential batterer.

1. Does a man report having been physically or psychologically abused as a child?
2. Was the man's mother battered by his father?
3. Has the man been known to display violence against other people?
4. Does he play with guns and use them to protect himself against other people?
5. Does he lose his temper frequently and more easily than seems necessary?
6. Does he commit acts of violence against objects and things rather than people?
7. Does he drink alcohol excessively?
8. Does he display an unusual amount of jealousy when you are not with him? Is he jealous of significant other people in your life?
9. Does he expect you to spend all of your free time with him or to keep him informed of your whereabouts?
10. Does he become enraged when you do not listen to his advice?
11. Does he appear to have a dual personality?
12. Is there a sense of overkill in his cruelty or in his kindness?
13. Do you get a sense of fear when he becomes angry with you? Does *not* making him angry become an important part of your behavior?
14. Does he have rigid ideas of what people should do that are determined by male or female sex-role stereotypes?
15. Do you think or feel you are being battered? If so, the probability is high that you are a battered woman and should seek help immediately.

These clues are certainly not definitive signs that a man is a batterer, only that he has the potential to become one. We need more research to understand what they mean. Much of the information that we have comes from already identified battered women and batterers. We know that they have all displayed some of these characteristics. There may be men who evidence these traits and are not batterers. If anyone who is reading this is in the latter category, it would be important that he get in touch with me at Colorado Women's College, Montview Boulevard and Quebec Street, Denver, Colorado 80220, in care of the Battered Woman Research Center, so that we can learn from his experiences.

An important issue in discussing a future free of battering is support for those people who are involved in violent relationships today. I am convinced that there is a generational cycle to such abusiveness, and the way to prevent violence in the next generation is to stop it today. I accept the theory that such violent behavior is learned behavior rather than innate aggression tendencies. Thus, it is not important to channel such aggression into legitimate modes of expression. Rather, I am more interested in finding ways of eliminating violence in its entirety. This means controlling the amount of violence that we experience in our daily lives. Violence on television is one such aspect. Eliminating the "machismo" image from expected masculine sex-role behavior is another. As I have stated before, observing violence will not necessarily cause someone to become violent; it is a much more subtle interaction than that. A person who has experienced violence becomes more accepting of violent behavior as a norm. Thus, we must be very intolerant of any expressions of brutality in order that the next generation not become inured to such situations.

Women who are being battered need to find a support system that can help them reverse the detrimental effects such victimization has had on their lives. Another question I am always asked when I speak to large audiences is "How can I find a support group to help me cope with the battering relationship in which I live?" It is difficult to answer that question specifically because the resources for battered women are growing every day in every place in this country and others. Thus, by the time this book is published, any list of resources will have become outdated. There are published manuscripts which list various resources in different parts of the country. I list several in the pages of this book. As I mentioned previously, to obtain specific up-to-date information, write to the Center for Women Policy Studies, 2000 P Street, N.W., Suite 508, Washington, D.C. 20036. The Center is funded by the Law Enforcement Assistance Administration in order to provide technical assistance to anyone involved in domestic violence. It keeps a constantly updated resource file in its office where people can learn of the resources closest to their homes.

Another way to find support groups is to write or call the local or state NOW chapter (National Organization for Women). NOW has developed extremely useful task forces on the local level to assist communities in providing support services for battered women. The probability that a local NOW chapter would know how to reach other community resources is very high. Look through the local yellow pages for the address. If you want to organize people in your community to begin such a support group, get in touch with NOW or read the excellent chapter on starting a safe house in Del Martin's book *Battered Wives*.

If you live in a college or university town, or near one, go to the campus women's resource center or your local community women's resource centers, which usually provide counseling, advocacy, and legal advice at little or no cost. Often they have a list of people willing to take in battered women needing emergency shelter. Many towns have one bookstore which carries a full line of feminist-oriented books. Any woman there would also know how to reach community resources to help battered women. A problem that keeps women from valuable assistance is that many battered women feel uncomfortable in going to feminist women for aid. They see themselves as more traditional and are not sure that they are in agreement with feminist goals. It is important to note that in every experience I have had with these feminist support groups, they do not insist that women espouse a feminist point of view in order to be helped. Rather, they attempt to accept the woman, whatever her views are, and help her understand her choices and then assist her in the ones she makes. Many communities have formed task forces on eliminating domestic violence, too.

Another way to find support is through local community mental health centers. These centers must provide consultation and education to community groups that offer resources for rape-assault victims. In many instances, they also have workers who are trained to work with battered women. It is important when first making a call to a local community mental health center to tell the intake worker that you are a battered woman and wish to see a therapist, preferably a woman therapist who has been trained in working with such problems. In that way, you alert the members of the center that they must provide specialized care for you. If they do not have such specialized services or refuse to help you select a therapist based on your specific needs, send a written complaint to the Department of Health, Education and Welfare, National Institute of Mental Health regional or Washington, D.C., office. They receive tax monies to serve you, and with assistance they can learn to do so.

It is more difficult to find specialized help when seeking a psychotherapist in the private sector. Getting in touch with the state psychological association, or other mental health professional state associations, and asking for a feminist-oriented therapist, or a therapist who is trained to work with rape victims, or other victims of violence, may produce the kind of help that you need. Do not settle for psychotherapy with a therapist who tells you that you have precipitated your own assaults. It is obvious that such a therapist has not yet had his or her consciousness raised in terms of working with battered women. Such therapy can do you more harm than good.

If you are eligible for social service intervention or financial aid for dependent children, do not be reluctant to seek such help. Too many middle-class women in this sample told of being embarrassed to apply for welfare, food stamps, or aid to their dependent children. All available services should be used during the period of time that the battered woman needs it. It has been my experience that most battered women do not need to stay on public assistance for long periods of time. They are usually women who readily accept job retraining. Many are already skilled but simply need time to pull themselves together and find a job. I hope that by the time you read this, social service departments across the country will have declared battered women a special class of citizens under the section of the law called Title XX, so that they will be eligible for public assistance immediately upon application. They then may receive rent money, food money, and emergency allotment money promptly, rather than waiting the several weeks it sometimes takes to determine eligibility. Currently, there are other classes of citizens, including geriatric men and women, and abused children, who can receive such speedy assistance in some states. Legislation in a new tomorrow will have been passed to enable women to receive temporary governmental funding as another way out of their violent homes.

Seeking adequate legal counsel is also an essential step for a battered woman. Often she fears her batterer's threats to sue for child custody, strip her of any claim to joint possessions, and leave her without financial support. Good legal advice will clarify what her rights are before she inadvertently gives them away to her batterer. Although the court system cannot be expected to dispense justice in marital disputes, a good lawyer teaches her/his client how to get the most of what she is entitled to. She learns to trust her/him to help her through the legal bureaucracy. Finding a good feminist attorney without assistance from the above-mentioned groups can be difficult. My legal friends advise that you should call the legal aid agency in your town and request to speak directly with the attorney who handles marital disputes or child abuse cases just to get advice on the telephone. Do not give them information that can determine financial eligibility to use their services first. Most legal aid offices only handle very poor women's affairs, owing to restrictions on income level that include husband's earnings even if a divorce is contemplated that would leave the woman penniless. Once you get to this lawyer on the telephone, ask for names of several lawyers who could handle your case.

In my fantasy world, the police department, the YWCA, religious groups, emergency rooms in hospitals, and other community resources would all be able to provide support services for battered women. All of these resources would provide non-sexist assistance. In fact, no one would really need to worry about whether or not help would be forthcoming. It would be there for the asking, and in some cases the women might not even need to ask. Benevolent workers, family, and friends would suggest resources that everyone knew existed. In this fantasy world there would be a self-help group much like Alcoholics Anonymous, Parents Without Partners, Parents Anonymous, which would deal with the battered women or their children in providing self-help support. The National Association of Human Rights Workers is discussing just such a project. Crisis hot lines are springing up everywhere. In the world of a new tomorrow, such telephone hot lines would be available twenty-four hours a day, not just from nine to five. I am hopeful and even optimistic that such a new tomorrow will come. It is my sense that a new tomorrow has already begun for the battered women who have shared their stories with you.

Resources

I have not attempted to provide names of available shelters or services for battered women because the frequent opening and closing of current facilities would quickly make such a published list outdated. Hopefully, if the proposed national legislation on domestic violence is passed, a national clearinghouse for such information will be established. Until then, these are two current sources of reasonably accurate information:

Betsy Warrior, *Working on Wife Abuse.* Available at a nominal charge directly from Ms. Warrior at 46 Pleasant Street, Cambridge, MA 02139.

Programs Providing Services to Battered Women. Available from The Center for Women Policy Studies, 2000 P Street NW, Washington, DC 20036.

If you are involved with a group that wishes to begin its own community program of services for battered women, there is a new publication that gives guidelines and discusses model programs. Several annotated bibliographies are also included in this monograph, which is entitled *Services to Battered Women: Program Development in the United States.* It is available, at a charge, from The Colorado Association for Aid to Battered Women, P.O. Box 136, Colorado Women's College, Montview Boulevard and Quebec, Denver, CO 80220.

Index